Available
Just Ask

THE ORGANIZATION OF THE FUTURE 2

Other Publications from the Leader to Leader Institute

The Five Most Important Questions You Will Ever Ask About Your Organization, *Peter F. Drucker with contributions from Jim Collins, Philip Kotler, Jim Kouzes, Judith Rodin, V. Kasturi Rangan, and Frances Hesselbein*

Leader to Leader 2: Enduring Insights on Leadership from the Leader to Leader Institute's Award-Winning Journal, *Frances Hesselbein and Alan Shrader, Editors*

In Extremis Leadership, *Thomas A. Kolditz*

The Leader of the Future 2, *Frances Hesselbein and Marshall Goldsmith, Editors*

Leadership Lessons from West Point, *Major Doug Crandall, Editor*

Leading Organizational Learning: Harnessing the Power of Knowledge, *Marshall Goldsmith, Howard Morgan, Alexander J. Ogg*

Be*Know*Do: Leadership the Army Way, *Frances Hesselbein, General Eric K. Shinseki, Editors*

Hesselbein on Leadership, *Frances Hesselbein*

Peter F. Drucker: An Intellectual Journey (video), *Leader to Leader Institute*

The Collaboration Challenge, *James E. Austin*

Meeting the Collaboration Challenge Workbook, *The Drucker Foundation*

On Leading Change: A Leader to Leader Guide, *Frances Hesselbein, Rob Johnston, Editors*

On High Performance Organizations: A Leader to Leader Guide, *Frances Hesselbein, Rob Johnston, Editors*

On Creativity, Innovation, and Renewal: A Leader to Leader Guide, *Frances Hesselbein, Rob Johnston, Editors*

On Mission and Leadership: A Leader to Leader Guide, *Frances Hesselbein, Rob Johnston, Editors*

Leading for Innovation, *Frances Hesselbein, Marshall Goldsmith, Iain Somerville, Editors*

Leading in a Time of Change (video), *Peter F. Drucker, Peter M. Senge, Frances Hesselbein*

Leading in a Time of Change Viewer's Workbook, *Peter F. Drucker, Peter M. Senge, Frances Hesselbein*

Leading Beyond the Walls, *Frances Hesselbein, Marshall Goldsmith, Iain Somerville, Editors*

The Organization of the Future, *Frances Hesselbein, Marshall Goldsmith, Richard Beckhard, Editors*

The Community of the Future, *Frances Hesselbein, Marshall Goldsmith, Richard Beckhard, Richard F. Schubert, Editors*

Leader to Leader: Enduring Insights on Leadership from the Drucker Foundation, *Frances Hesselbein, Paul Cohen, Editors*

The Drucker Foundation Self-Assessment Tool: Participant Workbook, *Peter F. Drucker*

The Drucker Foundation Self-Assessment Tool Process Guide, *Gary J. Stern*

Excellence in Nonprofit Leadership (video), *Featuring Peter F. Drucker, Max De Pree, Frances Hesselbein, Michele Hunt; Moderated by Richard F. Schubert*

Excellence in Nonprofit Leadership Workbook *and* Facilitator's Guide, *Peter F. Drucker Foundation for Nonprofit Management*

Lessons in Leadership (video), *Peter F. Drucker*

Lessons in Leadership Workbook *and* Facilitator's Guide, *Peter F. Drucker*

The Leader of the Future, *Frances Hesselbein, Marshall Goldsmith, Richard Beckhard, Editors*

THE ORGANIZATION OF THE FUTURE 2

Visions, Strategies, and Insights on Managing in a New Era

Frances Hesselbein

Marshall Goldsmith

Editors

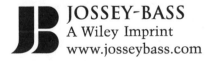

JOSSEY-BASS
A Wiley Imprint
www.josseybass.com

Published by Jossey-Bass
A Wiley Imprint
989 Market Street, San Francisco, CA 94103-1741—www.josseybass.com

Jossey-Bass books and products are available through most bookstores. To contact Jossey-Bass directly call our Customer Care Department within the U.S. at 800-956-7739, outside the U.S. at 317-572-3986, or fax 317-572-4002.

Jossey-Bass also publishes its books in a variety of electronic formats. Some content that appears in print may not be available in electronic books.

Library of Congress Cataloging-in-Publication Data

The organization of the future 2 / Frances Hesselbein, Marshall Goldsmith, editors. —1st ed.
  p.   cm. —(Leader to Leader Institute series)
Includes index.
ISBN 978-0-470-18545-2 (cloth)
  1. Organizational change.   2. Organizational effectiveness.   3. Industrial organization.
4. Management.   I. Hesselbein, Frances.   II. Goldsmith, Marshall.   III. Leader to Leader Institute.
HD58.8.O72842   2009
658.4'06—dc22
                                                                      2008041913

Printed in the United States of America
FIRST EDITION
HB Printing   10 9 8 7 6 5 4 3 2 1

About the Leader to Leader Institute

Established in 1990 as the Peter F. Drucker Foundation for Nonprofit Management, the Leader to Leader Institute furthers its mission—to strengthen the leadership of the social sector—by providing social sector leaders with essential leadership wisdom, inspiration, and resources to lead for innovation and to build vibrant social sector organizations. It is this essential social sector, in collaboration with its partners in the private and public sectors, that changes lives and builds a society of healthy children, strong families, good schools, decent housing, safe neighborhoods, and work that dignifies, all embraced by the diverse, inclusive, cohesive community that cares about all its people.

The Leader to Leader Institute provides innovative and relevant resources, products, and experiences that enable leaders of the future to address emerging opportunities and challenges. With the goal of leading social sector organizations toward excellence in performance, the Institute has brought together more than four hundred great thought leaders to publish twenty-three books available in twenty-eight languages, and the quarterly journal, *Leader to Leader*. This Apex Award–winning journal is the essential leadership resource for leaders in business, government, and the social sectors—leaders of the future.

The Leader to Leader Institute engages social sector leaders in partnerships across the sectors that provide new and significant opportunities for learning and growth. It coordinates unique, high-level summits for leaders from all three sectors and collaborates on workshops and conferences for social sector leaders on leadership, self-assessment, and cross-sector partnerships.

Building on its legacy of innovation, the Leader to Leader Institute explores new approaches to strengthen the leadership of the social sector. With sources of talent and inspiration that range from the local community development corporation to the U.S. Army to the corporate boardroom, the Institute helps social sector organizations identify new leaders and new ways of managing that embrace change and abandon the practices of yesterday that no longer achieve results today.

Contents

PREFACE

Frances Hesselbein

Peter Drucker said, "I never predict. I simply look out the window and see what is visible but not yet seen." And in the mid-1990s, the Leader to Leader Institute, then the Peter Drucker Foundation for Nonprofit Management, looked at leaders and organizations and the massive change, the challenges, and the opportunities of that last decade of the twentieth century and published three books: *The Leader of the Future, The Organization of the Future*, and *The Community of the Future*. Great thought leaders contributed chapters to this trio of remarkable resources for leaders of organizations and communities around the world, with global impact, in twenty-seven languages. The chapters in all three "future" books were a gift of the authors to our readers.

Sometime in the late 1990s, Peter Drucker wrote, "The next ten years will be a period of great political turmoil in many parts of the world, including the United States." We were in a lovely bubble at the end of that decade, and some viewed Peter's prescience as pessimism." Then came September 11, and that world is gone forever.

It's a new decade, with leaders, organizations, and society facing massive change and a future yet to be defined. It's time for a new, powerful, relevant, just-for-our-turbulent-times response, by the people of Leader to Leader Institute and the great thought leaders, who are part of this family tradition. A new decade calls. We respond.

In 2006, *The Leader of the Future 2* was published, with authors responding to our very different times with questions, challenges, observations, and prescriptions—the intellectual ferment of great authors, thinkers, and leaders responding once again to a difficult world and describing the future, how leaders will make it their own, in their own way, in their own times.

The Organization of the Future 2 is eagerly awaited by emerging leaders, the great leaders in organizations across all three sectors in the United States and around the world—leaders determined that, indeed, theirs will be the organization of the future. We are grateful for the vision, the wisdom, the generosity of all the authors of this new guidebook to the future.

Our authors "looked out the window," and what they saw is their gift to you, our readers, and to all those whose lives will be touched when they pick up this book, turn the pages, and find a new world. They will join you in moving forward to build the organization of the future that our societies require and deserve.

We are profoundly grateful to all our contributors, whose only recompense for their contributions is the opportunity to serve you. We express our appreciation to our coeditor Marshall Goldsmith, whose passion for the task, his vision and energy, help make this volume possible. Our gratitude goes to Jesse Wiley, Ruth Mills, and Jahkedda Akbar, who all contributed to this volume in many different ways.

We are grateful to you, our readers and supporters who cheer us on. We hope we have met your expectations with *The Organization of the Future 2.*

INTRODUCTION

Marshall Goldsmith

It has been more than twelve years since the Peter Drucker Foundation published *The Organization of the Future*. Although some elements of organization have remained the same, many have changed. In assembling *The Organization of the Future 2*, we have had the privilege of working with an amazing and diverse array of authors. In reviewing all the chapters, I am pleased that the thoughts of these distinguished experts are so different—yet so complementary!

This introduction provides a brief overview of each chapter. Although some readers like to "begin at the beginning and end at the end," others would prefer to skip around and begin with chapters that address their specific areas of interest. Either approach will work with this book!

The Organization of the Future 2 begins, as it should, with the first step that precedes the achievement of results: setting direction. Part One, "Strategy and Vision: Setting the Direction of the Organization of the Future," describes how tomorrow's organizations can chart the path toward growth and prosperity in rapidly changing times. Chapters with creative case studies show how organizations can—and have—gone well beyond "Strategy 101" in planning for the new world.

What better author to begin our journey than Jim Champy, who is widely recognized as one of the world's top authorities on strategy? Jim's chapter shares wonderful case studies of "creative guerrillas who thrive by outsmarting complacent companies in industries that run on tired ideas." He points out that "those who fail to adapt face extinction in a much shorter time frame than ever before," and he encourages organizations to look beyond the standard operating procedures in their industries—and to learn from other industries in completely different fields.

Dave Ulrich and Norm Smallwood are thought leaders in the area of leveraging human resources to create tomorrow's organizations. They are not only noted authors but also skilled practitioners who have worked with many of the world's major organizations. In Chapter Two, Dave and Norm point out that the organization of the future exists today when leaders shift their focus from "the organization in terms of its structure" to "the organization as a set of capabilities needed to execute the strategy."

Jim Kouzes and Barry Posner are the coauthors of *The Leadership Challenge*, which is not only one of the best-selling books about leadership ever written but also one of the most practical and useful. In Chapter Three, Jim and Barry share research from thousands of leadership survey respondents, research which shows that creating an exciting vision for the future is vitally important—and that leaders aren't doing it very well! They show how encouraging input from key stakeholders is critical for creating a shared vision because "It's not the *leader's* vision; it's the *people's* vision that matters most."

Srikumar Rao is the developer and instructor of Creativity and Personal Mastery—one of the most popular courses ever taught in three of the world's leading graduate business schools. Srikumar has had the opportunity to review more than a thousand essays in which his students—the future leaders of major organizations—describe what they are looking for from their potential employers, and Chapter Four shares this valuable information.

James O'Toole is one of the most noted professors and authors on organizational management. His Chapter Five argues that the race to the bottom, whereby American companies increasingly lower costs and outsource labor, is not the only path (or often the best path) to long-term corporate success.

In today's faced-paced, highly competitive world, there is the widespread desire for the quick fix or the easy answer. Chapter Six explains why "spot management"—attempting to fix immediate problems with short-term solutions—doesn't work. Paul Borawski, the chief strategic officer of the American Society for Quality, and Maryann Brennan, professor, consultant, and Baldrige National Quality Award judge, describe organizations that connect strong values with a systems approach to quality, in ways that deliver great products and services, top customer satisfaction, and long-term profitability for shareholders.

• • •

Part Two, "Organizational Culture: Values, Emotions, Hope, Ethics, Spirit, and Behavior," provides amazing examples of how organizations from completely different industries have created cultures that are transforming their employees and their communities. The authors in this part of the book challenge leaders to make a positive difference in creating organizational culture—and point out the consequences to individuals and to society when they don't.

Tom Moran is greatly respected as both the CEO of Mutual of America and a leader who has made a huge global difference through his support of the social sector. Chapter Seven illustrates how making employees know they are important—and focusing on training and diversity—can be combined to create a workplace that enables employees to achieve their dreams. Tom also shows how an organization can promote giving back to society in a way that builds employee pride while also making our world a better place.

Charles Handy is a writer, broadcaster, and master teacher. His unique ability to combine great wit and incredible insight has made him one of the most admired management thinkers in history. Chapter Eight deals with such "big questions" as *Can capitalism evolve to make a more positive difference for society?* Charles challenges leaders to move beyond just being driven by "financiers"—to provide meaning and reward both for the employees, who are providing knowledge and skills, and for the larger society, which is allowing the corporation to exist.

In Chapter Nine, Jon R. Katzenbach and Zia Khan provide a refreshingly different prescription for the organization of the future. Jon is a former McKinsey director, senior partner in Katzenbach Partners, and one of the world's most admired organization consultants. Zia is an expert on the informal organization—and how it can make a difference in long-term corporate success. Jon and Zia give compelling examples of how major companies have realized that "soft" variables, such as pride and commitment, can make all the difference in creating positive, lasting organizational change.

The Western world is undergoing a demographic revolution: by 2030, 80 percent of the U.S. workforce will be over fifty years old. Richard J. Leider is one of the world's most respected career and executive coaches and a leading spokesperson for positive aging issues. In Chapter Ten, Richard discusses how mature workers can make major contributions to the organizations of the future. He provides a road map that can help "new elders" experience living on purpose—instead of retiring in the traditional way.

Ira A. Jackson is the dean of Claremont University's Peter F. Drucker and Masatoshi Ito Graduate School of Management. In Chapter Eleven, Ira views today's world through the eyes of Peter Drucker, looking first at societal trends that Peter would approve of, such as the huge growth in the social sector and nonprofit organizations and organizations that are "doing good while doing well." Ira also challenges leaders to help create what Peter Drucker envisioned—"a functioning society: one that is well managed, well led, and respectful of the need for innovation and strength and accountability in each of its sectors, public, private, and philanthropic."

Lee G. Bolman and Terrence E. Deal are two of the most respected teachers and authors in the field of organizational behavior. Chapter Twelve offers a thoughtful analysis of how organizations can help provide meaning and value to human existence. Lee and Terry break the mold by pointing out that organizational leaders can also be spiritual leaders who "offer the gift of significance, rooted in confidence that the work is precious, that devotion and loyalty to a beloved institution can offer hard-to-emulate intangible rewards."

Chapter Thirteen is an inspiring chapter that shows how dedicated leaders can build organizations that create meaning and beauty from the depths of despair. Bill Strickland is the CEO of Manchester Bidwell Corporation (MBC) and a MacArthur Fellowship recipient for leadership and ingenuity in the arts. Regina Cronin is a freelance writer and friend of the MBC family. Bill and Regina describe how MBC has helped its underprivileged clients achieve fantastic success where other community organizations (some with much more funding) have failed. How? By creating an environment that produces pride—and communicates dignity—for all its members and clients.

• • •

Part Three, "Designing the Organization of the Future," offers varied and diverse views on the organization of the future—ranging from entrepreneurial organizations to large corporations, nonprofits, and colleges.

The organization of the future will have to change—to meet our changing times. Christopher Gergen and Gregg Vanourek are among today's leading authors, thinkers, and practitioners in the field of entrepreneurship. In Chapter Fourteen, they point out how five socioeconomic shifts have converged to create a "perfect storm" that will lead to the creation of more entrepreneurial organizations, and they share a variety of creative organizational strategies to illustrate these shifts.

Jay R. Galbraith is widely considered to be the world's authority on organization design: a noted author and practitioner, he has been on the forefront of changing the way that organizations are structured. In Chapter Fifteen, Jay describes the evolution of organizational design from the two-dimensional model of the 1920s to the multidimensional model that will be needed in the future, using Procter & Gamble and IBM as examples of organizations that recognize the true complexity of their businesses—and that have adapted and thrived by creating multidimensional organizational structures.

Edward E. Lawler III is a world authority on developing human resource practices, such as performance management systems and compensation; he and Chris Worley are colleagues at the USC Center for Effective Organizations. In Chapter Sixteen, they provide a compelling case as to why the organizational designs of the past—which focused on stability—won't work in the future. They then offer practical suggestions on how to create a "built to change" organization that will have the flexibility required to thrive in a world where the only certainty is change.

Although dramatic change can be easy to discuss eloquently, it is hard to execute! Kathy Cloninger is the CEO of the Girl

Scouts of the USA, and in Chapter Seventeen, she describes how she is currently leading a dramatic transformation in an important national institution that has experienced a series of ups and downs. With refreshing honesty, humility, and candor, she describes the challenges that she is facing and her plans for an exciting new future. Kathy provides a real-world example of organization change that can benefit leaders from any organization.

Chapter Eighteen, by Roxanne Spillett, CEO of the Boys & Girls Clubs of America, provides a road map for leaders in the nonprofit sector. (There are over one million nonprofit organizations in the United States alone!) Roxanne discusses people, funding, and strategy at a broad level, and then goes on to share some of the great successes that she has had in her leadership role—including a fascinating partnership with Bill Gates and Microsoft.

In Chapter Nineteen, Darlyne Bailey, dean of the College of Education and assistant to the president at the University of Minnesota, writes boldly about the college of the future. She issues a clear challenge to the status quo: "all our talk in education about setting 'world-class standards,' establishing 'globalized curricula,' and creating organizations that will thrive in our 'knowledge economy' is unfortunately becoming more *rhetoric* than *reality*." Darlyne then goes on to show how higher education is structured today, why it needs to change, and how she thinks it can.

● ● ●

Part Four, "Working Together," offers three different yet highly complementary views on inclusion, integration, and horizontal organization. Each author provides examples of how the old top-down, hierarchical structure is being replaced by more fluid and horizontal organizations and teams.

Lee Cockerell recently retired as executive vice president of Walt Disney World, where he was credited with developing and implementing Disney's "Great Leader Strategies." In Chapter Twenty, Lee shares his learning from years at Disney and outlines ten ways to foster an inclusive work environment. He points out how any organization can learn from Disney and create not only a great employee experience but also a great customer experience.

Edgar H. Schein is an icon in the field of organizational culture: he has taught at MIT's Sloan School of Management since 1956. In Chapter Twenty-One, Ed takes the concept of organizational culture to another level: most major organizations have very different subcultures, and effective managers need to integrate these subcultures to execute coherent corporate actions. He uses illustrations from several of the world's leading corporations (General Foods, Kaiser Permanente, HP, and more), and he describes how managers cannot *order* subculture alignment, but can help *build* subculture alignment.

Chapter Twenty-Two does a fantastic job of combining the "soft side" of team building with the "hard side" of achieving business results. Howard M. Guttman, noted author and expert on team building, declares that although the traditional hierarchical business model has worked well since the Industrial Revolution, it "is quickly becoming something of a dinosaur." He shows how several real-world executives have built a "radically different organization that is horizontal in structure, redefines the nature of leadership, and is driven by high-performance teams that are aligned, accountable, and focused on achieving an ever-higher measure of results."

• • •

Part Five, "Leadership," is the final section of the book and is focused on the leaders of the organizations of the future—and how they can make a critical difference in the success of their enterprises. Our authors cover the gamut of leadership thinking from historical leaders in Persia to duos running hypergrowth companies.

David G. Thomson is a best-selling author and researcher who (while with McKinsey & Company) launched a multiyear study to identify the success patterns of America's highest-growth companies. In Chapter Twenty-Three, David discusses the key factors that led to these companies' ultimate growth and success, including how "dynamic duos"—that is, leadership teams—can reinforce each other and build positive relationships both inside and outside the company. David also shares his "7 Essentials of Blueprint Companies" that helped lead to exponential growth.

Chapter Twenty-Four describes three phases in a leader's judgment process. Noel M. Tichy is one of the business world's top executive educators, professors, and authors, and Christopher DeRose is a top researcher and expert on organizational change. Noel and Chris describe how leaders can build the deep knowledge that they need and develop outstanding judgment. They share their extensive experience with major corporations in showing how judgment can lead either to the massive success or massive failure of an organization.

William A. Cohen is the president of the Institute of Leader Arts; in 1979, he was Peter Drucker's first executive PhD graduate—and he continued a relationship with Peter that lasted over three decades. In Chapter Twenty-Five, Bill builds on Peter's work to describe how leadership has remained a constant over time, how leadership has changed, and how leadership will change in the future. Bill describes the global and competitive challenges facing the leader of the future—and points out by explaining why "carrot and stick" leadership (by itself) will definitely not be sufficient for motivating the employees of the future.

Debbe Kennedy was a distinguished leader at IBM and is now an author and consultant specializing in leadership development. In Chapter Twenty-Six, Debbe begins by emphasizing the importance of *practice*—and learning through *doing*. She provides sound advice on how to turn experience into learning, and she shares five distinctive qualities of leadership for the organization of the future: making diversity an organizational priority, getting to know people and their differences, enabling rich communication, holding personal responsibility as a core value, and establishing mutualism as the final arbiter.

My final suggestion for you, our readers, is not only to think about what you have read but also to do what Debbe suggests: practice, practice, practice and apply what you have read. The messages contained in this book can help you in your efforts to create organizations that improve the lives of all their stakeholders, while at the same time making our world a better place.

PART ONE

STRATEGY AND VISION

Setting the Direction of the Organization of the Future

The six chapters that open this book cover a broad cross section of topics related to the direction that organizations should take in order to succeed in the future. Strategy guru Jim Champy shows how organizations of the future need to "change or die," and they can change by seeing new ways of doing things that their rivals have missed. He cites three companies as fascinating illustrations of this idea: for example, who would think that ER medicine could learn anything from the Jiffy Lube approach to servicing a car? Read Chapter One, and you'll find out!

Leadership consultants Dave Ulrich and Norm Smallwood describe five qualities that organizations of the future need to have. These have little to do with the *structure* of an organization (that is, the traditional "roles, rules, and routines"); instead, organizations of the future need to focus on their *capabilities:* their leadership, their agility, the talent of their employees, their relationships with stakeholders, and the strategic unity regarding their future goals and direction.

Leadership experts James M. Kouzes and Barry Z. Posner have surveyed thousands of people on what qualities their leaders should have, and "being forward-looking" ranks at number two. Unfortunately, Kouzes and Posner also found that "today's leaders stink at it." Fortunately, their chapter describes some of the reasons why, and they offer great ideas on how to overcome this challenge.

Business professor Srikumar S. Rao has surveyed more than a thousand of his students to ascertain what the "ideal job" is and what they seek in the organizations they work for. His chapter provides intriguing insight into what makes organizations great and successful—and it's not just about the bottom line. There are "good profits" and "bad profits," so an organization's success comes from its relationships with and attitudes toward its employees, customers, suppliers, and shareholders.

Business ethics professor James O'Toole focuses his chapter on organizations that pay lip service to their employees but then outsource jobs, cut employee benefits, and replace permanent employees with contract workers. O'Toole contrasts these companies, which claim that these tactics are necessary for keeping costs low and competing globally, with what he calls "high-involvement" companies, whose strategy is to treat their employees fabulously— and make money doing it.

Quality experts Paul Borawski and Maryann Brennan have seen too many companies focus on "spot management," trying to apply a quick fix to solve problems immediately, without considering any longer-term implications. They cite examples of Baldrige National Quality Award winners who have fought that tendency—including Ritz-Carlton Hotels, Boeing, a regional fast-food restaurant chain, a health care facility, and many others. These organizations have banished the "factory" approach to running their businesses in favor of a *holistic* approach that enables them to work better *and* be more successful. That's a vision worth pursuing.

CHAPTER ONE

OUTSMART YOUR RIVALS BY SEEING WHAT OTHERS DON'T

Jim Champy

Jim Champy is chairman of Perot Systems Corporation's consulting practice and head of strategy for the company. His latest book is Outsmart! How to Do What Your Competitors Can't. *Champy is also the author of the three-million-copy international best-seller* Reengineering the Corporation: A Manifesto for Business Revolution, *as well as* Reengineering Management, X-Engineering the Corporation, The Arc of Ambition, *and* Fast Forward. *He contributes regularly to leading publications and is in high demand as a speaker around the world. Champy earned a BS and MS degree in civil engineering from MIT, as well as a JD from Boston College Law School. He lives in Boston, Massachusetts.*

Seeing what others don't. It's a neat trick if you can pull it off. The companies I describe in my book *Outsmart!* have done just that by focusing on societal trends and unmet needs. And by sharpening their vision, they have achieved phenomenal growth rates and blown past competitors in a time of uncommonly rapid economic upheaval. They are literally changing the way business is done. Among this new breed of eagle-eyed entrepreneurs is MinuteClinic.

MINUTECLINIC SOLVES EVERYDAY HEALTH CARE PROBLEMS IN A NEW WAY

For entrepreneur Rick Krieger, the flash of insight followed an exasperating hospital emergency room experience one winter weekend in Minneapolis. His expanded view led him to conceive of the idea that became MinuteClinic, now a subsidiary of CVS Caremark following its $170 million acquisition in 2006. It's one of the companies featured in my new book, *Outsmart!*

After spending two hours waiting to find out if his son's sore throat was strep, which would require an antibiotic (and it wasn't strep), Krieger began thinking way outside the hospital. Why in this world of harried and hurried families wasn't there a quick and convenient way to get treatment for common medical problems like sinus infections, strep throats, and allergy flare-ups? Krieger's questioning of seemingly sacrosanct medical procedure—and his and his associates' willingness to buck the medical profession by applying retail practices to health care—spawned what is now a squadron of highly trained nurse-practitioners treating a range of ailments from kiosks located in scores of retail stores.

Why do the Rick Kriegers of this world spot opportunities where others see only obstacles? The answer begins with the human penchant for living in a bubble—an airtight cocoon of assumptions, beliefs, or worldviews. The exciting thing about business bubbles is that they invite inventive minds to insert pins.

MinuteClinic's original creators and veteran marketer Mike Howe are bubble bursters: their customer-centric ideas about responding to complaints helped expand the retail treatment concept into a national operation that serves half a million consumers annually. They are creative guerrillas who thrive by outsmarting complacent companies in industries that run on tired ideas. They see what others can't, and they act on what they see by applying proven practices from other fields that everyone else dismisses as irrelevant.

In MinuteClinic's case, the notion that you don't need a physician or a hospital emergency room to treat many common ailments sounds more like common sense than a revolutionary idea. In fact, the model owes a lot to Jiffy Lube's insight that you don't need a fully trained mechanic to change the oil in your car. But until Krieger came along, no one would have dared to suggest that health care could learn a thing or two from the car maintenance business. And with the addition of Howe's superb marketing acumen, a second bubble—the one that encapsulates medical providers and so often makes them oblivious to customer needs—collapsed with a loud pop as MinuteClinic personnel began focusing on how they delivered health care.

The success enjoyed by MinuteClinic presents not a business anomaly but, rather, a lesson for leaders in how to compete in today's ever-changing global economy. Like the founders of MinuteClinic, you must look beyond the parameters of standard operating procedure in your industry to see what you can borrow from the Jiffy Lubes of this world as they capture similar opportunities within their areas of expertise.

CHANGE OR DIE: GOOD ADVICE FOR ORGANIZATIONS OF THE FUTURE

MinuteClinic exemplifies the creative strategies that smart organizations are using to compete in a time of unparalleled change. Change, of course, is nothing new. It is one of life's givens. But today, those who fail to adapt face extinction in a much shorter time frame than ever before. "Change or die," as the saying goes—and to judge from the 157 million entries dredged up by a Google search of that phrase, no one from diet counselors to partisan political pundits doesn't believe it. But nowhere is change more rampant and potentially deadly than in the twenty-first-century, globalized business environment. Leaders are grappling with mind-boggling upheaval, and they're scrambling for every advantage against competitors that, just yesterday, were considered moribund and economically backward. Just a few short years ago, who would have named Brazil, China, India, and Russia as among the brightest stars in today's economic firmament? Yet in recent years, the so-called advanced economies have struggled to keep up with the astonishing rise of these economic powerhouses.

There is certain danger in this hypercompetitive world, but there is also a degree of excitement that is hard to quantify, as opportunity like that discovered by Rick Krieger and MinuteClinic shows itself in unlikely places. Innovation and expansion opportunities abound for leaders who know where to look and how to coax growth out of what they find.

Certainly, there's no shortage of powerful new business practices designed to hone a company's competitive edge. Or, as I often like to say, management theory may be stagnant, but there's plenty that is new and exciting in business practice. Take growth strategy, the linchpin of any successful company. What's out these days? The pronouncements of men with monogrammed cuffs reigning from secluded aeries. What's in? The hard-won strategic wisdom borne of in-the-trenches combat.

It's a trend I salute. In my more than three decades as a consultant and author, I've learned a few things, not least among them this simple and pragmatic notion: whatever works is the right thing to do. Moreover, I'm convinced that the very best management ideas come not from observers like me or from the old-style managers whose track records and egos make them resistant to change, but from the people who do the real work inside companies—people who are challenged on a daily basis and who not only survive but thrive in today's complex, volatile, and demanding global marketplace.

How do I know that this new breed of manager is leading the way today? They have the growth rates to prove it. Put another way, what they are doing works; therefore, what they are doing is right.

Keeping that proposition in mind as I set out to write *Outsmart!*, I could think of only one place to look for the best, most practical strategies, and that was inside companies whose plans of action have arisen organically in accordance with the opportunities grasped and challenges encountered. Hence, these creative companies are outsmarting and outgrowing their competitors by finding distinctive market positions and sustainable advantages in myriad ways. They are thinking innovatively, simplifying complex problems for customers, and finding ways to tap into the success of others. Better yet, their revenue-producing ideas don't require hundreds of millions of venture-capital dollars or IPO proceeds to get them airborne, and their strategies can be easily and immediately understood by any business leader.

SONICBIDS.COM FOUND A MUSIC MARKET NO ONE ELSE SAW

Boston-based Sonicbids.com is another new company that is thinking outside the music box. Sonicbids was founded by thirty-five-year-old entrepreneur Panos Panay in 2001; over the four years from 2004 through 2007, the company enjoyed a growth rate approaching 400%.

Panay, a guitarist who never made his mark on stage, became a successful online talent agent by parlaying his knowledge of the music business and his empathy for musicians hungry to connect with promoters into a $10 million enterprise. Taking advantage of new technology to span the world from the confines of his office, Panay now connects 120,000 musician-members with more than ten thousand promoters who have gigs to fill. The individual engagements may be small, but together they add up to a huge market: $2.5 billion annually for wedding bands alone, plus another $11 billion in bookings at small bars, clubs, coffeehouses, festivals, and such. Panay also helps his musician-members prepare electronic press kits that can quickly be placed in the hands of promoters via e-mail.

Panay's insight enabled him to connect the music industry's dots, or points of dysfunction. Having worked as a traditional talent agent, he knew it was impossible to listen to every tape and CD and view every video that pours into an agent's office, meaning that musicians—even great ones—may never get a hearing. And if they *do* get heard, they may still endure endless waits before they secure a booking. Panay knew that this frayed connection between musicians and their would-be audiences only worsened the struggle for struggling artists. For promoters, the promise of Panay's service was the help he could give in simplifying the often tedious search for the right artist to fill a gig and, in effect, do it at no cost, because Panay's fees come from the artist.

Often people who get caught up with a new business model or technology shortchange their customer service, and those who run technology-based businesses are particularly susceptible to this error. They seem to think that technology itself will solve customer problems. But you need only think of those despised customer service centers with no-service people and endless automated transfers to know just how wrong such assumptions are. Panay instinctively understood that an online business lacks the legitimacy that comes with a physical presence, so he insisted on a proactive customer service operation that emphasizes respectful and sympathetic human interaction with both promoters and musicians.

Struck by the disconnects in the music business and realizing that once-separate products and services could be brought together on the Internet, Panay conceived of Sonicbids and developed a whole new business model to profit from his revelations. And thanks to his knack for recognizing a market no one else saw, and then figuring out how to serve it efficiently and profitably, Panay's upstart now ranks eighty-eighth on *Inc.* magazine's list of the top five thousand privately owned businesses in the United States.

With far-reaching vision, Panay is looking to extend his business to other neglected markets. He's already signed up jugglers and magicians and has had inquiries from actors, models, freelance writers, and even video game companies looking to arrange cheaper and simpler deals with artists by bypassing record labels and publishers.

The lesson for leaders is that opportunities lurk in neglected fields everywhere, and especially in places where people accept dysfunction as the normal way of life. And as Panay's experience affirms, you don't need lots of money to find and exploit the opportunities. You need a sharp eye for an unmet need and a willingness to work hard to figure out how best to fill it

You can look in your own industry for the kind of opportunity Panay discovered. Map out the players: your customers, suppliers, business partners, even your competitors. Look at products, services, information, and money flows and determine where the breakdowns occur, where needs are going unmet. And don't forget to think globally. The Internet allowed a business based in Boston's South End to span the world. Sonicbids may have only one office, but it is rapidly building itself into a global giant. That's because Panos Panay never thought of the music industry as a business with borders. He knew that just as people in Turkey are eager to hear American music, musicians from Turkey would be thrilled to play for crowds in Brooklyn, New York, and people in Brooklyn want to hear music from Iceland, Turkey, Russia, or anywhere else on the planet.

Vision Isn't Limited to Upstarts: Older Organizations Can Reinvent Themselves, Too

About now, you may be thinking that because Sonicbids and MinuteClinic are start-up companies, their smart and smarter strategic moves don't apply to your older, established business. Not true. The Smith & Wesson Company (S&W) was halfway through its second century—and with a gun to its head—when Michael Golden brought the life-giving elixir of his hard-earned management and marketing expertise into the legendary company's sickroom. By leveraging the knowledge he had accumulated over twenty years in business at the Kohler Company, Stanley Works, and Black & Decker, he proved that smart strategy knows no age limits. Indeed, seasoned executives can muster extra firepower in the fight to outsmart competitors.

When Golden arrived at S&W in 2004, an NRA-led boycott was smothering sales, the stock price had fled so far south as to conjure visions of penguins on ice floes, and federal agents were scouring the books for accounting irregularities. Now a skeptic might ask what a fellow fresh from heading up Kohler's cabinetry division—and whose expertise presumably ran to wood finishes and mirrored lighting options—could do for one of the nation's oldest firearms manufacturers. Golden, who had never fired a gun and couldn't tell the difference between a revolver and an automatic pistol, was somewhat baffled himself when S&W came calling. But the more he learned about the company's problems, he told me, the more he realized that the management and branding skills he had acquired over the course of his career were just what S&W needed.

It didn't take long for Golden to spot the source of the gun maker's troubles. A lack of leadership was apparent the first day when someone told him that the company "kind of runs itself." Mike knew from experience that nothing can be further from the truth, and if management thinks the company can run itself, then no one really knows what's going on.

His initial assessment was confirmed a few days later when he asked his subordinates a very basic question: "How are we doing?"

He received a blank stare in response. The manufacturing division was turning out product without knowing whether it was needed—not surprising given that the sales staff had no targets, either. Within twenty-four hours, change was under way, as Golden, reverting to Management 101, held the first of his daily meetings with his vice presidents and their top people overseeing all major areas. He forced them to begin talking to one another and to report daily on orders received, products manufactured, and so forth, measuring the results against target numbers. Discrepancies had to be explained and plans outlined for fixing problems. As basic as Golden's approach sounds, it was all new to S&W.

From that beachhead of basic change, Golden began to re-imagine the company's strategy, starting by using the brand management skills he acquired at Kohler to take advantage of S&W's storied brand. His extensive research turned up an amazing fact: although the company had only $100 million in sales, it had an 87% public awareness level—no matter whether the interviewees liked guns or not, were male or female, or lived on the West Coast or the East. Golden knew he had an asset no money could buy: a brand name that conjured up the unique essence of America and the derring-do of its cowboys, soldiers, and lawmen.

The customer response was much the same. Whether hunters, marksmen, or sports enthusiasts, they loved the brand—even when the company didn't have an entrant in the race: asked what shotgun they would buy, respondents put S&W in third place, even though the company didn't make a shotgun!

Before Golden took over, S&W's strategy had centered entirely on dominating a niche market: handguns in the United States. With research in hand, Mike broadened the company's strategic goals. He not only planned a huge expansion in the handgun business but also set out to revitalize markets that had been left fallow, such as U.S. military and police sales, and to branch out to new markets, including the shotgun and long-gun market where S&W had a phantom presence. And to speed up S&W's entry into the premium rifle market, Golden acquired a company that already had the expertise he needed.

To attract local law enforcement agencies, he remembered how at Black & Decker, he had gone out on job sites to discover what potential customers wanted in the way of tools. Now he dispatched engineers and designers to talk to state and city police officers about the kind of pistol they needed. The result was the sleek yet powerful M&P 45, which has won more than 80% of the law enforcement evaluation processes in which it has competed and is used today by more than three hundred police departments in the United States.

It may seem obvious to solve problems by applying knowledge gleaned elsewhere, but doing so *takes discipline.* So often we forget what's gone before, even though we know that history has a way of repeating itself. But our tendency to compartmentalize issues leads us to overlook lessons learned in one context even when the problem at hand is remarkably similar. Michael Golden has the concentration and imagination needed to ferret out past experiences and apply them to present challenges. He forgets nothing and uses everything.

For example, to increase sales, he fell back on what he'd learned at Black & Decker about creating demand during the launch of a new power-tool division. Rather than spend money on television commercials, he engaged in what he called "hand-to-hand combat" at the retail level. Highly trained S&W salespeople showed dealers how to merchandise their products, suggesting that they organize special events at stores and shooting ranges to give potential customers the chance to handle and fire S&W guns. Golden well knew that giving customers such opportunities could create a need for his products.

The strategies Golden employed at S&W, the new processes he put in place, the thinking that led him to acquire the expertise needed to get into the premium long-gun market quickly—all were outgrowths of difficulties met and actions taken in his previous corporate life. Golden proves that using everything you know is an excellent way to outsmart your rivals.

Under Golden's leadership, S&W's revenues soared and nearly nonexistent profits rebounded (though the recent economic slowdown and turbulent markets have interrupted the company's recovery process). Nevertheless, as the editor of *Shooting* magazine was led to remark, "No company in modern history has come back from the dead like Smith & Wesson."

Several lessons can be drawn from Golden's story, but one of the most important is that any leader making a change in his or her company's strategy must know which assets can be leveraged and which need protecting. Knowing that Smith & Wesson was already a much-respected name in the gun world, Golden might have kept hands off the brand and focused solely on bringing sales and production operations into the twenty-first century. Instead, he ordered extensive brand research that led him to expand S&W's market footprint, with impressive results. Brand management was a skill he picked up at Kohler, and his prior experience paid big dividends.

CONCLUSION

The vignettes contained here, and the more detailed accounts found in my book, are intended to get you thinking about how to apply the strategic lessons to your own unique situations. It won't be simple, and there are no set formulas you can follow without changing how you operate. What all of my examples have in common, though, is their adherence to Peter Drucker's simple advice to know where you are, where you want to be, and how to get there.

The people and companies I've chosen to showcase have opened their eyes to opportunities that others have overlooked and dared to go places others shy from. And in making the journey, they have found the holy grail of strategy: an unmet customer need.

We live in a time of innovation and expansion, a world of smart and smarter strategic options. The race will not necessarily go to the swiftest, but it will go to the shrewdest competitors among us, those who can stake out new territory, define the boundaries, and even set new rules for the game. There's no reason why you and your organization cannot be among them.

CHAPTER TWO

ORGANIZATION IS NOT STRUCTURE BUT CAPABILITY

Dave Ulrich and Norm Smallwood

Dave Ulrich is a professor of business at the University of Michigan and a cofounder of the RBL Group, a consulting firm focused on helping organizations and leaders deliver value. He studies how organizations build capabilities of speed, learning, collaboration, accountability, talent, and leadership through leveraging human resources. He has helped generate award-winning databases that assess alignment between strategies, human resource practices, and HR competencies. He has published fifteen books and hundreds of articles, and he has consulted and done research with more than half of the Fortune 200 companies.

Norm Smallwood is cofounder of the RBL Group, where he specializes in building leadership and increasing strategic HR capabilities. He has coauthored six books. Ulrich and Smallwood's most recent book is Leadership Brand: Developing Customer-Focused Leaders to Drive Performance and Build Lasting Value *(Harvard Business School Press, 2007).*

The organization of the future exists today. But not in the traditional sense. Generally, when thinking about an organization, we turn to morphology (that is, the study of structure or form), and we define an organization by its roles, rules, and routines:

- *Roles* define the hierarchy of who reports to whom and who has accountability for work.
- *Rules* represent policies and prescriptions for how work is done.
- *Routines* reflect processes or cultures within the workplace.

Combined, these three traditional factors capture an organization's structure or shape. In the last decade, a lot of restructuring of organizations has been done to right-size, reshape, reengineer, redesign, de-layer, and rebuild organizations in terms of these three factors. However, organization design as encapsulated by roles, rules, and routines is only a small part of the complete organization of the future.

When we work with executives to define the organization of the future, we start with a simple question: "Can you name a company you admire?" The list of admired companies varies, but it often includes such well-known firms as General Electric, Apple, Disney, Google, and Microsoft. We then ask the executives, "How many levels of management are in the admired firm?" Almost no one knows.

More important, none of us really cares—because we do not admire an organization because of its roles, rules, or routines. Instead, we admire GE because of its capacity to build leaders in diverse industries; we admire Apple because it seems to continually design easy-to-use products; we admire Disney for the service we experience; and we admire Google and Microsoft for their ability to innovate and shape their industry. In other words, organizations are not known for their *structure*, but for their *capabilities*.

Capabilities represent what the organization is known for, what it is good at doing, and how it patterns its activities to deliver value. The capabilities define many of the intangibles that investors pay attention to, the firm brand to which customers can relate, and the culture that shapes employee behavior. These capabilities also become the identity of the firm, the deliverables of HR practices, and the key to implementing business strategy.

In previous books and articles, we have chronicled a menu of capabilities an organization might require to succeed.[1] In this chapter, we specify five key capabilities that organizations of the future must demonstrate (talent, leadership, agility, an "outside-in" connection, and purpose). We select these five because they are the capabilities required to cope in the business world of tomorrow. In this chapter, we highlight new business realities, review these five capabilities, and then discuss their implications for creating the organization of the future, today.

THE ORGANIZATION OF THE FUTURE FACES NEW BUSINESS REALITIES

What are some of the new business realities facing organizations today and in the future? Most are aware of these challenges, but here are just a few to remind us:

- *Globalization* has made the world a global village, with new markets offering new challenges and opportunities, especially in China, India, Brazil, and Russia. Therefore, global issues—including trade barriers, exchange rates, tariffs, and distribution—become important elements of managerial choice.
- *Technology* has increased accessibility, visibility, and connection. The connected world is smaller and rapidly changing, and has open information.
- *Employees* represent increasingly diverse demographic backgrounds, in terms not only of race and gender but also of personal preferences, global or cultural backgrounds, and orientation to work. In some parts of the world, birth rates have declined and there are more older employees than in other parts of the world. In addition, employee expectations are constantly rising as they gain in education and skills.
- *Customers* are increasingly segmented and demanding. With more choices, they are more selective about the businesses with whom they work.
- *Investors* are increasingly attuned to and concerned about not only financial results but also intangibles.
- *Competitors* are both traditional global players and smaller innovators.

Many management thinkers spend enormous amounts of time specifying these trends and their implications for business in general.[2] Most of these trends are outside the control of any individual or any company. They occur in predictable and unpredictable ways. They affect all aspects of business, including how to fund a firm, how to position the firm in customers' minds, and how to engineer and deliver products. They also help determine what capabilities the organization of the future should master. In recent decades, leaders have built organizations to succeed by being efficient, accountable, and innovative. We don't deny these are critical capabilities, but they are mere table stakes for survival in the world ahead.

Therefore, in this chapter, we propose five capabilities for dealing with the global trends of the future:

1. **Talent**—the ability to attract, retain, and deploy human capital, to assure competence and knowledge of the workforce
2. **Leadership**—the ability to build future leaders as an organizational capability, to turn customer expectations into employee actions and to increase leadership brand
3. **Agility**—the ability to respond quickly, change, be flexible, learn, and transform
4. **An outside-in connection**—the ability to turn outside expectations from customers, investors, and communities into internal organizational actions
5. **Strategic unity**—the ability to create a shared point of view and common behaviors in an increasingly diverse work setting

Let's look at each one in more detail.

CAPABILITY 1: TALENT

An organization with talent as a capability is good at attracting, motivating, and retaining competent and committed people. Ensuring that your company has a talent capability means going beyond such platitudes as "people are our most important asset" and "strategy follows people" and instead investing time and resources to source, secure, and engage superior talent. We believe there is a formula for talent: *competence $\times$ commitment $\times$ contribution.*

Competence means that individuals have the knowledge, skills, and values required for today's and tomorrow's jobs. One company clarified competence as the "right skills, right place, and right job."

Committed or engaged employees work hard, put in their time, and do what they are asked to do. In the last decade, commitment and competence have been the accepted definition of "talent."

However, we have found that the next generation of employees may be competent (able to do the work) and committed (willing to do the work), but unless they are making a real *contribution* through the work (finding meaning and purpose in their work), then their interest in what they are doing diminishes and their talent wanes. Contribution occurs when employees feel that their personal needs are being met through their participation in their organization.

Organizations are the universal setting in today's world where individuals find abundance in their lives through their work, and they want this investment of their time to be meaningful. Simply stated, *competence* deals with the head (being able), *commitment* with the hands and feet (being there), and *contribution* with the heart (simply being).

In this talent equation, the three terms are multiplicative, not additive. In other words, if any one is missing, the other two will not replace it. A low result in competence will not ensure talent even when the employee is engaged and contributing. Talented employees must have skills, will, and purpose; they must be capable, committed, and contributing. Leaders need to improve each of these three dimensions to respond to the talent clarion call.

Capability 2: Leadership

An organization with a leadership capability is good at embedding leaders throughout the organization who deliver the right results in the right way through crafting and carrying a leadership brand. A leadership brand exists when the leaders from the top to the bottom of an organization transfer customer expectations to employee actions. These leaders are identifiable. They are focused. This leadership identity and focus begins with the customer. Customer expectations define the criteria by which leaders are judged. When organizations have a leadership brand, they deliver results. We have identified five steps to building a leadership brand.

Step 1: Nail the Fundamentals

Any brand takes a long time to build and includes two major elements: the *fundamentals* and the *differentiators*. For example, a Rolex has the fundamentals of any watch: a watch face, minute hand, second hand, and crystal. It also has brand differentiators— its look and feel and the accuracy of its timekeeping—that bespeak high quality. Both the fundamentals and the differentiators must be carefully crafted, but the fundamentals must be in place first. We call leadership fundamentals the "Leadership Code," which consists of leaders' ability to demonstrate competence as

- Strategists—able to position the firm for continued success with internal and external stakeholders
- Executors—able to implement systems that deliver results and to make change happen
- Talent managers—able to get the most out of people in the short term by motivating and engaging them
- Human capital developers—able to find ways to develop tomorrow's talent and groom employees for future opportunities
- Personal proficiency experts—able to learn, act with integrity, exercise emotional intelligence, make bold decisions, and engender trust

A successful leadership development model should incorporate all elements of the Leadership Code. An individual leader may have a predisposition in some areas and should be strong in at least one of the leadership fundamentals. Once these fundamentals are established, companies can move on to shaping their organization's leadership brand.

Step 2: Connect Leadership Behaviors to the Firm's Reputation You're Trying to Establish

Building a leadership brand begins with a clear statement, somewhat similar to a mission statement, that connects specific leadership skills and behavior to what the firm wants to be known for by its best customers. For example, Apple wants to be known for its outstanding ability to innovate and design user-friendly technology; to that end, it hires the best technologists and designers and encourages them to innovate. In contrast, Wal-Mart wants to be known for its everyday low prices, so it hires managers who are frugal and unassuming themselves, who can drive a hard bargain, and so on.

Step 3: Assess Leaders Using the Statement of Leadership Brand

Once a company has crafted a statement of leadership brand, it needs to evaluate individuals against the statement to make sure that they are living up to it. Firms must ensure that executives continue to embody the brand values as these individuals develop over time and progress through the leadership pipeline. This requires firms to assess leaders from the *customers'* point of view, measuring results less by what the individual manager (or the company) produces than by how customers perceive and value the company and its offerings. Here are some examples:

- Instead of worrying about goods *shipped* on time, customers care about whether they *received* their goods on time.
- Instead of concerning themselves about the firm's product *error rates*, customers notice when products they receive *aren't fully operational* on arrival.
- Rather than measuring *employee engagement to the firm,* a company should try to assess *the impact of employee engagement on customers.*

Step 4: Invite Your Customers and Investors to Participate in Designing and Delivering Management Practices Consistent with Your Leadership Brand

If your best customers or investors could observe or participate in the training you offer your leaders, how would they respond? Likewise, to what extent does your company's hiring, performance management, communication, and other management practices reflect customer expectations?

Step 5: Track Your Leadership Brand Efforts

The result of a leadership brand focus is good management that is unmoored from individualism, yet it lasts over time. As companies begin to develop as "leader feeder firms" and to "graduate" excellent leaders, they engender a reputation for very high quality management—which is the essence of a leadership brand. Such leadership bench strength can easily be seen in the frequency with which leaders who leave the firm go on to top positions in other corporations.

Capability 3: Agility

An organization with agility is good at implementing important changes quickly. Gaining speed goes beyond merely changing to executing fast change. Speed that comes from agility means that the organization has an ability to identify and move quickly into new markets, new products, new employee contracts, and new business processes. Leaders embed this capability into the organization in the following ways:

- By being focused on making decisions rigorously
- By implementing change processes throughout their organizations
- By removing bureaucratic barriers to change
- By eliminating organizational viruses

Building agility takes time because inertia resists change, but when large firms can act like small and nimble firms, they have mastered the speed capability. We see five main issues that leaders need to address in their pursuit of speed.

First, emphasize smart agility. Speed matters, but only to relevant and important issues, not trivial ones. Being faster at a bad idea or incorrect solution only gets wrong things done sooner. Leaders do smart speed when they use speed as a way to help accomplish business goals rather than as an end in itself, and when agility varies by business issue.

Second, start small. Leaders working to increase agility need to turn large, complex problems into small, daily, and doable actions—and then be consistent and persistent about pursuing those actions until a tipping point is reached and change occurs more rapidly.

Third, recognize capacity. Capacity measures the amount of change an institution or individual can absorb. Leaders need to ensure that change aspirations exceed resources, but not by too much. Managing capacity begins with answering the questions, "What do we most want to do?" and "What are we doing that we don't need to do?" Separating high- from low-priority issues and being explicit about what will and will not be done serve to free institutional and individual time and energy. These actions also help prioritize the workload so that resources and energy may be directed to the things that matter most.

Fourth, identify agility targets. For institutions, leaders may create a number of key initiatives to accomplish business goals. Your company is achieving agility or speed goals when these initiatives (e-commerce, quality, customer service, and so on) are done faster with similar or better quality. An indicator of institutional speed would be a 20 to 30% reduction in cycle time for any and all key initiatives, such as the time to respond to a new business reality or change to a new business focus.

Finally, recognize that agility also affects individuals. It's useful to calculate a return on time invested index to track trends in employee productivity, commitment, and engagement in their work. Individuals experience agility and speed under the following conditions:

• When they are able to focus on work that matters most
• When they feel they have control over their work
• When they see how their work aligns with the overall goals of the company

Moreover, individual speed can have the following results:

• Employees will take appropriate risks.
• Employees will feel more responsibility for their actions.
• Employees will be able to focus their time on important and value-added work.
• Employee enthusiasm, commitment, and productivity at work will increase.

Agility must be both institutional and individual. Processes may be improved when there is institutional agility, but if individuals are not feeling engaged in the effort, they may not be committed and productive, and over time the speed will diminish. Conversely, if individual behaviors are performed with more agility but the institutional processes remain slow, people will become frustrated, and the institutional changes won't be sustained.

Capability 4: An Outside-In Connection

An outside-in organization is good at building enduring relationships of trust with targeted external stakeholders. An outside-in connection produces value when it translates expectations from customers, investors, or communities into employee and organization actions.

Customer Connection

This type of connection occurs when the identity in the customer's mind becomes the basis for creating an organization's culture. When a firm develops an external reputation for quality, service, or price, customers rely on this identity and do business with the firm based on it.

This identity of the firm in the mind of its best customers should also translate to employee behavior. When employees inside behave congruently with customers' expectations outside, a unique bond and connection are forged. An organization's culture begins from the outside and moves in, through an understanding of the firm's external brand.

Investor Connection

This type of connection occurs when those who directly invest in the firm's performance and those who analyze that performance examine not only tangible but intangible results. Investors may gravitate toward firms with favorable intangibles, such as

- Fulfilled expectations
- Strategic clarity
- Functional competence
- Leadership depth

Managers who act on and communicate these external investor intangibles build confidence in investors.

Community Connection

A connection with the community occurs when the organization's policies and practices are congruent with sustainable, socially responsible, and ethical standards. Increasingly, Generation

Y employees want to work for companies who demonstrate social conscience and good citizenship through their policies and practices. Managing energy, working on environmental issues, and serving a broader humanity become a part of an organization's social identity.

CAPABILITY 5: STRATEGIC UNITY

An organization with strategic unity has the ability to articulate a shared point of view about the future. More organizations have strategies than accomplish them. Often this happens because there is no unity or shared understanding of the desired strategy.

Three agendas go into creating strategic unity:

1. *An intellectual agenda* ensures that employees from top to bottom share both what the strategy is and why it is important. This agenda is delivered through simple messages repeated constantly.
2. *A behavioral agenda* ensures that the strategy shapes how employees behave by telling employees what to do and by asking employees what they will do on the basis of the strategy. When employees are allowed to define their behaviors relative to strategy, they become committed to that strategy.
3. *A process agenda* ensures that the organization's processes (such as budgeting, hiring, and decision making) align with strategy. These processes may be reengineered to ensure that they create unity.

When all three agendas are in place, strategic unity follows.

We are surprised to discover how many leaders can't answer the simple question, "What is your business about?" Many respond with an industry affiliation: "We're in the chemicals business." Or they come up with a high-level activity report: "We make and sell vacuum cleaners." What they don't have is an insight derived from paring the business down to its *core of viability*. Business focus describes what makes the organization tick at the elemental level, and without it, it's very difficult to attain strategic unity. An organization demonstrates strategic unity when employees at all levels know what the organization is trying to do, what they are personally expected to contribute, and how they can make a difference.

IMPLICATIONS FOR THE NEW ORGANIZATION

Leaders at all levels should focus on their organization in terms of its capabilities, not its structure. For example, in meetings of the board of directors, good governance is not just about fiscal responsibility, management succession, or corporate ethics, but about ensuring that management understands and builds the capabilities that will execute strategy. As leaders work to define their strategic direction, they should also be disciplined about how they will execute that strategy. Focusing on organizational capabilities ensures that desired strategies are realized.

As we have worked with dozens of companies to conduct capability audits, we have learned some lessons. The capability audit assesses these five (and other) critical capabilities to determine how important they are and how well they are being done. No two audits will look exactly the same, but our experience has shown us that in general, there are good and bad ways to approach the process. You'll be on the right track if you observe a few guidelines:

Get focused. It's better to excel at two to three targeted capabilities than to diffuse energy over many. Leaders should choose only a few on which to spend their time and attention. This entails identifying which capabilities will have the most impact and will be easiest to implement, and prioritizing accordingly.

The remaining capabilities identified in the audit should meet standards of industry parity. Investors seldom seek assurance that an organization is average or slightly above average in every area; rather, they want the organization to have a distinct identity that aligns with its strategy.

Learn from the best. Compare your organization with companies that have world-class performance in your target capabilities—and don't hesitate to look outside your industry.

For example, the lodging and airlines industries have many differences, but they're comparable when it comes to several driving forces: stretching capital assets, pleasing travelers, employing direct-service workers, and so on. The advantage of looking outside your own industry for models is that you can emulate them without competing with them. And they're far more likely than your top competitors to share insights with you.

Create a virtuous cycle of assessment and investment. A rigorous assessment helps company executives figure out what capabilities will be required for success. This audit helps them determine where to invest management resources of time and money to improve. Over time, repetitions of the assess-invest cycle result in a baseline for benchmarking.

Compare capability perceptions. Like 360° feedback in leadership assessments, organizational audits may reveal differing views of the organization. For example, it's instructive when top leaders perceive a shared mind-set, but employees or customers do not.

Therefore, involve your stakeholders in your improvement plans. For example, if your investors rank your firm low on a particular capability, the CEO or CFO should meet with the investors to discuss specific action plans for moving forward.

Match capability with delivery. Leaders need not only to talk about capability but also to demonstrate it in results; rhetoric shouldn't exceed action. Outline expectations in a detailed plan. One approach is to bring together leaders for a half-day session to generate questions similar to the following so that the plan will clearly address these issues:

- What measurable outcome do we want to accomplish with this capability?
- Who is responsible for delivering on it?
- How will we monitor our progress in attaining or boosting this capability?
- What decisions can we make immediately to foster improvement?
- What actions can we as leaders take to promote this capability? Such actions may include developing education or training programs, designing new systems for performance management, and implementing structural changes to house the needed capabilities. The best capability plans specify actions and results that will occur within a ninety-day window.

Avoid underinvestment in organizational intangibles. Often leaders fall into the trap of focusing on what is *easy to measure* instead of what is *in most need of repair.* They read balance sheets that report earnings, EVA, or other economic data, but they miss the underlying organizational factors that may add value. Don't fall into that trap.

Don't confuse capabilities with activities. An organizational capability is a bundle of activities, not any single pursuit. So leadership training, for instance, needs to be understood in terms of the capability to which it contributes, not just the activity that takes place. Therefore, instead of asking what percentage of leaders received forty hours of training, ask what capabilities the leadership training created. Attending to capabilities helps leaders avoid looking for single, simple solutions to complex business problems.

CONCLUSION

The organization of the future exists today when leaders shift their focus from the structure of their organization to the set of capabilities the organization needs in order to execute the strategy. We've described five critical capabilities that leaders can identify, implement, and track to help their organizations succeed. Leaders who build these capabilities today will be able to respond to a variety of potential futures.

Endnotes

1. Our work on capabilities can be found in our book *How Leaders Build Value* (Hoboken, NJ: Wiley, 2003) and in our article "Capitalizing on Capabilities," *Harvard Business Review,* June 2004.

2. Those who have studied business trends include Gary Hamel, *The Future of Management* (Boston: Harvard Business School Press, 2007); Adrian Slywotsky and Karl Weber, *The Upside: The 7 Strategies for Turning Big Threats into Growth Breakthroughs* (New York: Crown Business, 2007); and Thomas Davenport and Jeanne Harris, *Competing on Analytics: The New Science of Winning* (Boston: Harvard Business School Press, 2007).

CHAPTER THREE

THE LEADER'S MANDATE
Create a Shared Sense of Destiny
James M. Kouzes and Barry Z. Posner

Jim Kouzes and Barry Posner are the coauthors of the best-selling and award-winning book The Leadership Challenge, *now in its fourth edition, with more than 1.5 million copies sold, as well as more than a dozen other books on leadership. They are also the developers of the highly acclaimed Leadership Practices Inventory, a 360° questionnaire assessing leader behavior that has been administered to more than five hundred thousand leaders and more than three million observers worldwide.*

Kouzes is the Dean's Executive Professor of Leadership at the Leavey School of Business, Santa Clara University, and the Wall Street Journal *has cited him as one of the twelve best executive educators in the United States.*

Posner is both the dean and professor of leadership in the Leavey School of Business, Santa Clara University. He has received numerous teaching awards and the President's Distinguished Faculty Award, and is the author or coauthor of more than a hundred research and practitioner-focused articles.

The capacity to imagine exciting future possibilities is the defining competence of leaders. Today's leaders are custodians of the future, and they must be concerned about tomorrow's world and those who will inherit it. It's their solemn duty to leave their organizations in better shape than they found them.

This chapter is excerpted and revised with permission from *A Leader's Legacy*, by James M. Kouzes and Barry Z. Posner (San Francisco: Jossey-Bass, 2006). Copyright John Wiley & Sons, Inc. All rights reserved.

We've surveyed thousands of people on what they want in their leaders, and they tell us that being *forward-looking* is second only to *honesty* as their most admired leader quality. On average, 72% of respondents select it. In Asia, Europe, and Australia, the preference for forward-looking is a full 10 percentage points higher than it is in America. At the more senior levels in organizations, those selecting *forward-looking* constitute nearly 90%. This isn't just confirmed in our own studies. Every serious student of the subject asserts that leaders must have the capacity to envision an uplifting and ennobling vision of the future and to enlist others in a common purpose.

That's the good news.

Here's the bad news: *today's leaders stink at it.* Even though being forward-looking is a highly valued leadership competence, it's the one that leaders are least capable of demonstrating. And there's more bad news. Those of us who help leaders become better at creating and communicating visions of the future stink at it, too.

We know this because ever since we started measuring leadership practices, this is the competency that's the least understood, appreciated, and demonstrated. Leaders report that they're not very good at or comfortable with envisioning the future and enlisting others in a common vision. The feedback from their constituents is even more unfavorable. This is the skill set at which the vast majority of leaders need to become significantly more capable.

That raises two questions. If there's reliable evidence and general consensus that it's so important for leaders to articulate a vision and get others excited about it, why do leaders do so poorly at it? And if academics and practitioners alike agree on its value, why are we still struggling after so many years to develop this capacity in leaders—and what can we do about it?

WE'RE HOSTAGE TO THE PRESENT

Whenever we ask our clients and students about these low scores, the most frequent explanation is that people and organizations today are hostage to the present. They tell us that the demands of the business culture keep leaders focused on the quarterly profits, preventing them from spending enough time thinking *beyond* the next three months. In nonprofits and government agencies, it's the current crisis that consumes the majority of everyone's time.

Another thing that keeps people from thinking long term, we're told, is the pace of change. Things are just moving so fast that many believe it's impossible to know what's going to be happening in a year, let alone three, five, or ten years.

Then there's the increased complexity of problems. Everything seems to be related to everything else.

And there's also all the frightening uncertainty in the world. It's tough to get a clear picture of where you're headed when the landscape keeps shifting.

And finally, most of us feel overworked. How can you squeeze in time to think about the future when you're too tired to think about what you are going to have for dinner?

All these explanations have some truth to them. The workload is unlikely to get much lighter any time soon. Wall Street does apply constant pressure to meet or exceed investors' quarterly expectations, and it punishes organizations if they don't. Citizens want action now on critical issues that affect their lives. Customers want their needs met today. And you have only to look at the headlines to know how rapidly things change and how complex and uncertain our world is.

How can anyone possibly be more forward-looking when we're all driving under the influence of all these pressures?

WE JUST HAVE TO PAY MORE ATTENTION

We're sorry to say, but none of the pressures that are holding people hostage are going to go away. The likelihood is miniscule that investors, citizens, employees, or customers are going to stop insisting that leaders remain vigilant about current operations. New advances in technology will surprise us all daily. International disputes will still threaten our security, and natural disasters will create hardship and heartache. The world will continue to serve up unexpected challenges. That's just the way it is. Even so, people still want leaders to be forward-looking. That won't change either.

Despite the daily pressures that hold your mind hostage, you *can* be more future oriented. As counterintuitive as it might seem, the best place to start creating the future is by *being more mindful in the present*. The failure to be forward-looking may be due more to your mindlessness in the present than to any other factor. You may be operating on automatic pilot, not really noticing what's going on around you, believing that you know everything you need to know, viewing the world through preestablished categories, and operating from a single point of view. You're not really "present" at all. Your body may be in the room, but your mind has been shut off, become distracted, and lost perspective.

To increase your ability to conceive of new and creative solutions to today's problems, you have to *stop, look,* and *listen.* You have to *stop doing* for some amount of time *each* day. You have to remind yourself that most of the disruptive electronic devices have an off switch. Turn off the cell phone, the pager, the instant messaging, the e-mail, the PDA, and the browser. Stop being in motion.

Then start noticing more of what's going on around you right now. To notice things, you have to be present, you have to pay attention, and you have to be curious. Look around. Most innovation is more about noticing what's going on in the here and now than it is about gazing into some crystal ball. The best leaders are and have been those who are the best observers of the human condition. They just pay more attention than everyone else to all that's around them. So look at the familiar in novel ways. Look for differences and distinctions. Look for patterns. Look at things from multiple perspectives. Look for unmet needs.

And listen to the weak signals. Listen to the unheard voices. Listen for things you've never heard before. When you stop, look, and listen, you will always be amazed at all the possibilities.

Explore Future Possibilities

Even as you stop, look, and listen to messages you're being sent in the present, you also need to raise your head and gaze out toward the horizon. Being forward-looking is not the same as meeting the deadline for your current project. Whether that project ends three months, one year, five years, or ten years down the road, the leader's job is to think beyond that end date. The leader has to ask the question, "What will we be doing *after* the project is completed?" If you're not thinking about what's happening *after* the completion of your longest-term project, then you're thinking only as long term as everyone else. In other words, you're redundant! The leader's job is to think about the next project, and the one after that, and the one after that.

And remember: you don't have to do this all by yourself. Just because your constituents expect you to be forward-looking doesn't mean you can't ask for help. For example, our colleague Joel A. Barker—futurist, author, and filmmaker—uses an historical analogy to provide insight into how leaders can enlist others in their quest to discover what lies ahead:

> Before a good wagon master rolled the wagons, he sent out scouts to see what was over the horizon. Rapid exploration by scouts provided crucial information that allowed the wagon master to make quicker decisions with higher confidence and move the wagons forward at a faster pace.
>
> Twenty-first century leaders need their own scouts. But instead of searching the geography of place, your scouts need to search the geography of time. The most important frontier for you is the next five to 10 years.[1]

Get everyone involved in asking, "What's next?" Where is this assignment right now taking us *in the future?* And talk out loud about the implications of the things you anticipate. Joel also offers this important lesson from his work: "I have found that the most important implications of any change are rarely those that spring immediately from the initiating event, be it an innovation, an emerging trend, the introduction of a competitor's product, a strategic objective. Instead, the most important implications are usually found several orders out from the initiating event. That is, they are the implications of the implications of the implications of the initial event that cascade out in all directions. This is where unintended consequences lurk."

Ask another crucial question: "What's better?" What's better than what you're now doing or anticipate doing in the foreseeable future? The leaders we have talked to share the perspective that helping people find meaning and purpose in their current situations by focusing on making life better in the long run is a key ingredient in getting extraordinary things done.

All enterprises or projects (big or small) begin in the mind's eye; they begin with imagination and with the belief that what's merely an image can one day be made real. In order for you to meet your constituents' expectations that you scout the geography of the future, you have no choice as a leader but to take yourself on journeys in your mind to places you have never been before.

It's imperative that you spend *less time on daily operations* and *more time on future possibilities.* Doing so is one of the very few things that make leadership different from other roles, and you must make it a priority. This is also where the creation of legacies begins—in the process of deciding how you want the world to be different from what it is today.

It's Not Just the Leader's Vision

At some point during all this talk over the years about the importance of being future oriented, however, leaders got the sense that they were the ones who had to be the "visionaries." Often with the encouragement of a lot of leadership developers (including us), leaders came to assume that if others expected them to be forward-looking, then they had to go off all alone into the wilderness, climb to the top of some mountain, sit in a lotus position, wait for a revelation, and then go out and announce to the world what they foresee. Leaders have assumed that it's *their* vision that matters and that if it's *their* vision, then *they* have to create it.

Wrong! This is *not* what constituents expect. Yes, leaders are expected to be forward-looking, but they aren't expected to be prescient or clairvoyant. Exemplary leadership is not about uttering divinely inspired revelations. It's not about being a prophet. It's actually much simpler than that.

What people really want to hear is *not* the leader's vision. They want to hear about *their own* aspirations. They want to hear how their dreams will come true and how their hopes will be fulfilled. They want to see themselves in the picture of the future that the leader is painting. The very best leaders understand that it's about inspiring a *shared* vision, not about selling their own idiosyncratic view of the world.

Maybe your constituents don't tell you this quite so directly. Maybe they don't tell you this at all. But we're quite certain that very few grown adults like to be told in so many words, "Here is where we're going, so get on board with it." No matter how dressed up the message is in all kinds of fine and fancy language, most adults don't like being told where to go and what to do. They want to feel part of the process.

Buddy Blanton, a principal program manager at Rockwell Collins Display Systems, learned this lesson firsthand. He got his team together one morning to ask them for some feedback about his leadership. He specifically wanted to learn how he could be more effective in creating a shared vision. What they told him helped him understand that it's the process and not just the vision that's critical in getting people all on the same page:

> One of the team members that I most respect . . . spoke first. She is very good at telling it like it is, but in a constructive manner. She provided me the following feedback: "You have all of the right skills," she said. "You have global vision and understanding. You're a good, sincere listener. You're optimistic, and you command respect and trust of team and colleagues. You're open and candid, and you are never shy about saying what needs to be said to team members." Then she gave me this advice, "You would benefit by helping us, as a team, to understand how you got to your vision. We want to walk with you while you create the goals and vision so we all get to the end vision together."

> Another team member said that sharing this road map would help him to feel more ready to take the initiative to resolve issues independently. A couple of other team members stated that this communication would help them to understand how the goals are realistic. One of the team members said that they would like to be a part of the vision-building process so they could learn how to better build visions for their team.

> I looked at the group, and it was clear that they were in agreement that they wanted to be a part of the vision sharing and development process. We launched into a discussion on our vision for the program, and each person contributed to the discussion.

> Previously, I believed that the team would benefit more by my setting the road map and vision and then just letting them give me

feedback when they thought that I was off base—which they have done on numerous occasions. From our discussion, it was clear that the team wants to be included in the process. I asked them if it would be useful if we got together every two weeks to discuss and build our program vision, similar to what we did that day. The feedback was a resounding Yes.

The vast majority of us are just like Buddy's team members. We want to walk *with* our leaders. We want to dream with them. We want to invent with them. We want to be involved in creating our own futures. This doesn't mean you have to do exactly what Buddy did, but it does mean that you have to *stop taking the view that visions come from the top down.* You have to stop seeing it as a monologue, and you have to start engaging others in a *collective dialogue* about the future.

YOU HAVE TO SEE WHAT OTHERS SEE

Take a look at some data for a minute and see what it tells you. On our thirty-item assessment instrument, the Leadership Practices Inventory,[2] six items measure a leader's effectiveness in "Inspiring a Shared Vision." Three of these six items are in the bottom four lowest-scoring items, making inspiring a shared vision the leadership practice that leaders consistently do least effectively. (The item at the very bottom of the list is on seeking feedback.) Here are the three items in question:

1. "I describe a compelling image of what our future could be like."
2. "I appeal to others to share an exciting dream of the future."
3. "I show others how their long-term interests can be realized by enlisting in a common vision."

Examine these three statements for a moment. What do you notice? Do you see that each of these is about how well a leader engages others in the vision? Do you see that these statements are about "us" and not "me," "we" and not "I"? The underlying reason for such a poor showing on Inspiring a Shared Vision doesn't seem to be because leaders aren't talking about the future or that they don't have personal conviction about the future. What leaders really struggle with is *communicating an image of the future that draws others in*—that speaks to what others see and feel.

To be able to describe a compelling image of the future, you have to be able to grasp hold of what *others* want and need. To appeal to others and to show them how their interests will be served, you have to know *their* hopes, dreams, motives, and interests.

That means you have to know your constituents, and you have to speak to them in language they will find engaging. If you're trying to mobilize people to move in a particular direction, then you've got to talk about that future destination in ways that others find appealing. It's got to be something that *they* care about as much as—or even more than—you do.

Getting others excited about future possibilities is not about creating better PowerPoint presentations. It's not about better public speaking skills, although that would help. And it's certainly not about being more charming or charismatic.

It's about intimacy. It's about familiarity. It's about empathy. The kind of communication needed to enlist others in a common vision requires understanding constituents at a much deeper level than most of us normally find comfortable. It requires understanding others' strongest yearnings and their deepest fears. It requires a profound awareness of their joys and their sorrows. It requires experiencing life as they experience it.

Being able to do this is not magic, nor is it rocket science. It's really all about listening very, very closely to what other people want.

Now some of you at this point may be saying to yourselves, *All well and good, but what about breakthrough innovations? Aren't leaders supposed to focus on the next new thing? Nobody ever said they wanted a hybrid car or an iPod or a Google search function.* True, but people did say they wanted to clean up the environment for their kids, take their music with them on the road, and access information more quickly and globally.

We submit that these innovations were not and are not the result of hermits' coming up with ideas in isolation. In fact, they are the result of superb and attentive listening. They are the result of being highly attuned to the environment. They are the result of a deep appreciation of people's aspirations.

And what if people don't know what they need? This is all the more reason to be a stellar listener. Listening is not just about the words. It's also about what is unspoken. It's about reading between the lines. It's about paying attention.

What breakthrough innovators and exemplary leaders understand is that *all* of us want a tomorrow that is better than today. We don't necessarily all want exactly the same thing, but whatever we want, we want it to be an improvement. The critical skill is in discovering just what "new and improved" means to others.

If you're going to stir the souls of your constituents, if you are going to lift them to a higher level of performance, then this is what you need to know: it's not the *leader's* vision; it's the *people's* vision that matters most.

Endnotes
1. Joel A. Barker, "Scouting the Future," 2005. Available online at www.implicationswheel.com.
2. James M. Kouzes and Barry Z. Posner, *The Leadership Practices Inventory (LPI): Facilitator's Guide Package, 3rd Edition* (San Francisco: Pfeiffer, 2003).

CHAPTER FOUR

A DIFFERENT KIND OF COMPANY

Srikumar S. Rao

Srikumar S. Rao conceived Creativity and Personal Mastery, a pioneering course that was one of the highest rated at Columbia Business School, London Business School, and the Haas School of Business at the University of California at Berkeley. It is believed to be the only course at a top business school to have its own alumni association. He also created the Advanced Leadership Clinic, an innovative and intensive leadership workshop offered to senior executives. His book, Are YOU Ready to Succeed? Unconventional Strategies for Achieving Personal Mastery in Business and Life, *was published by Hyperion. Rao has been featured and quoted widely in the media. He is currently an adjunct faculty member at both the London Business School and Haas School of Business at the University of California at Berkeley. More information on his work is available at www.areyoureadytosucceed.com.*

In November 2007, I had dinner with Mohan Mohan, a former top executive of Procter & Gamble. When he retired seven years ago, he was running a big chunk of the company's international business and also played a major role in recruiting and training talent.

His success story was not atypical in the world of expatriate Indians. He came from a background of struggle but was highly intelligent. Education was his way out of birth circumstances and into a global world. He had spent virtually his entire working life at P&G, and the company polished him into a world-class executive and gave him status and wealth. I had met many such people, and each had fond memories of the organization that lifted them, and had kind words for it.

But Mohan had more than mere affection for his old employer. His eyes shone when he talked about the company and what it stood for. He had war stories galore of how multiple bosses went out of their way to prop him up when he was hit with personal adversity. Later, I heard from others about how inspiring a boss Mohan himself had been and why they remained in touch with him decades after they had left and achieved prominence in their own right.

It was this last characteristic that had led to the dinner. He was serving—pro bono—as the executive in residence at one of the top business schools in the world, and I had heard from countless students that he had helped them solve knotty career problems and led them to understand that unless they could convert a job into a calling, they were setting themselves up for a life of frustration and stress. Where and how, I asked him, had he developed his unusual worldview?

His eyes lit up. It was all from P&G, he explained. With the practiced flair of a conjuror performing a trick, he produced a somewhat dog-eared card—the P&G purpose statement. It explicitly called for prosperity to engulf the "communities in which we live and work." This was not PR hokum, as is the case with countless mission statements, Mohan explained. The company indeed lived by its credo, and that was where he himself was shaped and where he learned what he did.

I nodded. What really impressed me was that this multitalented executive—who could have written his own ticket as CEO at any number of companies—coached students for no fee. And that nearly a decade after he retired, he still carries around the company mission statement and refers to it several times a week.

I am still not sure whether this deep loyalty is a function of Mohan's peculiar upbringing and character or whether it is a natural by-product of P&G's culture. What I am sure of is that the organization of the future, if it is to survive and thrive, will have to be able to engender similar feelings in the vast majority of its workforce.

Describing the Ideal Job

I am in the unique position of knowing exactly what the company of the future will be like. More accurately, I know exactly what the employees of the future would love the companies they work for to be like. They are a highly intelligent, deeply driven, and fiercely ambitious bunch, and I have no doubt that, one way or another, they will bring their collective vision into being.

For many years, I have taught a course called Creativity and Personal Mastery at many of the top business schools in the world. It is a deeply introspective course, and one of the exercises calls for each participant to mentally craft and report on his or her "ideal job." They are required to consider every aspect of this job in excruciating detail, and many reports are fifteen to twenty pages or more. They are also encouraged to repeat this exercise every few months, and many send their later efforts to me as well.

I have read more than a thousand such reports and so can speak with some authority about what these highly desirable employees are seeking. I can also speak with the same authority about what they find distasteful about the organizations with which they are currently affiliated—and these are some of the largest and best-known firms in the world.

The Mission of the Organization of the Future

The mission of an organization is where it all starts. There is complete unanimity that the company has to stand for something greater than itself, that its existence serve the common weal.

There is much cynicism here. Virtually every major commercial organization today has a carefully crafted mission statement that promises to honor employees (which many organizations claim are "our greatest asset"), honor customers, serve society, and be a force for good. In the vast majority of cases, this statement hangs unnoticed on the wall of the boardroom. Most senior executives do not even know it, and it is rarely, if ever, brought up as the touchstone that shapes major decisions.

Instead, *expedience* is the driver, and the objective is to report financial growth that propels share price ever higher. In fact, growth in share price is quite often used to define success, and CEOs are lauded in the business press for increasing the market capitalization of their company. "Maximization of shareholder value" is what managers are supposed to accomplish, according to business school dogma; some academics even assert that managers are derelict in their duty and misguided if they let other considerations—such as the social desirability of the consequences of business actions—affect their decisions.

This viewpoint is roundly rejected by the vast majority of students. The "double bottom line" (that is, profits as well as social good) and the "triple bottom line" (profits, social good, and safeguarding the environment) are the concepts that resonate deeply with them.

They look for authenticity. Corporate social responsibility is PR window dressing in many companies, and these young people are aware of this. When crucial decisions have to be made and in a hurry, do managers instinctively check to confirm that what they are considering jibes with the mission? Are potentially profitable opportunities rejected because they do not mesh with what the company stands for?

In short, does the company walk the talk? I see a strong desire—indeed a hunger—to be a part of something that is noble, that is of service to a greater cause. There is a willingness to commit to an enterprise where a glorious mission is not a framed statement on a wall but a living, breathing expression of purpose that serves as a guidance device at key junctures. For example, Google founders Larry Page and Sergey Brin were painfully aware of the damage that can be caused by arrogant and unthinking behavior by an industry leader. So they came up with an injunction to "First, do no evil," which has resonated strongly with many people. Somehow it rings true, and the company has become larger than life as a beacon for those seeking a humane workplace. It remains to be seen whether it can retain its mystique as it continues growing.

The idea of business serving a social cause is a counterpoint to the notion that the business of business is to be profitable, with the "hidden hand" working to deliver benefits to society. Thus profits are important, but so is the well-being of various stakeholders, such as employees, customers, suppliers, shareholders, and the community at large.

An even more radical viewpoint is just starting to be raised and is perhaps best articulated by Nobel prize–winner Muhammad Yunus in his book *Creating a World Without Poverty*. This notion is that the function of business is to serve society. Profits are a by-product and should be plowed back into the enterprise to expand its reach and depth. Shareholders move to the back of the bus, if they are on it at all.

Most of my students (and remember, I teach at top business schools!) do not agree entirely with this. They do believe, and strongly, that profits are important and should be distributed to "owners." But they also believe, and even more strongly, that companies have obligations to employees, customers, and society and that these cannot and should not be subordinated to the interests of stockholders.

On the basis of what I have heard from so many, I can confidently state that the classical idea of capitalism—where each person acts solely in his or her self-interest, and market forces somehow magically transform this selfish activity into social good—is dying. There are far too many instances of market break-downs, and these cause incalculable human misery.

What will emerge is a different take on capitalism—one where intent is important, where the stated objective of commercial ventures is the alleviation of poverty and human suffering. Markets will still have a big role to play, but they will not be allowed to reign unchecked, and there will be interventions to prevent the untrammeled excess so common today.

HOW EMPLOYEES SHOULD BE TREATED IN THE ORGANIZATION OF THE FUTURE

How employees are treated is the single most important touch-stone of how a company is regarded. This is hardly surprising, because virtually all the program participants are employees or in the process of becoming employees.

Practically every company boldly states that its employees are its "most valuable" assets. Nevertheless, at the slightest hint of a downturn, these valuable assets are thrown overboard with more alacrity than ballast. This hypocrisy is quickly noted, and employees reciprocate with their own form of revenge. Unfortunately, this revenge is terrible for both the individual and the organization. They react by becoming disengaged and disheartened, with the attendant physical and emotional damage. And the organization gets only a fraction of the innovative ideas and dedicated service it could have obtained.

The following paragraphs describe what the best and brightest employees are looking for, and organizations that will flourish tomorrow will provide all these qualities to some degree and quite a few to an exceptional degree.

Trust. This is hugely important. Each employee needs to know that he or she is trusted and that the company not only gives autonomy to each employee but also expects each employee to use initiative.

Lack of trust manifests itself in many ways, from close scrutiny of expenses and time sheets to hoarding of relevant information. There are sound legal and business reasons why some information cannot be shared, and this is fine. What is important, however, is that employees know what cannot be revealed and why, and they should be kept informed about other matters. Employees should be given discretion to act on their own, and the occasional mistake should be treated as a learning opportunity, instead of as a reason for punishment.

Justice. Employees need to know that there exists a set of values and rules that apply to everyone regardless of rank. They need to know that these rules are applied uniformly and openly. And they need to know that there are mechanisms in place to prevent abuse of rules, that appeals are also open, and that resolution is speedy.

Transparency. In any organization, decisions need to be made— marketing decisions, financial decisions, personnel decisions, technology decisions. The process by which these decisions are made is what counts. Do employees feel that any relevant information they have is solicited and used appropriately? Do they feel that they can participate in the process if they have anything relevant to contribute? "Black box" decisions produce alienation and disengagement.

Learning. Do employees feel that they are learning? Do colleagues and supervisors care whether their employees are being stretched without being overwhelmed? Obviously, whether a person learns or not is as much a function of individual curiosity and determination as it is of organization design. But what is obvious is the intent—or lack of it—to provide a challenging environment, where employees are constantly upgrading skills and given the tools with which to do so.

Competence. Are most persons, by and large, competent? Do they have the requisite domain knowledge and interpersonal skills? Employees need to know that the people they are dealing with have been screened, are regularly evaluated, and are fully capable of performing the tasks with which they are charged. This is a simple and intuitively appealing concept, but is extremely difficult to pull off.

If an employee is not performing well, is that person going through a bad period? Should he or she be cut some slack, or should that employee be terminated for the greater good of the company? How such decisions are made obviously has implications for justice and transparency as well.

Fun. Is there a sense of jollity, an understanding that we are all humans in this predicament called life and that we might as well have a blast while traversing our respective paths? Does laughter come spontaneously and often? Is hilarity encouraged? There is a place for decorum, but if the environment is a grind, then there will be no long-term loyalty and commitment. It is important to be serious, but it is even more important not to take oneself too seriously.

Flexibility. We live in complex times, and the lives of many employees are complicated. Traditional family support structures don't exist for many, and there are demands from children, parents, and spouse, not to mention nontraditional connections, such as parents of a former spouse who remain grandparents of children. When an employee needs accommodation, what is the company attitude? Is it "Let's see if it is possible to make your request happen"? or is it "Sorry, that's against procedure and sets a bad precedent"? The former is the wave of the future.

The Progressive Organization's Attitude Toward Its Employees

On a par with mission in terms of importance—and stemming from it as well!—is the company's attitude toward its employees. Does it view employees as a means of accomplishing its goals? Or is it dedicated to helping each person reach his or her highest potential? Proper alignment can ensure that these are not distinct and contradictory aims. But it does take an enlightened leadership even to understand this, let alone achieve it.

Far too many organizations try to "motivate" dispirited and disengaged employees. Bluntly speaking, this is an attempt to manipulate people into doing what they find distasteful and would not otherwise do. Motivation is not something that needs to be inculcated. It is built into the DNA of every worker. No worker on the first day in a new job thinks, "In six months, I look forward to being a disgruntled clock-watcher, counting the minutes until Friday evening." Instead, a new employee is usually afire with enthusiasm and eager to get started. Disillusionment happens gradually.

The organization of the future will not even attempt to "motivate" workers. Instead, it will go to great lengths to find out what is demotivating them and try to get rid of whatever that is. When the company mission is crafted as described earlier, members inherently resonate with it. There is more than abundant motivation.

Managers continually remind everyone of the mission and make sure that it is followed in spirit at all times. It is also revisited frequently and updated as necessary and as the world changes. Involvement by all workers in this process is what keeps motivation high. It is a natural by-product of the process, not an end.

Countless firms have found that investing in their employees is sound business practice in addition to being the proper thing to do. For example, the early success of Starbucks owed much to Howard Schultz's decision to offer health insurance to part-time workers. He did it because of his own experience with poverty, and the happy by-product was that employee turnover dropped precipitously, as did training costs. Similarly, Costco's Jim Sinegal pays his employees significantly more than his parsimonious rival, and the company enjoys considerably higher sales per square foot.

HOW CUSTOMERS SHOULD BE TREATED BY THE ORGANIZATION OF THE FUTURE

What is the company's attitude to customers? There is certainly recognition that without customers, the company will not survive, but how does the organization view its customers? Are they a necessary evil? Or are they "the reason why we exist"? Where is the explicit focus? Is it on delivering outstanding value, or is it on extracting the maximum possible cash?

It is amazing how quickly the attitude of leadership becomes apparent to the rank and file and is adopted by them; shortly afterwards, customers will note it too.

The organization of the future recognizes that providing superlative customer service has little to do with the customer. It has much more to do with the employee. When an employee delivers such service, that employee knows it deep inside and comes alive. Such employees love their jobs and are brimming with energy. There is never a problem with their "motivation."

The function of leadership is to make sure that every employee has the tools and training to provide such service. Leaders should also ensure that each employee is attuned to the market and quick to spot and report on any changes in the market or operating environment. Each employee also needs to be empowered to make the requisite changes in products, services, and delivery systems that are appropriate responses to such changes. Such rapid action by multiple employees is an organic self-correcting and regenerative process. And it works fabulously as long as the underpinnings of mission and leadership attitude are strong.

Frederick Reichheld articulated the concepts of good profits and bad profits in *The Ultimate Question,* his book on customer loyalty. *Good profits* come when the customer is delighted with the transaction and walks away with good feelings and a sense of satisfaction. Do you remember having a delightful meal at a restaurant, when the food was good, the service great, and the experience memorable enough that you still remember it? That restaurant earned good profit.

For example, when L. L. Bean started his company, he offered an unconditional lifetime money-back guarantee. He trusted his customers. There are tales of people who came in years after buying a piece of clothing and returning a threadbare garment, and they got their money back, with no questions asked. And, of course, the company earned hundreds of millions of dollars of good profits from countless customers who bought from it again and again and again.

In contrast, *bad profits* come when customers are annoyed with the transaction and resent paying for what they did. They walk away with a residue of ill will, and they'll defect at the first available opportunity. Have you ever cried "Foul" when you looked at the long-distance charges for a short phone call you made from your hotel room? That is an example of bad profit.

And, of course, there is a huge amount of *mediocre profit*, resulting from transactions with which the customer is neither thrilled nor mad. This possibly represents the majority of commercial transactions.

The company of the future works hard to ensure that its personal balance is skewed strongly toward good profits and that its bad profits are minimal or nonexistent. Delighted customers keep coming back, and there are other benefits as well. Good profits come when an organization is so aligned with its stakeholders that employees feel fulfilled and alive, and the organization becomes a vibrant and fun place to be a part of.

HOW SUPPLIERS SHOULD BE TREATED BY THE ORGANIZATION OF THE FUTURE

How does the company view its vendors? Are they the enemy to be defeated by beating them down on price and terms? Or are they trusted partners in a holistic enterprise that ultimately leads to delighted customers and a better society? Is it a transactional relationship easily abandoned when someone else comes along with a better price or more favorable terms? Or is it a longer-term association based on warm mutual interests?

The organization of the future does not view negotiations with a supplier as a zero-sum game and never tries to seize an unfair advantage. Instead, it leaves a tidy pile on the table. It recognizes that even an attempt to extract that last bit of value leaves a legacy of bitterness that poisons the well for employees of both companies.

Instead, this organization enters into a partnership where it readily shares information and technical know-how to improve its supplier's operations and profitability, even as it seeks to lower its own costs by asking for lower prices.

This is a delicate balance, and it is quite easy to get the steps wrong in this dance. The only thing that will make it work is the intent of the company and the trust that has been built up over time.

And this again leads back to the mission. Suppliers are no different from employees. They too are energized and motivated to be a force for good. If they see that this is your sincere reason for existence, they will rally around and cut you a lot of slack.

For example, Honda buys more than 80% of every car from external suppliers. Unlike U.S. car companies, it does not "squeeze suppliers to the point that their survival is threatened," notes Raj Sisodia, coauthor of *Firms of Endearment*. Instead, it partners with its vendors in a Best Partner program that has earned it production improvements averaging 48%, as noted in the book.

How Shareholders Should Be Treated by the Organization of the Future

Shareholders are the "owners" of our public companies. And financial markets reward short-term performance and do not distinguish between good profits and bad profits. It's a major challenge for organizations to recognize the legitimate need for solid returns by shareholders and to refuse to cave in to the demands for short-term earnings, which may cause spikes in share price but cannot be sustained.

There is no easy answer to this one. However, transparency and authenticity make the task easier. When the mission is articulated clearly and is repeatedly held up, investors get the picture. Some will be drawn to it because they too want to be part of this effort. However, others will bail out, if they subscribe to the idea that profits are paramount and that companies have no business being concerned about social good.

Those who stick with the company know that earnings will be reinvested for the long term. They know that employees and other stakeholders will have their interests preserved. And they will be comfortable in the knowledge that this also bodes well for the value of their investment over the long haul.

And so, over time, the organization will attract investors who resonate with its values. For example, Berkshire Hathaway is perhaps the gold standard for shareholder satisfaction. There have been no stock splits, people scramble to buy one share, and many view it as a lifetime investment to be bequeathed, not sold. In no small part, this is because of CEO Warren Buffett's detailed, no-holds-barred letters in which he is candid about his thoughts, his mistakes, and his plans.

CONCLUSION

So there you have it: a picture of the organization of the future, drawn by so many bright and dedicated future employees. This chapter has described what they want to see, and that vision already exists in bits and pieces in various diverse entities. The organization of the future is dedicated to a cause greater than itself, determined to improve the well-being of a significant chunk of society. It lifts all those associated with it—employees, vendors, shareholders, and others—to a higher plane of self-actualization.

Its success stems from the deep identification with all its stakeholders and their collective knowledge that the *organization's success* is also *their success*.

CHAPTER FIVE

FREE TO CHOOSE

How American Managers Can Create Globally Competitive Workplaces

James O'Toole

James O'Toole is the Daniels Distinguished Professor of Business Ethics at the University of Denver's Daniels College of Business. Previously, at the University of Southern California, he held the University Associates' Chair of Management, served as executive director of the Leadership Institute, and was editor of New Management *magazine. O'Toole received his doctorate in social anthropology from Oxford University, where he was a Rhodes Scholar. He is the author of sixteen books, including* The Executive's Compass, Leading Change, *and* Creating the Good Life, *and coauthor (with Warren Bennis and Daniel Goleman) of* Transparency *and (with Edward Lawler) of* The New American Workplace, *on which this chapter is based.*

Judging from what they say in their annual reports, corporate executives believe that the success of their businesses rests heavily on the efforts, initiative, commitment, and motivation of "our people." Most major employers are sincere in this, as they are in their desire to treat "their people" right. Nonetheless, American executives increasingly outsource and offshore jobs, cut employee benefits, substitute contingent or contract workers for regular or permanent employees, eliminate traditional career paths, and reduce expenditures on worker training. When U.S. employees aren't losing their jobs to lower-paid workers in Asia, their salaries and benefits are being drastically cut by corporate executives who believe that the way to boost productivity is continually to reduce labor costs. In particular, many seek to lower those costs by reducing—or eliminating entirely—the health care benefits of "their people."

Why the apparent contradiction between word and deed? The executives' stock answer: "We have no choice." For example:

- In a 2005 interview on MSNBC, Wal-Mart's CEO argued that to serve the desires of customers for the lowest-priced goods, Wal-Mart's business model precluded offering higher wages, greater health insurance coverage, or more training to front-line workers.
- In 2003, when IBM announced plans to offshore the jobs of thousands of its American white-collar employees, the director for global employee relations explained, "Our competitors are doing it, and we have to do it."
- In 2006, when Boeing announced it would offshore 60 to 70% of components of its new 787 commercial jet, a leading aviation consultant explained, "If a company can go to China and get a widget for 10¢ an hour, and it costs $1 an hour in the U.S., what's the company to do?"
- When Delphi Corp. (General Motors' major parts supplier) called on the UAW to renegotiate the contract with its thirty thousand hourly workers—requesting wage and benefit give-backs on the order of 50 to 60%—the company's CEO said it had no choice: the alternative was bankruptcy, the loss of U.S. jobs, and the forfeiture of pension commitments. (Indeed, when the concessions weren't forthcoming, Delphi did declare bankruptcy.)

Many executives believe they are prisoners of iron economic laws which dictate that they have no choice but to match working conditions offered by their lowest-cost competitors. Unfortunately, increasing numbers of American managers have no alternative because they have strategically painted themselves into a corner: when their labor costs exceed the value their product commands in the market, there is little choice but to downsize, outsource, or offshore. Decades of poor strategic choices eventually do make it "too late" for managers to pursue positive employment practices that, had they been adopted earlier, might have led to better organizational performance.

But are top managers really as handcuffed as they assume? Do they have no viable option but to lower their working conditions to the level offered by their lowest-cost competitor, or to offshore jobs? After a yearlong review of hundreds of academic studies, my colleague Ed Lawler and I concluded that in fact, managers of most U.S. companies are free to choose workplace practices that would have *positive* future consequences for both their companies and employees.[1] We found numerous businesses that have created competitive advantages by adopting productive alternatives to the standard workplace practices in their industries. These companies have significant labor productivity advantages over competitors in their respective industries who, typically, pay their employees less and offer fewer benefits. We found not only that managers have *more* alternatives than they commonly assume but also that many are actually shortchanging their shareholders, not capturing the opportunity to differentiate themselves from their competitors by turning employees into strategic assets.

EMERGING EMPLOYER MODELS: LOW-COST COMPANIES AND GLOBAL COMPETITORS

American workers are increasingly employed by what we call "Low-Cost Companies"—that is, large grocery, discount, fast-food, and mall-store chains like Wal-Mart, where the customer is king. To keep prices low, employees in these companies face this unhappy situation:

- They are paid at (or close to) the minimum wage.
- They receive few if any benefits.
- They have no job security.
- They are given only the amount of training needed to do jobs that have been designed to be simple and easy to learn.

Because there is little opportunity for workers at the bottom in these companies to make a good living or to do interesting work—much less to make a career in them—these jobs mainly attract employees who cannot find other employment: retirees, students, and less educated workers with few other options.

Although Low-Cost Companies are the fastest-growing sector in terms of numbers of workers employed, the best-paid jobs in America are at what we call "Global-Competitor Companies." Characterized by their enormous size and geographic reach, these corporations compete in terms of the financial capital, skills, knowledge, and technology they are able to command. They are the glamour companies of the age—that is, industry leaders in information and telecommunications technology, consumer products, pharmaceuticals and biomedicine, financial and professional services, media and entertainment. These agile organizations move products, services, capital, jobs, operations, and people quickly and frequently across borders and continents.

Although workers are well paid in Global-Competitor Companies, they enjoy precious little stability or security, because these companies

- Increasingly hire people on a contractual basis and, where possible, outsource and offshore work.
- Offer their "contingent" workers no security beyond the time limits of their contracts, and no promise of a continuing employment relationship.
- Often look outside to hire even permanent and top-level employees, carefully limiting how much they spend on developing managers and professionals, let alone on the training of workers.
- Frequently offer "the new employment contract," in which they commit to telling employees what their strategy is and where they think future jobs in the organization will be, and workers then are told that their continued employment depends on their performance and the fit between their skills and the needs of the business.
- Are constantly searching for workers with the skills needed for today's challenges. And although they pay top dollar for that talent, they expect employees to work long hours and, especially, to be productive.

The relationship between these companies and their employees is thus transactional, not based on loyalty. The rewards are interesting work and high pay, not being part of a community or in a long-term employment relationship. Because they are global enterprises, these companies are adept at offshoring work; hence, they are not a source of domestic job creation, and they actually employ a *declining* portion of the total U.S. labor force.

The net effect of the growth of these two models is relentlessly grim for American workers: since 2000, labor's share of the gross domestic product has declined despite rising productivity, and it stems largely from the mistaken managerial assumption that low wages are the key to corporate competitiveness. A great many business executives believe that the way to boost productivity and profits is to continually reduce labor costs. But that strategy can be taken only so far: at a certain point, salaries and benefits can't be slashed any further, and, in the long term, comparative economic advantage then must be realized through the effective mobilization of an educated, engaged, and productive workforce. If America is to maintain its precarious position atop the world economy, its business executives must recognize that providing good jobs is not just a "nice thing to do": it is a competitive necessity for both their companies and their nation.

HIGH-INVOLVEMENT COMPANIES: THE THIRD WAY

Although many Americans are very familiar with Low-Cost and Global-Competitor Companies, they are less aware of a small number of businesses that understand that comparative advantage in a global economy must be realized by effectively deploying their workforces. These "High-Involvement Companies" are found in services as well as manufacturing industries, and they offer their employees

- Challenging and enriched jobs
- A say in the management of their own tasks
- A commitment to low turnover and few layoffs
- A relatively egalitarian workplace, with few class distinctions between managers and workers and relatively small ratios between the salaries of the CEO and the average worker
- Jobs organized in self-managing teams

- A strong sense that every employee is a member of a supportive community
- Extensive, ongoing training and education to all
- Salaries rather than hourly wages
- Employee participation in company stock ownership and a share in company profits

Moreover, the performance of these High-Involvement Companies is overwhelmingly consistent: the productivity of their workers more than justifies the high pay and good benefits they receive. In fact, *when managed correctly,* highly paid American workers prove to be *far more productive* than the low-wage overseas workers they compete against.

Research shows that managers at High-Involvement Companies organize work processes and systems in ways that allow employees to contribute significant amounts of "added value" to the products and services they make and provide. When managers give employees the organizational structure, resources, and authority needed for them to contribute their ideas and efforts, American workers almost always are able to compete effectively against their overseas counterparts. Workers in less developed countries routinely are outproduced through the ingenuity, initiative, and efforts of their American counterparts making steel at Nucor, motorcycles at Harley-Davidson, consumer goods at Procter & Gamble, and high-tech products at W.L. Gore and Associates. The evidence shows that the comparative advantage of having educated, motivated, and committed workers can be realized by a wide variety of businesses, both high-tech and low.

THE ECONOMIC DISADVANTAGES OF THE LOW-LABOR-COST STRATEGY

In a radical cost-cutting move, Circuit City announced in 2007 that it was dismissing thirty-four hundred of its most experienced employees. Although (in a surreal twist) the company offered to rehire many of those salespeople at lower wages, this is a common approach of many companies trying to gain competitive advantage. However, such bottom feeding may not be the most effective strategy. In fact, low wages paradoxically generate a variety of negative employee behaviors that add to the overall cost of doing business. Although managers rarely calculate these costs, they often turn out to be substantial:

Higher turnover. Employees at low-wage companies have significantly higher turnover rates than those at well-paying companies: for example, Wal-Mart has nearly a 50% turnover rate, and at many fast-food, retail, and service companies, the rates are even higher. Researchers have computed the total costs of such turnover as equal to one month's salary for unskilled workers and more than a year's salary for skilled ones.

More absenteeism. High rates of absenteeism are common at low-wage companies because employees don't lose much pay when they fail to show up for work (when absent, they often are out looking for better jobs!). Absenteeism has a negative impact on productivity: because low-wage employees rarely give notice that they won't be showing up, companies must overstaff in order not to be caught shorthanded. Absenteeism also negatively affects customer care: if enough workers aren't on the job to serve customers, or if customers can't find the same employee who helped them on their last visit, absenteeism drives business away and reduces customer loyalty.

Increased theft by employees. Added to these hidden costs is the readily measurable one of employee pilferage. In retail establishments, employee theft is higher when wages are lower. It's not clear how much of this is due to employees' justifying their criminal behavior because they are poorly paid, and how much results from the fact that employees willing to take low-wage jobs are more prone to theft; still, the cost directly hits the company's bottom line.

Increased focus on preventing unionization. Realizing that union organization means higher wages and more expensive benefits, low-cost employers hire consultants to develop antiunion tactics, conduct "educational" sessions for their employees, incur legal and court costs associated with fighting unions, and, in the case of Wal-Mart, even shut down operations to avoid a fate they see as worse than lost business.

Inability to attract talent. The most significant negative consequence of a low-wage strategy may well be that talented, hard-working, and motivated individuals simply do not interview for jobs at low-wage companies. Such companies thus end up with employees who are below average in their ability to perform on the job, with resulting low productivity and poor customer service.

Clearly, when all these costs associated with low wages are added up, paying low wages is a classic example of being penny wise and pound foolish.

HIRING EMPLOYEES WHO ADD VALUE

In almost all industries, the most profitable companies are those with the lowest overall operating costs, *not* those that pay the least. Put another way, the issue is not how much a company pays each worker; instead, it is how much its total labor costs are. The distinction is subtle but important.

For example, researcher Wayne Cascio examined 2004 data from retailer Costco and its competitor, Sam's Club (Wal-Mart's upscale brand),[2] which showed that

- Costco employees, on average, were paid $33,218 per year, and an additional $7,065 in benefits
- The average Sam's Club employee earned only $23,962, with $4,247 in benefits

However, *total* labor costs were actually *lower* at Costco, largely because Costco's 68,000 employees produced roughly the same amount in sales as did Sam's Club's 102,000. When the lower costs of turnover and pilfering and the higher rates of productivity were reckoned, setting aside the thousands of innovative ideas generated by its employees, it was "cheaper" in the long run for Costco to pay its people more.

These figures illustrate that labor rates do not simply equal labor costs. Costco's hourly labor rates are almost 40% higher than those at Sam's Club ($15.97 versus $11.52), but when employee productivity (sales per employee) is considered, Costco's total labor costs are significantly lower (9.8% versus 17%). James Sinegal, Costco's CEO, concludes that "Paying your employees well is not only the right thing to do, but it makes for good business." To make its high-wage strategy work, Costco constantly must look for ways to increase its efficiency, by repackaging goods into bulk items to reduce labor costs, speeding up just-in-time inventory and distribution systems, and boosting sales per square foot through being the industry leader in innovative packaging and merchandising. Costco employees have incentives to come up with such new ideas (even labor-saving ones) and to cooperate with management when the ideas are introduced.

In contrast, Wal-Mart's low-wage strategy brings undeniable benefits to customers: low prices. The company also has been a great long-term investment for shareholders, although they have not fared quite as well as Costco's in recent years. (In mid-2005, Wal-Mart's stock was selling at nineteen times earnings, compared to a multiple of twenty-three at Costco.) Yet Wal-Mart could not be the low-price leader in its industry if it simply paid the same high salaries and offered the same training and benefits package to its employees that Costco does. Costco's business model works because, unlike those at Wal-Mart, Costco's workplaces are organized in ways that allow employees to add value. At Costco, there is a deep managerial understanding that the correct metric to be used with regard to labor productivity is *total overall* labor costs and not *unit* labor costs.

BARRIERS TO ADOPTION OF HIGH-INVOLVEMENT PRACTICES

Given the manifest benefits to shareholders, employees, and society alike, why aren't there more High-Involvement Companies? Although American managers often say they would like to pay their employees more, they argue that they can't afford to do so and simultaneously keep the prices of their products competitive. As one CEO explained, "I would treat my employees as well as Starbucks treats theirs, *if* I could charge the equivalent for my product of $3 for a cup of *latte!*"

But managers who assume that higher profits drive better working conditions have their logic *backwards:* there are companies in virtually every industry that are profitable *because* they provide good jobs. As Starbucks' CEO, Howard Shultz, explains, the high-quality customer service that makes it possible for his company to charge a premium for its coffee *results from* the investments it makes in employees. He says Starbucks is able to offer its employees—even part-timers—"health coverage, stock options and discounted stock purchase plans, retirement savings plan, extensive training, a fun, team-oriented work environment . . . and tuition reimbursement for eligible employees with one or more years of service" not because the company charges a lot for a cup of coffee but, rather, because its highly productive, customer-sensitive employees allow Starbucks to do so. Ditto the productive contributions of employees at such diverse companies as UPS, Whole Foods, and Goldman Sachs.

The reason high-wage High-Involvement Companies have lower total labor costs than their low-wage competitors is thus misunderstood. It is commonly assumed that the greater a company's profitability, the greater the benefits it can provide. In fact, the opposite is—or can be—true. It often is *because* companies involve their workers in decision making, reward them fairly for their efforts, and provide them with good training and career opportunities that their employees reciprocate in terms of much higher productivity than workers in comparable, but low-wage, companies.

For example, there is a virtuous circle at High-Involvement Company SAS: this software producer offers more security and lifestyle-friendly benefits than its competitors, and, in turn, its employees seek to build long-term relationships with customers instead of going for one-off transactional sales. Obviously, treating employees well doesn't always produce better business results, but there are numerous examples of the two factors being mutually reinforcing.

The ability of American companies and workers to compete in world markets is greatly hampered by the widely held, but mistaken, managerial assumption that businesses need to be successful in order to be able to offer good jobs. Until more executives understand that companies need to offer good jobs in order for them to be able to succeed, the nation will be underemploying its most important resource: the American worker.

HOW ORGANIZATIONS TREAT WORKERS IS A MATTER OF CHOICE

Such companies as Nucor, W.L. Gore, SRC Holdings, Alcoa, Costco, Whole Foods, SAS, Southwest Airlines, Harley-Davidson, and UPS illustrate the benefits that arise when companies create workplace practices that meet the legitimate needs of workers, as well as those of managers and owners. These companies are at least as profitable as their competitors, typically more so, and that profitability in great part results from their leaders addressing the three deepest needs of workers:

1. Financial resources and security
2. Meaningful work that offers the opportunity for human development
3. Supportive social relationships

These examples also illustrate that some bad jobs can be turned into good ones *if there is the executive will to do so.* For example, whereas Delphi downsized and off-shored thousands of jobs and reduced the pay and benefits of its surviving American workforce, Harley-Davidson—in the same industry and with the same union—increased its U.S. manufacturing business, added jobs, and operated profitably *because* it turned Rust Belt manufacturing jobs into "good work" for its nearly ten thousand blue-collar employees. The company now competes successfully in the global export market against companies from low-wage countries. It is able to do so because its leaders were willing to create a viable business model based on High-Involvement practices. The top managers at Harley-Davidson and Starbucks should be regarded not as exceptions but as *role models* for other leaders who choose to change their employment models.

The statement "I have no alternative" is one of the surest indicators of leadership failure. Great leaders create viable options where others see none: they look for alternatives that haven't been tried, or for ones that others assume "won't work." They take the extra step and search for actions that serve all their stakeholders.

Recall that the CEO of Wal-Mart said that he has "no choice" but to pay his workers poorly in order to keep his costs down. Yet Wal-Mart's business model wasn't etched on stone tablets. Instead, it resulted from numerous choices made by Wal-Mart executives over many years. When the company's founder, Sam Walton, was alive, he made the following choices:

- He involved his employees in a generous stock ownership program.
- He encouraged his employees' engagement in making the enterprise successful.

- He personally continued to live frugally in the same middle-class neighborhood where he had begun his career.
- He took a relatively small salary, compared to other CEOs at the time.

In contrast, subsequent executives at Wal-Mart have made different choices in each of those regards.

Wal-Mart has chosen to favor investors over workers when it could have chosen to meet the needs of both, as Costco does. To be fair, Wal-Mart's executives are under constant pressure from Wall Street to make pro-shareholder choices. Indeed, Costco executives face the same pressure: in a 2005 *New York Times* article, a financial analyst argued that Costco should stop mollycoddling its workforce by paying such a large percentage of their health care premiums and, instead, reduce the company's contribution and then pay the savings out to its investors.

Much as Wal-Mart executives have chosen to accede to pressures from the investing community, Costco's leaders have chosen to reject them. In turn, investors are free to choose which of those, or other, companies to invest in. And workers also have a choice among employers . . . and Costco's High-Involvement working conditions give it an edge in competition with its rivals for the most productive employees. Such choices are the essence of a free-market economy.

The clearest demonstration that managers are free to choose occurred in 2007 when Wal-Mart's CEO suddenly—and surprisingly—announced the following changes:

- The company would offer health insurance coverage to more of its workers.
- It would support legislation to raise the minimum wage.
- It would henceforth be a global leader in its environmental practices.

What had changed? The primary reason for the CEO's about-face was the negative publicity the company had been receiving. But apparently the company did learn the positive lesson that in fact their hands were *not* tied when it comes to how they manage.

Experience shows that it is the options *not* considered that come back to haunt managers. When companies get into serious trouble, it is seldom because they have mistakenly chosen course A over course B; rather, they failed to consider option C. Executives who fail to consider creating High-Involvement workplaces are simply limiting their own range of options.

WHAT YOU CAN DO IN YOUR OWN ORGANIZATION

Clearly, not every company can benefit from adopting High-Involvement practices: there is simply no way in which the mass manufacturing of clothing can be done profitably in a postindustrial, high-wage economy such as America's. Yet American executives will find they have more room to choose the type and form of working conditions their companies offer than they commonly assume. Remember, it once was widely assumed that no airline could trust its employees to decide how best to serve customers—until Southwest did. It once was assumed that no company in the discount retail industry could succeed while paying its employees decent salaries and offering them full benefits—until Costco did. It was assumed that poorly educated blue-collar workers in old-line manufacturing firms could not be taught managerial accounting and then left to be self-managing—until SRC Holdings did. Once the conventional wisdom was that employees must be closely supervised and governed by rules—until W.L. Gore proved otherwise. And it was assumed that the first thing a company must do in a financial crisis is to lay off workers—until Xilinx discovered alternatives.

Today, some say that America has no choice but to export jobs to the developing world in order to remain competitive in world markets, and some say that America has no choice but to build protective barriers around the U.S. economy in order to prevent the export of jobs. In fact, we have a third, and better, alternative: by choosing to adopt High-Involvement practices, America can compete through the efforts and ingenuity of its workers and managers.

Endnotes

1. All data and quotes in this chapter from James O'Toole and Edward
    E. Lawler III, *The New American Workplace* (New York: Palgrave-
    Macmillan, 2006).
2. Wayne Cascio, "The Economic Impact of Employee Behaviors on
    Organizational Performance," in Edward E. Lawler III and James
    O'Toole (eds.), *America at Work: Choices and Challenges* (New York:
    Palgrave-Macmillan, 2006).

CHAPTER SIX

MANAGING THE WHOLE MANDATE FOR THE TWENTY-FIRST CENTURY

Ditching the Quick-Fix Approach to Management

Paul Borawski and Maryann Brennan

Paul Borawski, CAE, is executive director and chief strategic officer of the American Society for Quality, with thirty years of association management experience. He serves on the boards of several nonprofit organizations, including the Center for Association Leadership. Borawski was awarded the Georges Borel Medal by the European Organization for Quality for his contributions to quality in Europe. A past president of the Council of Engineering and Scientific Society Executives, Borawski has also been honored with its Leadership Award.

Maryann Brennan is principal for Brennan Worldwide. Previously, she served as quality manager for Chase Bank, as faculty for the Quality Management Master's Program at Loyola University, New Orleans, and as treasurer for ASQ. Since 1994, she has served as an examiner and is currently serving as a judge for the Baldrige National Quality Award and California Award for Performance Excellence programs. Borawski and Brennan are coauthors of "The Baldrige Model: An Integrated and Aligned Systems Approach to Performance Excellence" (Journal of Association Leadership, *April 2008*).

Issues for leaders at the dawn of the twenty-first century have not changed much since the days when the American Society for Quality (ASQ) was formed in the mid-twentieth century. ASQ's work with organizations from all sectors across the globe confirms key themes that keep being repeated—that organizations are challenged to

- Gain market leadership in the face of rapidly expanding yet crowded markets
- Improve contribution to profit by lowering costs
- Deliver remarkably good products and services to ever more discriminating consumers
- Stoke innovation to develop new and better products and services that edge out the competition

Moreover, these issues remain relevant as the shift of economic power and competition expands to such countries as China, India, Korea, Brazil, and Vietnam.

Over the past two decades, we've observed another key theme: too many organizations attempt to address these challenges through "spot treatment" management. In other words, they go for the quick fix. There is a hidden danger in getting on the treadmill of spot treatment management. Cite a problem—fix it. If you simply treat this and treat that, you have no idea whether your overall organization is becoming more fit over time or whether you are building organization-wide capabilities to achieve goals. In the twentieth century, when organizational change cycles were longer, you might have survived by putting out the fires you unwittingly set and relying on time for the benefits of improved processes. But that approach won't work in a future changing as rapidly as it is and destined to change faster.

Spot treatment thinking has limits. The problem is, you can't effectively improve a process in isolation from other processes in the system or without consideration of how a change in one process contributes or detracts from achieving the overall strategic goals of the organization.

For example, before Ritz-Carlton adopted a systems approach to management, it operated, like most hotels, using a *factory concept* with functional departments (for example, food and beverage, rooms, and purchasing). In a factory approach, if a change in a task in one function causes a problem in another, it most likely isn't identified until it reaches the customer.[1] Today, in contrast, Ritz-Carlton's systems approach uses a *nine-step quality improvement process* to ensure that changes planned for one task involve all those impacted in other tasks. Ritz-Carlton's commitment to a systems approach resulted in the company's exceeding the industry average for revenue per available room by more than 300% and nearly doubling pretax ROI and earnings.[2]

Here's another example. Before Caterpillar Financial Services takes on a Six-Sigma improvement project, it conducts an analysis to ensure that the project is linked to corporate strategy, is aligned to customer and market requirements, and reflects financial and operational needs and risks. Furthermore, Caterpillar Financial involves suppliers in improvement projects because Caterpillar views the role of suppliers as an essential element of its system. As a result of its focus on fixing a problem within the context of the whole, Caterpillar Financial has outperformed the S&P 500 even in times of recession.[3]

Why aren't more leaders thinking like that?

Overcoming the Addiction to Spot Management

One answer might be that the quick fix offers nearly instant gratification. Reliance on quick fixes can become addictive. It is easy to get hooked on them because they are easier to underwrite, and offer immediate results. Why select a more arduous and higher-cost longer-term fix when you can embrace an investment that is certain to yield an immediate return? Although a quick fix might alleviate some problems for a while, without a systems approach, those same problems often reemerge with even greater force and tenacity.

Another key theme that we are witnessing is that the tenure of leaders is declining. You need only to listen to the business news to note that in reaction to reports of disappointing results, stakeholders seek to remedy poor performance with their own quick fix by changing out the leader. Given the tyranny of the stockholders' demand for quarterly gains, no wonder leaders forgo longer-term and systemic solutions for the promise of immediate, albeit short-lived, relief.

The point is that organizations that choose spot management strategies to the exclusion of deploying a systems approach jeopardize the capability of the organization to sustain success in the future. And—this is important—applying spot treatments in the absence of system understanding almost certainly ensures that the treatments will have limited success.

Systems thinking is an essential ability for leaders who want their organizations to outperform and outlast competitors in the twenty-first century. The mandate for leaders is to develop a capacity to think about their organization as a system. They must understand the organization as a whole rather than as a collection or sum of its functions, departments, or problems.

VIEWING THE ORGANIZATION AS A WHOLE

Systems thinking, a not-so-new idea, is a management revolution that began in the mid-1940s, led by W. Edwards Deming, Joseph Juran, and Russell Ackoff, and further developed by Peter Drucker, Chris Argyris, Peter Senge, and other quality gurus.

Systems thinking calls for a paradigm shift. A systems perspective demands that you look at the big picture. Viewing an organization as a whole allows you to see patterns and make cause-and-effect connections at a higher level. It helps you understand the consequences, sometimes unanticipated, of tampering with a part of the system. Anything less than a systems approach, Dr. Deming told us, is simply meddling.

Russell Ackoff uses the analogy of a car to explain systems thinking: "If you take the best parts from each automobile manufacturer and put them together, you wouldn't have a car that works. It's the fit of the parts that determine the function of the whole system."[4]

In systems thinking, it follows that before you can fix one part of the system, you need to know how the parts of the organization fit together and how these interactions drive the performance of the whole.

The good news is that leaders don't have to reinvent the wheel to adopt a systems approach. In 1987, the notion of managing the organization as a system was codified (oddly enough) by an act of Congress. To improve competitiveness of U.S. companies,

Exhibit 6.1. Baldrige Criteria for Performance Excellence Framework.

Congress created the Baldrige National Quality Award program to promote best practices shared by high-performance organizations. Exhibit 6.1 illustrates the systems framework on which the award criteria are based. The systems operations are composed of the six Baldrige categories in the center of the figure that define an organization's operations and results. All arrows point to the integration and alignment of processes within a system and emphasize that all actions point toward results.

Developing Systems Thinking and a Learning Organization

Not all organizations using the Baldrige system framework seek award recognition. Most use Baldrige as a basis for becoming a learning organization. Organizations that rely on quick fixes don't necessarily learn from their endeavors. To avoid making the same mistake, you need to share knowledge about what worked and what didn't throughout your organization so that other functional areas with similar problems can apply the solution. Too often, a problem is solved by one department, but because the solution isn't shared with other departments, only one part of the system benefits, while the rest struggle on. Peter Senge points out that systems thinking is a necessary component of a learning organization.

This is not the case at Boeing Aerospace Support, which shares best practices at process councils. Councils provide process leadership and communicate horizontally across Boeing business units to ensure that the latest processes, procedures, and tools are shared. Organizational knowledge is shared so that "decisions are made in the best interest of the company as a whole."[5] As a result, Boeing Aerospace Support leveraged its aircraft design, development, and production capabilities to deliver quality support solutions that met 100% of the customer requirements on time (95 to 99% of the time) and at a competitive price.

Systems thinking works as well for a small business such as Pal's Sudden Service, a quick-service restaurant, as it does for a behemoth such as Boeing. Pal's has grown to become a major regional competitor, providing a commodity menu of hamburgers and hot dogs at seventeen locations in Tennessee and Virginia. Customer scores for quality averaged 95.8%, as compared with 84.1% for its best competitor.[6] So how does Pal's successfully compete with large national chains with much larger marketing budgets?

Pal's systems approach is embedded in the design and use of its automated information management system. On a daily basis, the company collects and analyzes store-level and company-wide data on sales, customer count, product mix, and food and material costs. Using correlation analyses, the system converts that data into meaningful information that is used to identify cause-and-effect relationships among different functional areas, processes, and performance measures and to provide a basis for decision making. With this analytic tool, Pal's is able to do all of the following:

- Identify how changes in one performance area impact all other areas
- Make accurate performance projections

- Provide a basis for identifying root causes
- Solve problems
- Capture improvements and learning to be shared
- Take action across the whole company

The success examples of Baldrige recipient organizations, such as Caterpillar Financial, Boeing Aerospace Support, and Pal's, simply touch the surface of results produced by the seventy-six exceptional organizations that have adopted a systems approach and have been recognized by Baldrige for performance excellence. What their successes demonstrate is that systems thinking produces dramatic profits, better products and services, delighted customers, and a more engaged and satisfied workforce. The "parts" improve as a result of improving the whole.

Whereas organizations following a systems path have revolutionized the way they manage, other organizations are struggling. Given that a systems approach works so well, why haven't more leaders adopted it? Why isn't every organization embracing this tried-and-true solution for better performance? Is it going to take another twenty years of sharing Baldrige success stories to convince leaders that organizations capable of sustaining success and outlasting their competitors in the twenty-first century will be those that manage the whole organization through a systems approach? Why aren't more leaders seeing it? What is getting in their way? What do leaders need to do to join the parade of system zealots that do "get it"?

OVERCOMING THE ACCOUNTABILITY HURDLE

One reason a systems approach has not been quickly adopted is that systems thinking requires that the tasks of an organization be accomplished in work systems that go beyond existing business unit or departmental boundaries. Work system design has been traditionally focused around business unit analysis, profit and loss accountability, and resource allocation. The focus of traditional work system design is on a functional task (vertical) instead of on the whole operation (horizontal). Perhaps there was a day when you could make a profit even if one work area was running in a different strategic direction than other areas; not so today.

Today, making a profit requires more careful thought. It is essential to align work systems to ensure that the work in every part of the organization optimally aligns with strategic goals.

Don't worry. The traditional business unit and department aren't going away. Nevertheless, the way we organized people into work systems in the past may not make sense for the future. This is especially the case as organizations turn to alternative strategies for getting work done, such as outsourcing or colocating vendors at their work sites. The line between an organization's work system and its vendor's work system is becoming blurred.

Two examples include Xerox Business Solutions, which colocates its document copying services at its clients' sites, and Federal Express, which provides dedicated point-of-service employees at its customers' shipping departments. More and more companies are outsourcing their information technology management, customer service, and purchasing functions as a strategy to reduce operational costs by taking advantage of a vendor's economies of scale.

Another solution to work system design that evolved out of systems thinking is to organize people into work teams that cut across functional areas. For example, SSM Health Care (SSMHC), a private, not-for-profit health care system, is recognized as a role model in the health care industry. SSMHC is committed to a systems approach that relies on cross-functional teams to address work-related issues and promote communication and cooperation as well as knowledge and skill sharing. Physicians work together with other caregivers, administrators, and staff using an innovative team model called "clinical collaboratives" to make rapid improvements in patient care. For example, improvements identified by clinical collaboratives for patients with congestive heart failure and ischemic heart disease produced results that exceed national benchmarks.[7]

However, as soon as you shift a leader's span of control from managing a department to managing a cross-functional work team, you put that leader out of his or her comfort zone. Work systems not bounded as profit-loss or cost centers are generally unpopular, and even the hint of changing the rules of accountability garners resistance.

Therefore, leaders must diligently help managers move beyond their comfort zone and make it over the hurdle to embrace shared accountability. For example, at SSMHC, president and CEO Sr. Mary Jean Ryan and her extended leadership team of nearly two hundred executives from across the enterprise personally role-model the team process for building consensus and making decisions. To enable people to successfully work together on teams at the work unit, department, and systemwide level, SSM leaders ensure that employees participating on teams are trained in a common language and with a common set of improvement tools. To reinforce expectations for shared accountability and decision making at the team level, SSMHC leaders use meetings, conferences, teleconferences, and learning sessions to share lessons learned and best practices.

THE SYSTEMS APPROACH MUST BE VALUE DRIVEN

Without values, a systems approach is sterile and barren of direction on how leaders and employees should behave with each other, with customers, and with suppliers and partners. Values drive belief systems. If the belief system of an organization reinforces a focus only on quick fixes (instead of longer-lasting solutions), how will employees behave? Will they forgo sharing an innovative idea because they fear that the time frame for seeing results may be viewed as too long? If the belief system rewards individual performance and not team performance, how can an organization hope to enlist an employee to join a team?

A set of values that drives behavior is the keystone of an effective systems approach. Leaders must find a way to make sure that everyone understands the values that drive individual behavior and how individual behavior affects the whole. To do so, leaders need many channels of communication, some formal and some informal.

For example, at Ritz-Carlton, leaders set out the shared values of trust, honesty, respect, integrity, and commitment, and they articulated a work environment where diversity is valued, quality of life is enhanced, individual aspirations are fulfilled, and the Ritz-Carlton mystique is strengthened. These values are embodied in the Employee Promise. The Ritz Credo further describes how employees are to behave by pledging to provide the finest personal service and facilities for guests. The Promise and Credo are personally reinforced by leaders and managers in a variety of forums, including a daily line-up meeting, new employee orientation, and values training conducted by leaders. Ritz leaders provide opportunities for two-way communication. Dialogues with employees help Ritz leaders understand whether employees are translating values into their day-to-day behavior. To ensure that leaders are effectively communicating values and gaining the full support of the workforce, a semiannual employee survey is conducted to provide leaders with feedback. Gaps in leadership effectiveness are addressed with development and systemwide training. Ritz-Carlton Hotels was twice recognized as a Baldrige recipient for its role-model performance.

MAKING IT HAPPEN: HOW TO CHANGE TO A SYSTEMS APPROACH TO MANAGEMENT

Assuming you have decided to change to a systems approach to management, change efforts require buy-in to ensure success. Winning the support of leaders, managers, and employees is essential in any change effort. How are you going to make this happen?

A key theme that ASQ has observed is that if the effort to adopt a systems approach falters, it is because the organization focuses its buy-in strategy on addressing the *why* we need to change and not the *how* we are going to make the change.

It is not sufficient just to establish agreement on why an organization should shift to a systems approach. In general, there is little resistance to "why." The facts speak for themselves in terms of customer, workforce, financial, and market success of organizations using a systems framework to achieve performance excellence. So why is there resistance to change?

The problem arises when an organization does not gain agreement on exactly *how* this change should be accomplished. That's where the pushback comes into play. True buy-in and engagement occur when a leader can also gain agreement on the key steps for how the change to systems thinking is going to be accomplished.

So how do you change to a systems approach? There are stages.

First, as a leader, you have to *decide you believe in a systems approach.* You have to make a sufficient investment in your own knowledge and commitment. Get a dose of inspiration by speaking with the CEO of a Baldrige or state quality award recipient company. For example, Horst Schulz, former CEO of Ritz-Carlton, followed this path. He is now the president and CEO of West Paces Hotel Group. It has been nearly a decade since he left Ritz-Carlton, yet during a recent occasion to speak with him, it was clear that he is an even stronger zealot for a systems approach to excellence than ever before.

Second, *help your organization build broad support to view the organization as a system.* This requires a discovery process, which may involve conducting an assessment to explore how the organization is working now and how the different components might look from a systems perspective. For example, all the companies cited in this chapter took this step and conducted an assessment using the Baldrige criteria. Another method for personal immersion is to download a copy of the Baldrige Criteria for Performance Excellence[8] or attend the Quest for Excellence to hear how leaders and employees talk about how their organizations used Baldrige.

So prepare for two things: the investment of your time to learn, experiment, and learn more, and a commitment to a journey toward performance excellence that will take years. Oh, you'll get results sooner than that, but they won't take the form of a quick fix. Instead, the results will be reflected in your organization's strengthened capability to sustain longer-term success.

Third, working with the findings of the assessment, you must *craft a plan on how your organization is going to move from its current state toward a systems approach.* Then you have to deploy these ideas throughout the organization. Over time, the systems framework will mature, and the strategy will become firmly embedded. It will no longer be a change strategy, but the way the organization operates.

Every organization is facing a changing economic environment. With every tick of the clock, new organizations are created and others fade out. From our vantage point, it is clear that organizations capable of sustaining success and outlasting their competitors in the twenty-first century will be those who break their addiction to spot management and turn to managing the whole by using a values-based systems approach.

Endnotes

1. "Ritz-Carlton Hotel Company Baldrige Application Summary," National Institute for Standards and Technology Web site: www .quality.nist.gov/PDF_files/RCHC_Application_Summary.pdf, 1999, p. 1.

2. "Ritz-Carlton Hotel Company Baldrige Application Summary," National Institute for Standards and Technology Web site: www .quality.nist.gov/PDF_files/RCHC_Application_Summary.pdf, 1999, pp. 1, 7, 18.

3. "Caterpillar Financial Services Corporation Baldrige Application Summary," National Institute for Standards and Technology Web site: www.quality.nist.gov/PDF_files/Caterpillar_Application_ Summary.pdf, 2003, pp. 5, 36.

4. Ackoff, Russell, "Systems Thinking and Implications to Management," speech presented at Wharton West Leadership Conference (San Francisco, March 23, 2004), "Leading in an Era of Change and Uncertainty," white paper published by The Wharton School of the University of Pennsylvania, www.cheneydavidson.com/ Portfolio/Docs/Lead_Conf_3_04_Summary.pdf, pp. 9–10.

5. "Boeing Aerospace Support Baldrige Application Summary," National Institute for Standards and Technology Web site: www .quality.nist.gov/PDF_files/Boeing_Aerospace_Application_ Summary.pdf, 2003, pp. 4, 21.

6. "Pal's Sudden Service Baldrige Application Summary," National Institute for Standards and Technology Web site: www.quality.nist .gov/PDF_files/Pal's_Application_Summary.pdf, 2001, p. 15.

7. "SSM Health Care Baldrige Application Summary," National Institute for Standards and Technology Web site: www.quality.nist.gov/ PDF_files/SSM_Application_Summary.pdf, 2002, pp. 24, 38.

8. "Baldrige Criteria for Excellence," National Institute for Standards and Technology Web site: www.quality.nist.gov/Criteria.htm.

ORGANIZATIONAL CULTURE

Values, Emotions, Hope, Ethics, Spirit, and Behavior

Part Two focuses on some of the so-called softer issues of running an organization—topics that are just as important as being visionary and setting strategy.

Mutual of America's chairman Thomas J. Moran sets the tone with his chapter on the values he learned working in his first jobs—as a janitor, fry cook, cab driver, and office assistant. He learned the importance of a strong work ethic, pride and joy in one's work, self-respect, integrity, hard work, positive reinforcement, ongoing training, and workplace diversity. Organizations that embrace these values are the ones that will survive in the future.

Charles Handy has been an executive, professor, lecturer, and author. In his chapter, he describes how many offices today "seem to be prisons for the human soul for many of their occupants." He shows how organizations need to change, how capitalism needs to be redefined, and how a good business is a *community* with a *purpose*.

Organizational performance consultants Jon R. Katzenbach and Zia Khan show how organizations can survive and thrive if they tap their employees' emotions. Their chapter describes the amazing turnarounds of a GM plant that was slated to shut down, a failing NYC public school, Aetna when it was near financial collapse, and Bell Canada's shrinking profit margins and market share—all organizations whose leaders turned them around by creating emotional bonds with their teams.

Executive coach and consultant Richard J. Leider looks at the value older workers bring to organizations. Rejecting the idea of traditional retirement, he discusses how the one hundred million people over the age of forty-five *want* to work longer, and notes that 80% of workforce growth will be in the category of workers over fifty. Moreover, mature workers have much to offer: experience, reliability, knowledge, loyalty, and stability. Organizations of the future need to know how to capitalize on the talents of the "new elders."

Dean and management professor Ira A. Jackson considers how Peter Drucker would view today's organizations that encourage their employees to be creative, to connect with people in new ways, and to be socially conscious and give something back. Jackson describes a wide variety of organizations that do this: Google, organizations that develop teachers to work in inner cities, and others that bring together businesses, governments, and nongovernmental organizations to make the world a better place.

Professors Lee G. Bolman and Terrence E. Deal identify four ways to create ethical communities: a *factory* approach that rewards excellence and individual authority; a *family* approach that offers caring and love to its workers; the corporate *jungle,* where justice and power govern but can be used effectively and for good; and the *temple,* where employees are tied together by their shared faith in an organization that is doing something significant.

The final chapter in Part Two looks at the success of a vocational and arts school for economically disadvantaged and underserved students, founded forty years ago by Bill Strickland. He describes his goals for the school and how he has achieved them—and he provides ideas for other organizations in education, community development, and the social sector.

CHAPTER SEVEN

THE VALUES THAT BUILD A STRONG ORGANIZATION

Thomas J. Moran

Thomas J. Moran was appointed chairman of the board of Mutual of America Life Insurance Company in 2005 and has served as president and CEO since 1994. Mutual of America is among the most highly rated life insurance companies in the United States, specializing in providing retirement and long-term savings plans to small- and medium-size organizations. Moran is recognized for his caring leadership style and has been quoted in BusinessWeek *on the subject of "what leaders owe." In addition to his extensive business experience, Moran is an active supporter of the social sector. Over the last several years, he has traveled to the Democratic Republic of Congo, Rwanda, Niger, Sri Lanka, Ethiopia, and Haiti in his role as the chairman of Concern Worldwide (U.S.), an international humanitarian relief organization, which operates in twenty-nine of the poorest countries of the world.*

One of the more challenging aspects of the future is that it is unpredictable. Organizations of the future may have to deal with situations that none of us can even imagine today. So how do you prepare for this level of uncertainty? In giving this question some thought, I realized that organizations and people face that same challenge of not knowing what is waiting around the next corner. In life and in business, we see individuals and organizations that are able to accommodate almost anything and others that are devastated by the first bump in the road. So what is it that prepares us for the uncertainty of the future? As I searched for the answer, I found it close to home: one more life lesson learned from my parents' example.

THE STRENGTH OF AN ORGANIZATION—AND ITS EMPLOYEES—DETERMINES ITS SUCCESS

I've watched over the last three years as my father has lost virtually all of his physical ability to the ravages of the degenerative neuromuscular disease ALS, commonly known as Lou Gehrig's disease. This is obviously not something that any of us could have anticipated or planned for. Yet I've seen in both of my parents the same great strength that I have always admired and respected. It is their spirit and character that has allowed them to deal together with my dad's terminal illness. They have demonstrated that genuine strength does not come from how tall a person can stand or if he or she can stand at all. It comes from the spirit and character of the individual. I believe that an organization's ability to deal with the uncertainty of the future must also come from its own internal strength, as embodied by its employees. In this chapter, I explore the qualities of the organization of the future that will assure its success and its ability to respond properly to unexpected future events.

The successful organization of the future will have to be able not only to attract and retain talented employees but also to inspire those employees. My view of the organization of the future does not come from any experience I might have had if I were a university professor or a management consultant. Instead, my perspective comes simply from my own life experience as the chief executive of a company that competes successfully in the highly competitive financial services industry. It has also been largely influenced by my work experiences as a very young man.

THE VALUE OF A STRONG WORK ETHIC

At the age of fourteen, I began my working career, starting with a job as a janitor at my high school. The lessons I learned from the full-time janitors, Arty, Frank, and Dominic, provided me with a foundation that I believe has been invaluable to me and will be important to the successful organization of the future. As you can imagine, at the age of fourteen I was young, energetic, and eager to prove myself and make sure I was worthy of that $10 per day salary. Most of all, I was eager to learn. I watched and learned as my three generous mentors taught me the skills I needed to do my job.

What I saw were men who were true professionals and who treated their job with respect. I found that although they seemed ancient to me at the time (I now doubt that any of them had yet reached fifty), I could not complete what would appear to be a simple task, such as mowing the football field lawn, with the same precision or efficiency as these three professionals. Their work had reached the level of art, with its own rhythm that only comes from respect and commitment to excellence.

The successful organization of the future will need to have employees at all levels of the organization who truly understand and appreciate the importance of their role to the organization's overall success. Also important, it must have leadership that accepts each individual as being essential to his or her organization.

The Importance of Pride, Joy, and Respect at Work

Following my janitorial experience, I worked as the French-fry man at Nathan's, as a short-order cook at a dental factory, and as a cemetery worker. All these experiences reinforced what I had already learned at the age of fourteen. At Nathan's, I worked alongside Benny the hot dog man. In addition to being the very best at his trade, Benny knew how to make his job fun, singing out "a pound of bread, a pound of meat, all the mustard you can eat, give your tongue a sleigh ride." The sense of pride and joy in his job was infectious and made all of us enjoy our own jobs that much more.

What I also learned over those early years was that respect for the work you do also translates into respect for yourself, and that true self-respect makes all parts of your life better. I feel fortunate to have worked in those early years with people of great talent and passion.

The Power of the American Dream

Working as a taxicab driver in New York City during my college years, I learned about the power of the American dream. My years of driving a cab were during a time when many college-age students were out protesting the Vietnam War. But my college experience was quite different. Everyone I met at the garage while I was waiting for my cab to come in from the day shift was hoping for something more from life, either for himself or his children. And, in the United States of America, those dreams can be realized. Strangely, it might have been while driving a taxi at two o'clock in the morning that I developed my passionate belief in the greatness of our country. I came to understand how hard people are willing to work under what can at times be extreme conditions, just because of the promise offered by that American dream.

The successful organization of the future will not look at where you came from or what you look like. The organization's leadership will understand that what is important is that you believe in the American dream and that you know that your dream can be realized in that successful organization.

INTEGRITY AND HARD WORK WILL GET YOU FARTHER THAN ANY SHORTCUT

Being of Irish descent, I can tell no story without some mention of an Irish pub. I probably spent more time than I should have in my youth seeking inspiration in those pubs. But there was one lesson that I have always remembered. One late night, a fellow decided to have some fun: he threw all of his change into the crowd and then stood back watching as everyone scrambled for his money. I watched and held my place, deciding then that it was much more rewarding to make my own way rather than stoop to pick up someone else's money.

The successful organization of the future will, in my opinion, comprise individuals who rely on their own integrity and hard work and do not look for the easy shortcuts. As I've already noted, the fight among organizations for talent will intensify in the future. Strangely, the smaller organizations will have the advantage. Young people with talent will be looking for opportunities that are more personal and exciting. They will fear getting lost in the bureaucracy of the larger organizations. Small organizations will offer the promise of a more intimate work environment and an array of experiences. All organizations striving to be successful will have to demonstrate that their organizations offer opportunity and an exciting personal environment.

MAKE SURE YOUR EMPLOYEES KNOW THEY'RE IMPORTANT TO THE OVERALL ORGANIZATION

My own experience is one that I believe represents the possibilities that must exist in the successful organization of the future. Almost from the start of my business career in 1975, I was made to feel important to the organization. My immediate supervisor, Juana Luna, led by example and challenged me to commit myself to learning the pension business. And she did this with a great deal of knowledge and personal warmth. From the first day, I knew she believed in the importance of the services provided to our customers and genuinely cared about me and my having a future with the company. I felt that I had an important job with great opportunity for advancement. Of course, when you start as the person who attaches paper clips to contract pages where they have to be signed, it is a little easier to see "great opportunity for advancement."

It wasn't just Juana Luna who made me feel as if I were important to the company. It was also the president and CEO at that time, William J. Flynn. Those pages that I paper-clipped were to be ultimately signed by Mr. Flynn. When I had a stack of contracts ready for signature, Juana Luna would send me over to the president's office to ask him to sign the documents at the spots I had designated with my paper clips. He always welcomed me into his office and not only made me feel comfortable but also took the time to make me feel as if I were an important part of the company. While he was signing, he would talk with me and ask how I thought the company was doing. It was clear to me at the time that he genuinely cared about me and was interested in hearing my thoughts. He later became a close friend, and, even after he retired as CEO in 1994, he remained a great mentor. Throughout our company, it was always known that Bill Flynn would be there for you if you ever had a problem. That level of care and commitment to the employees instilled loyalty throughout the organization.

Today the signatures on the contracts are, of course, all computer generated, and there is no one with the awesome responsibility of paper-clipping pages for signing. But we still try to make working at our company a personal experience with concern for each employee's well-being and a clear interest in the advancement of our employees. On their first day, employees are given a warm welcome from the human resources department and a briefing on the array of employee benefits that are available. Also important, on that first day we discuss the various activities in which they can get involved, beyond their business responsibilities. These include a variety of sports programs, a theater program, and the charitable events that are a hallmark of our company. There are also occasions throughout the year for employees to come together and enjoy each other's company, such as one of the anniversary celebrations or the sports and recreation reception, where all the teams are recognized for their efforts and success in representing the company. All officers of the company are invited to these events, and they mix with the other employees, especially those who are new to the company.

The most important event is our annual employee meeting, in which the results of the prior year are communicated to every employee of the company. Also communicated at this meeting are the company's strategic plan and the goals for the upcoming year. This meeting is also an opportunity to reinforce the values that are the foundation on which the company is built and that are the underpinning of our mission statement.

ONGOING TRAINING IS CRITICAL TO SUCCESS

Training will continue to be a vital element of success for the organization of the future. When made an integral part of an organization, training can serve as the bond that secures the future of the organization. It is an opportunity to emphasize the importance that the organization places on each employee, and it allows the employees to develop personal relationships that extend beyond their own immediate work group.

Initially, this training takes place as an orientation program and can be the source of relationships that will develop over the long term and introduce employees for the first time to the mission and goals of the company. As training continues over the years, it becomes more specialized, while still continuing to emphasize the importance of each employee and the expansion of understanding that is essential to the successful fulfillment of the organization's mission and goals. Organizations can capitalize on this investment by challenging their employees to use their in-depth knowledge of the organization to identify innovative opportunities to improve the competitive position of the organization and enhance the products and services provided to customers.

Every employee is essential to the organization and must have the opportunity to participate in training. In successful organizations, leadership is nurtured and developed as a part of the training program. It is not the exclusive province of the senior-level officers but of *all* employees. Training needs to focus on the development of job skills, while also emphasizing the importance of ideas and having the ability to properly communicate those ideas and work collectively.

Training also highlights the important distinction that exists between bosses and leaders. In my opinion, anyone can be a boss. All you need is a loud voice and a certainty that you are never wrong. Bosses can ruin an organization. Leaders, in contrast, *share* their ideas and *communicate* their vision in a way that co-opts others to join with them in support of that idea. Leaders are not afraid to seek out differing opinions and opportunities for improvement. At any given moment, leadership may be required from any one person within the organization. At that time, the employee involved must fully understand the ethos of the organization and have the training needed to make the right choices.

Another important aspect of training is that it demonstrates an organization's loyalty to its employees and their future. Successful organizations of the future will have capable employees who are confident of their positions and their future within the organization. This requires that every employee understand and accept that change is part of the culture of the organization. They must also understand that the organization is committed to preparing them for the changes that lie ahead, but that it is up to them to embrace those opportunities.

The preparation of employees for the changes that are necessary in every successful enterprise are often ignored, leaving the organization with groups of individuals who may be *willing to commit* themselves to the organization but who are *unable* to participate in its future success because of a lack of training and preparation for change. Ultimately, these employees become redundant and can be the eventual target of downsizing. Training helps assure employees of their role in the organization's future. I would describe this as the loyalty that the organization owes to its employees. This is a clear reflection of the organization's commitment to the personal development and security of its employees. It also assures the employees of a challenging and exciting work environment and their participation in the continuing success of the organization. The combination of a personal interest in the welfare of the employees and the excitement of learning results in a workforce that is more productive, stable, and secure.

DIVERSITY IMPROVES ORGANIZATIONS

Successful organizations of the future will embrace diversity not only because it's the correct practice but also to reap the benefits it brings to an organization. Diversity strengthens organizations by allowing for a melting pot of experience and a larger pool of talent from which to choose. Each individual's unique experience will serve to enrich the overall culture of the organization and provide for a more interesting work environment.

The diverse work environment should include the often overlooked talent of physically challenged individuals. The physically challenged offer the same benefits to the organization that can be found in all other groups. For a variety of reasons, too many organizations often overlook the opportunity of hiring talented individuals who have already shown the strength of character needed to overcome the challenges of their physical ability. The skills and talents of these individuals can make a powerful contribution to the overall success of the organization. As competition for talent becomes even more important, successful organizations will develop the skills to hire the best talent available, including those who are physically challenged. Broadened diversity will also enhance the organization's ability to better understand its customers, who will also likely represent the increasingly diverse nature of our country.

YOUR ORGANIZATION'S VALUES MUST BE VISIBLE

As previously mentioned, the successful organization of the future will not only attract quality employees but also excite those employees in ways that will make the organization a more attractive choice for employment. Profits and share price are always important, but they are the *result* rather than the *cause* of employee satisfaction. The organization must have demonstrable values that go beyond the need to increase profits or raise share price. These values must be visible and clearly understood by the employees and should demonstrate the power of the organization to be an influence for good. And, when you live these values, there are several things that begin to happen. The organization will be a better place to work and will become more successful. Something else will also happen: the organization and its employees will want to play a larger role in shaping society.

Mutual of America's values and ability to be an influence for good can be seen immediately in the composition of its board of directors. They are individuals of diverse and celebrated backgrounds who have a broad perspective and proven record of leadership and accomplishment in various sectors, including business and management consulting, legal and public affairs, economics and finance, health care, and education. Various members of the board have been recognized in their personal and professional lives for their own positive contributions to the betterment of society. Collectively, they have encouraged the company's support of and involvement in numerous opportunities that help define us and create a sense of pride among our employees. Over the years, we have been involved in and supported financial literacy programs, meetings of Nobel laureates, health care and educational programs organized by several of the large national charities, international relief efforts, the Public Broadcasting System, and the peace process in Northern Ireland.

For more than a decade, our foundation, through its Community Partnership Award, has identified organizations that have created a partnership of the private, governmental, and social sectors with a program that can be easily replicated and that successfully addresses a need in our society. Each year, an awards dinner is organized that includes the top three Community Partnership Award recipients, our board of directors, and our senior officers. A video of the top program along with a brochure highlighting each of the top ten programs is also distributed around the country and at luncheon ceremonies held in the hometowns of each of the top ten award recipients. The Community Partnership Award is a highlight of each year's Mutual of America annual employee meeting. It is introduced along with an overview of the other philanthropic programs in which the company and its employees participate.

GIVING BACK HELPS EVERYONE

Virtually 100% of Mutual of America's employees participate in philanthropy, whether through financial support, volunteering their time, or both. The passionate commitment made by the employees to giving something back is a hallmark of our company and is an important part of our success. Successful organizations of the future will understand the importance of this level of volunteerism toward the creation of a caring work environment that both attracts and retains the highest-quality employees. Philanthropy on the part of the corporation and its employees is another important aspect of ensuring that employees are given an opportunity to look beyond the walls of the organization in a manner that will excite them and make them proud of the organization for which they work.

CONCLUSION

So, again, what is it that prepares us for the uncertainty of the future? None of us can ever be certain of what is waiting around the next corner, but with committed, talented, and motivated employees, organizations of the future will be able to adapt effectively to whatever the challenges may be, and to expand and prosper. The organization that is prepared in this way will be professional in every aspect of its business and passionate in its commitment to its employees, customers, and society at large.

Respect, ethics, excellence, pride, joy, opportunity, and loyalty will be much more than words. These will be the values by which the organization is guided each and every day. Employees will provide the inner spirit and character of the organization and will allow it to continue its mission and to thrive. And, finally, if it does all these things, the organization of the future will be respected for its products and services and admired for its contributions to society.

CHAPTER EIGHT

REVISITING THE CONCEPT OF THE CORPORATION

Charles Handy

Charles Handy is a writer, broadcaster, and lecturer. His books on the changing shape of work and its effects on our lives and organizations have sold more than a million copies around the world. He recently published a book with his wife, Elizabeth, a portrait photographer, titled The New Philanthropists: Making a Difference, *which is a sequel to their earlier book,* The New Alchemists, *which profiled successful entrepreneurs in all walks of life. In addition,* Myself and Other More Important Matters, *a series of reflections on his life, was published in 2008. He has been an oil executive with Shell, a business economist, a professor at the London Business School, the Warden of St. George's House in Windsor Castle (a study center for social and ethical issues), and the chairman of the Royal Society of Arts. He is also known in Britain for his "Thoughts for Today" on the BBC radio breakfast show* Today.

It is often wise to look back in order to move forward. I once lived and worked in Windsor Castle; our home was originally part of the palace of King John. It was from our courtyard that he rode out in 1215 to put his seal on the Magna Carta—an early version, perhaps, of a stakeholder contract (and note that he agreed to this contract only under extreme pressure). I ran conferences there on societal ethics, and I used to ask the participants to look around them. There had been a castle and a monarch in that place for nearly a thousand years. The castle was still there, a monarch still resided in it, and the sovereign's flag still flew above it. Like it or loathe it, you had to give the monarchy full marks for resilience.

But although things still looked the same on the outside, what was happening on the inside was very different. Change, I suggested, was often easier if you *kept the form* but *changed the substance* when the world around you changed.

I would then take my conference participants into the great and wonderful chapel of St. George across the courtyard, where the kings of England are buried. I would ask them to stand beside the tomb of King Charles I, the one who was beheaded because he refused to change the substance of his role to meet the needs of a changing society.

TO SURVIVE, ORGANIZATIONS NEED TO CHANGE

Could the same fate befall the corporations that have served us so well in the past if they do not change their ways? They were extraordinary social inventions back in 1550, when the twin ideas of the joint stock company and limited liability were first conceived and applied in Britain. Down the centuries, however, those good ideas have had some unintended consequences. To drive through the old communist countries of Eastern Europe, as I did during the summer of 2007, is to see history recorded in the city skylines, a very visible example of how power is transferred as society changes.

There are the old castles of the kings and the barons, which are now museums. Then came the huge concrete edifices of the communist regimes, parliaments of the people today, but even these are now hidden behind the glossy new glass towers of the corporate businesses. To the average passerby, it seems clear where much of the real power now lies in most societies. The organization of the future has to balance that power with the responsibility that inevitably comes with it. That is the challenge, and it begs the ultimate question: For whom and for what does an organization exist? The old answers are not enough anymore. The organizations of the future can no longer live in a world of their own making. They are too important to the rest of us for that.

Those towers, today, are full of uncomfortable paradoxes. They are clothed in glass, yet you can't see into them. Proud symbols of the new democracies, they are as centrally controlled as the communist regimes they displaced. The names on their doors, which are often paraded on their rooftops, are, as often as not, a set of meaningless initials. They are, of course, no different from—and are often offshoots of—their counterparts in our older democracies of the West.

To the layman, in every country, these are anonymous organizations, run by anonymous people, themselves the appointed agents of anonymous investors, represented, as often as not, by anonymous institutions in similar towers. You cannot blame that passerby for thinking that power and wealth had somehow gotten out of his or her control, that somehow the individual's concerns and those of the wider society were in danger of being ignored. That is, if the person thinks about it at all. Perhaps the real problem is that too many people don't, that they just assume that it is the way it was ordained to be—rather as our forebears thought of slavery until its social and moral flaws were brought to their attention.

MANY WORKPLACES ARE PRISONS FOR THE HUMAN SOUL

Office towers are the knowledge factories of the new economy. Cleaner and more elegant than the factories of old, they can still seem to be prisons for the human soul for many of their occupants. For example, even lawyers in smart firms can be required to deliver three thousand billable hours per year. When forty hours per week for fifty weeks totals only two thousand hours, it is clear that there is not much of life left to such people outside their factory. It may be well-paid and voluntary servitude, but it's still servitude—and these lawyers and other professionals in similar situations are the fortunate ones. Others are not even well paid! It is time to ask, "What are we doing to ourselves, and why?"

Of course, those towers may not last. The office in one of them where I once sat is now the living room of a smart apartment block, because who needs so many people in one building anymore in this age of the virtual? It is fashionable, too, for some organizations to prefer a campus to a tower, looking more like a university and often structured like one as well, with semiautonomous groups bonded into a federalist whole. But even these campuses will be surrounded by high fences, with guards at the gates, still off-limits to the ordinary citizen, still mysterious, still answerable to no one save themselves and their investors. The *cui bono?* question—for whose benefit do they exist?—is still begging. Of course, that is not the way all those mostly well-meaning people on the inside see it. They are just doing their best in a difficult world. That's what King Charles I thought, too.

Corporations Need a Cultural Shift

The questions get bigger. Francis Fukuyama and others have argued, and many statesmen have assumed, that a combination of liberal democracy and open-market capitalism would be the ultimate answer for a successful society. But democracy and capitalism can be uneasy bedfellows. If capitalism is not seen to be working for the demos, the demos could destroy it. Not by revolution, but by entangling it in so many restrictions and requirements that its vigor would be irreparably damaged. To passersby, those towers or barricaded campuses do not seem to be working for anyone's good but their own. Ironically, that feeling is strongest in the developing world, where the beneficial effects of capitalism are most needed.

We do urgently need a cultural shift in the way corporations behave and the way they are perceived in the wider society. That is why this book is so timely and so important, for governments typically do not move until they believe that their moves will be welcomed by a substantial section of the voting public. Therefore, change must initially come from the outside, from the key participants, from opinion formers and activists, from people like the authors of this book.

How did it get this way? How did such historically good ideas get corrupted? How can we rescue the good and eliminate the bad? There is a pile of good ideas already on the table. Transparency, accountability, and governance structures are probably at the top of the list, but I worry more about the big question that sits underneath these more technical issues. What is a business for, or even, perhaps, *who* is it for? More concretely, how should a business define success, and how measure it?

We need also to pay heed to two other reminders from the past, this time from Adam Smith, the Scottish moral philosopher turned economist. Most businesspeople will know of his theory of the invisible hand, which appears to legitimize self-interest. They do not realize that Adam Smith had assumed that his readers would also know about his earlier book, *The Theory of Moral Sentiments,* in which he argued that what he called "sympathy" was essential to bond a society together. We need both self-interest and sympathy in business and society—and in our organizations.

Adam Smith also said this: "A profitable speculation is presented as a public good because growth will stimulate demand, and everywhere diffuse comfort and improvement. No patriot or man of feeling could therefore oppose it. But the nature of this growth, in opposition, for example, to older ideas such as cultivation, is that it is at once undirected and infinitely self-generating in the endless demand for all the useless things in the world."

Adam Smith would, I think, despair of the way in which the creativity and energies of our businesses today are so often directed to such trivial ends. Can we insert a touch more cultivation into our corporate charters along with more sympathy? The organizations of the future will, more than ever, hold the main levers of change in society. Governments pass laws and regulate; organizations make things happen. Increasingly, they are the main communities, however fragile, in most people's lives. It behooves them to think more deeply than before on what sort of world they want us to live in.

The future is not all bleak. Legal experts assure us that the corporation has much more freedom than some would previously have granted it to define its own destiny, and there is a growing body of different models to choose from. It is even possible that the spate of scandals in recent years and the looming problems of climate change are helpful, in that they have begun to arouse the interest of the previously unconcerned. Cultural change needs triggers to get it started, then it needs its advocates.

THE BIG QUESTION: WHO AND WHAT IS A BUSINESS FOR?

If we cast history and preconceptions aside, it does seem odd (to say the least) that those who provide the money for an enterprise should have more clout and power over its destiny than those who actually create its wealth. The idea that those who provide the finance are the rightful owners and therefore entitled to decide the purposes of the business, rather than being just its financiers, dates from the early days of business when the financier was genuinely the owner and usually the chief executive as well.

Now that the value of a company largely resides in its intellectual property, in its brands and patents, and in the skills, creativity, and experience of its workforce, it can seem unreal to think it right to treat these things as the property of the financiers, to be disposed of if they so wish. This may be the law, but it hardly seems like justice. Surely those who carry this intellectual property within them, who contribute their time and talents rather than their money, should have some rights, some voice, in the future of what they also think of as "their" company? A good business is a community with a purpose. Communities are things you *belong to,* not things you can *own.* They have members, members who have certain rights, including the right to vote or express their views on major issues. It would seem only equitable, too, that dividends should be paid to those who contribute their skills as well as to those who have contributed their money (most of whom have not, in fact, paid any to the company itself but only to previous owners of the shares).

The Rise of Performance-Based Pay

It may only be a matter of time. Already, those whose personal assets are highly valued—for example, bankers, brokers, film actors, and sports stars—make a share of the profits, or a bonus, as a condition of their employment. Others, such as authors, get all their remuneration from a share of the income stream (in the form of royalties). This form of performance-based pay, where the contribution of a single member or a group can be identified, seems bound to grow along with the bargaining power of key talent. We should not ignore the examples of those organizations, such as sports teams or publishing houses, whose success has always been tied to the talents of individuals and who have had, over the years or even the centuries, to work out how best to share both the risks and the rewards of innovative work. In the growing world of talent businesses, employees will be increasingly unwilling to sell the fruits of their intellectual assets for an annual salary.

As it is, a few smaller European corporations already allocate a fixed proportion of after-tax profit for distribution to the work-force. This then becomes a very tangible expression of the rights of the members. As the practice spreads, it will then only make sense to discuss future strategies and plans in broad outline with repre-sentatives of the members so that they can share in the responsibil-ity for their future earnings and for the type of organization they would like it to be. Democracy of sorts will have crept in through the pay packet, bringing with it (one would hope) more under-standing, more commitment, and more contribution.

That may help remedy the democratic deficit in capitalism, but it won't repair the image of business in the wider community. In fact, it might be seen as only spreading the cult of selfishness a little wider. Two more things need to happen, and they may actu-ally be starting to happen already.

FIRST, DO NO HARM

The ancient Hippocratic oath that doctors used to swear upon graduating included the injunction "Above all, do no harm." The antiglobalization protesters claim that global business today does more harm than good. If their charges are to be rebutted, and if business is to restore its reputation as the friend, not the enemy, of progress around the world, then the chairmen of those companies need to bind themselves with an equivalent oath.

Doing no harm goes beyond meeting the legal requirements regarding the environment, conditions of employment, good community relations, or ethics. The law always lags behind best practice. Organizations of the future need to take the lead in such areas as environmental and social sustainability, instead of forever letting themselves be pushed onto the defensive.

SECOND, FIND A CAUSE

In the new world of the knowledge economy, however, sustainabil-ity also has to be interpreted at a more human level, as concerns grow over the deteriorating work-life balance for key workers and the stress of the long-hours culture. Some people worry that an executive life is becoming unsustainable in social terms. One would have to be the modern equivalent of a monk, forsaking all else for the sake of the calling. If the modern business, based on its human assets, is to survive, it will have to find better ways to protect its people from the demands of the jobs it gives them. A neglect of environmental responsibility may lose customers, but a neglect of this type of social responsibility may lose key members of the workforce. More than ever, a modern business has to see itself as a community of individuals, with individual needs as well as very personal skills and talents. They are not anonymous human resources.

More corporate democracy and better corporate behavior will go a long way to alter the current business culture for the better in the eyes of the public, but unless they are accompanied by a new vision of the purpose of the business, they will be seen as mere palliatives, a way to keep the world off their backs. It is time to raise our sights above the purely pragmatic. Article 14(2) of the German constitution states, "Property imposes duties. Its use should also serve the public weal." There is no such clause in the U.S. Constitution, but the sentiment has its echoes in some company philosophies. Dave Packard once said, "I think many people assume, wrongly, that a company exists simply to make money. While this is an important result of a company's existence, we have to go deeper and find the real reasons for our being. . . . We inevitably come to the conclusion that a group of people get together and exist as an institution that we call a company so that they are able to accomplish something collectively that they could not accomplish separately—they make a contribution to society."

The contribution ethic has always proved to be a strong motivating force in people's lives. To survive, even to prosper, is not enough for most. We hanker to leave some footprint in the sands of time, and if we can do that with the help and companionship of others in an organization, so much the better. We need a cause to associate with in order to provide real purpose to our lives. The pursuit of a cause does not have to be the prerogative of charities and the not-for-profit sector. Nor does a mission to improve the world make business into some kind of social agency.

Business has always been the active agent of progress, through innovation and new products, by encouraging the spread of technology, by lowering costs through productivity, and by improving services and enhancing quality, thereby making the good things of life available and affordable to ever more people. This process is driven by competition and spurred on by the need to provide adequate returns to those who risk their money and their careers, but it is, in itself, a noble cause. We should make more of it. We should, as charitable organizations do, measure success in terms of outcomes for others as well as for ourselves.

You can, however, also make money by serving the poor as well as the rich. As C. K. Prahalad has pointed out, there is a huge neglected market in the billions of poor in the developing world. Companies like Unilever and Citicorp are beginning to adapt their technologies to enter this market. In India, Unilever can now deliver ice creams at just 2¢ each because it has rethought the technology of refrigeration, and also in India, Citicorp can now provide financial services to people who have only $25 to invest, again through rethinking the technology. In both cases, they make money, but the driving force was the need to serve these neglected customers.

REDEFINING CAPITALISM

There are more such stories of enlightened business in both American and European companies, but they still remain the minority. Until and unless they become the norm, capitalism will still be seen as the rich man's game, interested mainly in itself and its agents. High-minded talent may start to shun it and customers desert it. Worse, democratic pressures may force governments to shackle the independence of business, constraining its freedoms and regulating the smallest details of its actions. Capitalism will have become corroded, and we shall all be the losers.

Alas, cultural change is a slow process. We need great examples, and we need good interpreters to spread the news of their work. We also need new words—or, rather, old words in new contexts—because words often seem to be the bugles that herald social change. For example, if more organizations talked of their *members* rather than their *employees,* or if they described their whole business as *having a social purpose,* or if they measured success by *what they achieved for others* rather than for themselves, it would signal a change of priorities.

Ultimately, any changes may need to be bolstered by changes in company law, but even as those laws now stand, there is great freedom for the directors of a company to define their purposes and to decide the allocation of their resources. If they can agree to pay out hundreds of millions of dollars in compensation to a parting chief executive without reference to the shareholders, they can also pay out appropriate rewards to their other members or contribute to the social fabric of their community. Shareholders have only the right to elect the directors; what these directors then decide to do is up to them. Of course, if those directors neglect their shareholders, the market will punish them, but to make them the priority is to mistake a necessary condition for a sufficient one—a logical error and, maybe, a moral one. Even shareholders, or their agents, can be persuaded that sustainability of all types is, in the long term, good for them as well as for society.

We have more freedom than we think to redefine the nature of capitalism, to make it more plainly something that works for all. To do so needs only the will and the energy from those who will lead the organizations of the future.

CHAPTER NINE

MOBILIZING EMOTIONS FOR PERFORMANCE

Making the Most of the Informal Organization

Jon R. Katzenbach and Zia Khan

Jon R. Katzenbach is senior partner of Katzenbach Partners, a consulting firm that helps leading global companies achieve breakthrough organizational performance. He is the author of several articles and books, including Why Pride Matters More Than Money, Peak Performance, Teams at the Top, Real Change Leaders, The Discipline of Teams *(with Douglas K. Smith), and the best-seller* The Wisdom of Teams *(also with Douglas K. Smith). Before founding Katzenbach Partners, he was a director with McKinsey & Company for more than thirty years. Zia Khan leads the San Francisco office of Katzenbach Partners and advises clients in a range of industries on strategic and organizational issues. His recent research focuses on how different kinds of organizations achieve their goals. He has authored several articles on the "informal organization" and its connection to performance drivers, such as leadership team effectiveness, customer service, innovation, and operational productivity.*

Jon R. Katzenbach and Zia Khan are writing a book that expands on the ideas in this chapter. It is about how leaders create an informal advantage by getting their formal and informal organizations "jumping together."

Organizations of the future will increasingly live in a world that is flatter, faster, and much more chaotic. They will need to respond in the marketplace before headquarters realizes the game has changed. They will need employees to provide service that is consistently excellent but flexibly suited to each customer. They will need to innovate at all levels—big bets on new products along with constant small-scale operating improvements. These needs already exceed the capabilities of the formal elements of organizations— the strategies, structures, processes, and metrics—that managers drew on heavily in the twentieth century to align behaviors rationally. Instead, these needs will be increasingly served by highly responsive organizations that emulate aspects of Southwest Airlines, Google, and Apple. Each of these companies complements its formal constructs with a strong "informal organization"—the values, networks, and working norms—that mobilizes emotions in ways that drive higher performance. Our research over the past five years suggests that leading organizations of the future will rely less on their increasingly undifferentiated formal organizations and compete more through their informal uniqueness.

Yet a strong informal organization is not enough. The work and wisdom of Mary Parker Follett, whose organizational insights have stood the test of time for over a hundred years now, point us to an even stronger solution. Follett (who lived from 1868 to 1933) was a Radcliffe-educated management and political theorist and author of several books about organizations and communities; her ideas on negotiation, power, and employee participation were influential in the development of organizational studies. One of Follett's most compelling notions was her relentless pursuit of integration versus compromise, consensus, and "either-or." She argued that integration is the ability to obtain the "best of both" with respect to conflicting and overlapping approaches—that, in contrast, compromise and consensus lead to the *lowest* common denominator of agreement, and either-or simply rejects one for the other.[1]

In that spirit, we believe that the most successful organization shapers of the future will need to work very hard to create organizationally dynamic approaches that can *integrate* the informal organization with the formal, finding ways to use seemingly conflicting approaches to get the best of both. We believe that this notion is at the heart of future organizational performance. In our view, the most important element for obtaining that kind of integration is in making more effective and purposeful use of the informal elements of organization. Only thus can the emotional determinants of behavior be fully mobilized to support the rational elements driven by the formal organization.

RATIONAL AND EMOTIONAL INTEGRATION

Most organization designs are created to accomplish one or more rational purposes, such as operating efficiency, marketing position, financial return, or competitive advantage. The rational approach to organization design assumes that clear structures and processes will ensure that the decisions and actions required will achieve their shared purpose. Success is measured rationally against the competition by comparing economic results and returns for various constituencies over time. This rationale explains the success of many leading enterprises of the past, such as General Motors, General Electric, Citicorp, and Wal-Mart, to name a few of the more obvious.

However, an organization's performance is highly dependent on people whose attitudes and behaviors are influenced at least as much by *emotional feelings* as they are by *logical reasoning*. Yet most enterprises design organizations based primarily on rational factors, and they assume that the necessary emotional forces will follow—or that they don't matter. In situations where urgency prevails, this assumption sometimes holds true. Increasingly, however, it is the emotional dimension that determines critical behaviors and, therefore, enterprise success.

HOW EMPLOYEE PRIDE TURNED AROUND A GM PLANT

Consider the classic story of the General Motors (GMC) manufacturing plant in Wilmington, Delaware, in 2000 or so.[2] For sound rational reasons, GMC corporate leadership had decided to close the more than forty-year-old plant over a two-year period because the investment required to fit the company's current product strategy did not make economic sense. The decision was announced at a gathering of plant employees by a corporate executive who explained the rationale, expressed his sorrow and concern for the workers, and, in the spirit of honesty, added that "there is really nothing anyone here can do to change this decision."

When the plant manager, Ralph Harting, addressed the employees afterward in a very emotional session, he acknowledged that the plant closing decision could not be reversed. However, he also issued a compelling emotional challenge that "we still have two years to demonstrate how wrong that decision was." With no promise of either job security or nearby plant opportunities, the Wilmington workforce set about "proving the bastards wrong."

And so they did. Within the two-year death sentence, the plant's productivity went from the *last* quartile to the *first* quartile among GMC's seventy-plus plants in North America. In fact, their death sentence was finally "commuted" for nearly fifteen years, and the plant is still in modified operation. During the two-year miracle turnaround, a lot of "rational changes" were made in the operating processes and procedures of the plant, but the major difference in its performance came from the incredible emotional commitment that Harting's leadership team created throughout the workforce. For several years afterward, at major employee gatherings, they played a tape of the "nothing you can do about it" message followed by Harting's "proving the bastards wrong" message. And it was usually greeted with standing applause and open emotional feelings.

In this case, Ralph was able tap into his plant's unrealized performance potential by using elements of the informal organization to instill pride in the day-to-day work—and thereby create a tighter emotional connection to rational performance metrics. Truly successful leaders do this all the time, even if their actions on the formal side are given more press than the informal.

Turning Around Aetna by Creating a New Corporate Identity

Jack Rowe was a highly respected doctor and hospital administrator with little business experience before he was named the new CEO of Aetna in March 2000. Aetna was near financial collapse due to "a perfect storm" of external pressures and internal confusion. Rowe was hardly an obvious choice; in retrospect, however, it is clear that he was a very wise choice. Within five short years, Aetna rose like a phoenix from the ashes of near-bankruptcy to increase its return to shareholders by more than 700% and go from a $1-million-per-day loss in 2000 to realizing $1.4 billion in operating income in 2005. In 2006, when Rowe turned his CEO role over to Ron Williams, his executive partner in the effort, Aetna was widely heralded as one of the most successful turn-arounds in recent North American business history.

The Aetna turnaround story has been told many times in the business press, but almost always with a focus on the standard formal elements of their success. These are what the business press instinctively looks for: strategy reformulation, top leadership changes, broad organizational restructuring, cost and headcount reduction, balance sheet strengthening, budgetary control, and operating rigor. That, of course, is where every turnaround story starts—and usually where it ends. Not so with the Aetna story.

Rowe knew that the *informal identity* of Aetna needed as much repair as the formal. To that end, he created informal interactions, councils, forums, and networks whose purpose was sharply focused and whose membership and working approach were highly flexible. Aetna's historical cultural values were also injured, but rather than res-urrect an old corporate value statement (there had been many over the years), Rowe opened a companywide dialogue with employees at every level to craft a new "Aetna Way." As comprehensive and impres-sive as Aetna's formal efforts were, they would not have been nearly as effective without the accompanying informal support that motivated critical behavior changes in essential parts of the company. These net-works, communities, and forums created new flows of knowledge and a resurgence of the pride that people felt in their day-to-day work.

• • •

Jack Rowe and Ralph Harting were basically doing the same thing: mobilizing emotions to motivate higher levels of performance than can be realized simply through the rational side of organizations. They accomplished this largely through the informal organization.

FORMAL AND INFORMAL INTEGRATION

Of course there are many similar stories of great leaders who seize moments of crisis to engender widespread, somewhat irrational, emotional commitment. Well-known examples include Southwest

Airline's early "survival wars" against Braniff, the USMC's "restoration of the warrior spirit" after a demoralizing Korean War experience, and KFC's recovery after global icon Colonel Sanders died. Such crises have always produced emotional as well as rational commitment—and always will. However, the real question for "organizations of the future" will be how to systematically and consistently capture the performance benefits driven by emotion when there is no crisis to draw on.

We believe the answer lies in more conscious efforts to marshal and integrate elements of the informal organization with the formal. In the past, most organizations left the informal elements to instinct and chance; in contrast, today's peak-performing enterprises increasingly develop innovative approaches and mechanisms to influence the informal, by doing all of the following:

- They consciously enforce value-based behaviors to support strategy.
- They supplement their organizational structures with networks of interaction as well as communication.
- They motivate through metrics as well as by instilling pride in the day-to-day work.

This kind of integration is often difficult to see, because the formal organization is more visible than the informal. Howard Shultz, the CEO and chairman of Starbucks, was quoted in a 1998 *Fast Company* article, "You can't grow if you're driven only by process, or only by creative spirit. You've got to achieve a fragile balance between the two sides of the corporate brain."[3] We could not agree more.

Turning Around a Troubled School

Lily Din Woo is known as a "fast-fixer" principal at the Hernando DeSoto School (PS 130) in Manhattan's Chinatown. Some people might see her as someone who bends the rules, but New York's best educators know the truth: she is a savvy and talented innovator who knows how to use the informal elements of her organization to get what her school needs.

When Lily took over as principal of PS 130 in 1990, the school was in dire need of a turnaround—it was barely passing minimum performance requirements and in serious danger of facing state-mandated takeover. Over the next eighteen years, Lily pulled off the incredible educational feat of turning PS 130 into one of New York's best public elementary schools. Today, students at her school score in the top 10% of the city.

Lily succeeded because she has found creative ways of integrating the informal with the formal elements of organization. New York City's Department of Education (DOE) has a long history of unwieldy bureaucratic measures that have frustrated and discouraged many well-intentioned principals who tried to change things while adhering to the rules. In marked contrast, Lily has steered through and past the piles of paperwork and exhaustively extensive protocol policies. In addition, she has focused on creating emotional bonds with her teachers, reaching out to parents, and connecting with people from all over the city who can help her achieve her goals.

When Lily became principal of PS 130, she walked blindly into a hornet's nest. Although she had decades of preparation working as a teacher, staff developer, and administrator, she came to PS 130 as an outsider. She had always been part of the Chinatown community, but no one at PS 130 seemed ready for a shake-up, and she instantly felt unwelcome. In fact, the community literally protested her appointment. The school's assistant principal, a man who had already devoted over thirty years to PS 130, was the favorite candidate, and parents and teachers were appalled to discover that an outsider had landed the job over him. The protests made it clear to Lily that she faced an uphill battle to win over the faculty, the administration, the union, and the parents.

To gain trust, Lily made tough sacrifices on her end, such as by cutting the number of school secretaries from three to one. She communicated her standards to teachers, continually energizing them to try new methods, learn from each other, and get involved in students' lives. She worked indefatigably to target the school's areas of weakness. As she quickly realized, the problems for the children at PS 130 stemmed from language issues. Both the union and the administration were resistant to change, but she argued that PS 130 had unique problems and needed a unique solution. Her persistence allowed her to supplement the district's math curriculum, which parents had complained was too easy, and also to obtain extra resources toward improving language skills.

In our view, "fast-fixer" is just another way of saying that Lily has a high level of what we call "organizational intelligence quotient" (or OQ). She understands what the formal organization can and cannot do. When it is found wanting, she consistently finds creative ways to mobilize the informal organization to get what she needs and achieve the goals of her students and her school. She somehow always seems to get the difficult job done, whether it's obtaining funding for a new initiative or having the flexibility to design special training programs for her teachers. For example, she built trust with parents by teaching free adult English classes on weekends. Over the years, the tide has shifted so strongly in Lily's favor that she is able to use an informal network of supporters to help raise funds for enrichment programs, especially arts classes, which are traditionally underfunded by the city. For the past six years, the Parents Association has hosted an annual Chinese banquet to raise funds and celebrate the school's success. Using strong parental support to raise extra funds is one more example of how Lily navigates the informal waters to sneak through or squeak past the roadblocks of the formal organization.

Clearly, PS 130 is markedly different from the school it was eighteen years ago. With very high test scores, the DeSoto elementary school is a model for all of New York. According to one third-grade parent, "The credit lies with Principal Lily Woo, who manages to combine a genius for fiscal management with the hands-on involvement that finds her sitting at the door of the school every morning greeting her one thousand-plus students by name."

Although Lily worked her magic by outwitting the limitations of the DOE's formal organization, the chancellors in charge of New York's public schools have begun to recognize the opportunity presented by Lily and other fast-fixer principals like her. Realizing that principals are slowed down by excessive red tape and administrative roadblocks, the administration has begun several initiatives that focus on managing the informal more effectively. For example, the city of New York is instituting programs that allow principals to exert more control of their budgets and hiring processes in order to take better advantage of the informal organization as well as reshape the formal organization to better accommodate informal elements.

Turning Around Bell Canada

In the commercial world, similar initiatives are emerging. For example, like most companies in the telecommunications industry, Bell Canada found itself in the midst of a major technological and cultural change effort in 2003.[4] The old methods of communicating through telephone lines and copper cables were (and still are) rapidly giving way to broadband wireless connections and Internet protocols. For Bell Canada, this meant shrinking profit margins and diminishing market share.

When we first met Michael Sabia, Bell's CEO, at a dinner that year, he described the Bell change challenge as follows: "We have worked with various internal and external experts to develop our new strategy, organization, and operating approaches. We have also strengthened our leadership and planning processes, and launched a number of formal programs to reduce costs and build the new capabilities we will need going forward. But we are still not getting nearly enough traction across our thirty-five-thousand-person workforce. Many remain confused, frustrated, and anxious—almost like 'deer in the headlights'—about the changes we need them to make. We simply must find a better way to motivate and energize them in new directions, and we don't have much time."

Sabia was a dynamic and analytical strategist. His long, successful career included government positions, and he had engineered the turnaround at the Canadian Railroad before joining an ailing Bell Canada. The previous Bell CEO had jumped on the multimedia bandwagon and diverged into many different businesses. When Sabia stepped into the office, his first job was to sharpen the strategy, redesign the supporting structures, and align the leadership to pursue a new vision. But even after these achievements, he knew he was far from done.

Over dinner, Sabia lamented how few employees were motivated to change behaviors. For example, every year Bell Canada conducted an Employee Value Index survey that measured employees' engagement, and the most recent scores were results that most companies would welcome. Sabia, however, was disappointed because it was clear that high engagement scores were not leading to the behavior change he needed. Nor was the collective impact of several recently launched HR initiatives doing the job yet. He continued to feel pressure to move faster.

Moreover, Sabia was particularly frustrated because he and his leadership group had rigorously applied every *formal* element of organization they could think of. Yet they were still lacking enough people momentum to realize their strategic imperatives. At that point, he decided to seek out a dozen of his best frontline motivators, and start *informal* interactions with them. He wanted to learn what managers who were well known for delivering results were actually doing differently from most other "good" managers in the system.

So Sabia and his team turned to a few frontline managers who were motivating their people to do what had to be done. It turned out that these managers were concentrating almost solely on making their people *feel good about the work itself*—before, during, and after the task at hand. Surprisingly, they were also behaving very differently from the comprehensive approach outlined in the company's formal leadership model and training programs. They were delivering the desired results by *motivating their people*, not by *mastery of process*.

However, contrary to the popular image of the "people person" manager who seeks workforce approval by trying to make the work environment engaging, these so-called pride-builders were extremely demanding. They were focused on results and held their teams to high standards. In essence, they rejected the conventional wisdom about having to choose between making people feel good about their work and delivering results; instead, they did both. Exhibit 9.1 illustrates how these different kinds of managers compared.

The rather unexpected "Aha!" for Sabia now seems obvious to him: if he could get a critical mass of managers across the company to simply *focus on instilling pride in the work itself*, it would make a big difference. Now that he understood what those managers were doing, the question was, how could he get more managers to do that?

Well, why not just realign the management priorities, metrics, and monetary rewards to implement necessary behavior changes?

EXHIBIT 9.1. COMPARISON OF MANAGEMENT STYLES.

	A "Good" Manager	A "People Person"	A "Pride-Builder"
Is passionate about . . .	Measurable results	Personal feelings	Connecting company needs to individual definitions of "success"
Makes decisions by . . .	Being fair and rational; focusing on efficiency and impact of decisions	Talking through issues with his team; explaining the "why" while remaining hands-on	Actively involving staff in finding solutions; empowering people to pursue ideas even if not in full agreement
Develops people by . . .	Helping those with higher potential progress along formal development paths	Using his contacts to create development opportunities for all his people	Acting as a powerful agent for her people's development
May be described as . . .	"A solid manager—I'm confident with her at the helm . . . [She] gives me the tools to get the job done."	"Easy to work with—believes people matter more than numbers."	"Someone you never want to disappoint . . . She trusts me in ways that make me a better worker—she supports me to go above and beyond."

Time and money were the reasons why not; it would take many months, if not years—and a ton of money—to realign the formal management system again. Nor was there any guarantee that such a realignment would provide more traction the second time around. Alignment mechanisms in the formal organization are based on the premise that all employees are similarly motivated.

In truth, every employee has his or her own definition of success and what matters most. Unless employees are able to see their work through their personal lens, behavior change is minimal at best. Sabia needed a lot more a lot faster than the formal system could provide. So he asked his small group of frontline motivators to help him find a better way.

Over the next few years, Michael Sabia and his team set the stage for one of the biggest transformations Bell Canada would see in its 120-year history. He drove this change by integrating key elements of the informal with the formal organization, counting on the informal's organic responsiveness and fluidity to accelerate change. The timeline highlights of Bell Canada's plan included the following:

- In spring 2004, Sabia identified twelve managers who were exceptional at motivating their people to higher levels of performance results and called them "pride-builders." As he learned what they did, it was clear that they sometimes behaved differently from how they were formally instructed. Moreover, it was clear that they were doing several things more spontaneously and personally—things that merely good managers were *not* doing.
- In summer 2004, he engaged with them directly as a group, and he asked them to be change agents and to help spread their management approach across the company without waiting for changes in formal training or management manuals. This direct involvement came as a surprise to the group, and as one pride-builder, Angel Prescott-Brown, remarked, "I want to go back and tell my team: 'This came from the powerhouse of our company, and this is how you make a difference.' . . . It's definitely the way the company needs to go, and I'm very excited to be a part of it."
- In fall 2004, Sabia identified another fifty pride-builders, brought all of them together, and created an informal network; it soon became the nucleus of a pride-builder "community of practice." "The employees were just given the time to sit around a room and talk to each other," said team member Christian Broussard. "Once you create that team spirit, it doesn't go away." These kinds of communities provided an environment where members could connect,

share best practices, and draw emotional motivation to continue the hard work of change.

- In winter 2004, Sabia engaged with 30 out of 120 VP-level executives, and he empowered them to take ownership of the change effort as well, particularly in mobilizing collaboration across formal organizational barriers. This group had never worked together before, but according to Domenica Maciocia, it "enabled us to create links and synergies across teams. And when those synergies come together, the solutions are very different—they're much richer." The relationships they built in ongoing quarterly meetings created a strong informal network that permeated the most senior levels. Collectively, they reached out to help the pride-builders, helped each other, and provided Michael and his team with honest and sound advice.

This community of emerging pride-builders grew to more than two thousand members in just two short years. There are other parts of the story, but what we want to highlight here is how Michael and his team tapped into the informal organization to catalyze a significant change effort.

CONCLUSION

Some argue that current technology and methodology for mapping informal networks and relationships make it possible to "organize the unorganizable." For example, because we can easily determine the nodes and densities of informal networks, why not simply get them organized? Let's design the optimal network, put someone in charge, hold him or her accountable, and enforce the interactions with metrics. In some cases, that may be a good thing to do. The problem, of course, is that it simply transfers the "informal network" into the "formal system." Sometimes this is the right path to take, but only with the recognition that the "converted" informal elements will be replaced. Rest assured, no matter how tightly you design and control it, there will still be informal elements on the loose. You simply cannot corral them all.

You can, however, mobilize informal networks in ways that retain the basic advantages of responsiveness, flexibility, and emotionality. And therein lies the secret to the organization of the future. It will excel at understanding and integrating the elements of the informal organization in ways that preserve its unique ability to influence emotional connections that support and energize the formal. One is not intrinsically better than the other.

Endnotes

1. Davis, Albie. "Dynamic Conflict Management: The Wisdom of Mary Parker Follett." Speech given at Beyond Mediation: Strategies for Appropriate Early Dispute Resolution in Special Education conference, Consortium for Appropriate Dispute Resolution in Special Education, Washington, DC, 2002.
2. Katzenbach, Jon. *Why Pride Matters More Than Money*. New York: Crown Business, 2003.
3. Muoio, Anna, "Growing Smart: Unit of One." *FastCompany*, July 1998, no. 16, p. 76.
4. Reingold, Jennifer, and Yang, Jia Lynn. "The Hidden Workplace." *Fortune*, July 23, 2007, pp. 98–106.

CHAPTER TEN

BEYOND RETIREMENT

Mature Workers Are Essential Talent for Organizations of the Future

Richard J. Leider

*Richard J. Leider is founder and chairman of the Inventure Group in Minneapolis, a coaching and consulting firm specializing in helping leaders and individuals discover the power of purpose. He is the author of eight books, including three best-sellers—*The Power of Purpose, Repacking Your Bags, *and* Whistle While You Work—*and his work has been translated into twenty-one languages.* Repacking Your Bags *has sold more than half a million copies and has been on the best-seller lists in Japan, Germany, and Sweden. His most recent book,* Something to Live For: Finding Your Way in the Second Half of Life, *has been touted as a breakthrough book on "purposeful aging." As a spokesperson on positive aging issues, Leider appears in the* Wall Street Journal, *the* New York Times, *and* USA Today, *and on television and public radio. He is widely recognized as a pioneer in the field of coaching, and* Forbes *ranks him as one of the top five most respected executive coaches.*

What is "beyond retirement"? What is the new way to do retirement? What is the purpose of retirement today? The nature of retirement is changing dramatically and profoundly in ways that are little understood. At the same time, mature workers are becoming the essential talent of the organizations of the future.

We're living longer and working longer. The longevity revolution is uncovering new questions for organizations and new choices for individuals. Breakthroughs are needed, and choices must be made.

We need new language and new maps for the territory normally called "retirement." We need to re-create retirement as we know it.

The workforce is aging. During the next twenty years, 80 percent of workforce growth in the United States—and even more dramatically in Europe—is going to be in the over-fifty age group. As the seventy-six million baby boomers start retiring, there simply won't be enough younger people entering the workforce to make up for the loss. Both the quantity and quality of talent leaving will be a competitive loss for organizations that are unprepared.

Our culture offers us precious little guidance on living the second half of our lives. Turning fifty or sixty is a milestone that for many people elicits feelings of apprehension, if not outright depression. Their parents' generation assumed that these years involve getting ready for retirement. But for many people in this age group, retiring to a full-time life of leisure looks neither emotionally nor financially satisfying.

Part of the problem is that our culture lacks a clear picture of what we are meant to be doing during our second half. We assume that these years are likely to be an extension of the commitments and enterprises we undertook earlier—an extension that for all too many people feels increasingly devoid of meaning. Our cultural glorification of youth further distorts the picture. Despite the fact that most of us are still full of life and energy, we are subconsciously entering the second half of life with an outdated script.

The good news, however, is that there are interesting new scripts at hand to help "new elders" re-create retirement.

WHO ARE THESE NEW ELDERS?

In a survey by the MetLife Mature Market Institute, almost 70 percent of working people over age fifty said they expected to continue to work for pay after retiring from their current career.

Many people age fifty and older are "new elders"—people who are motivated to work in the second half of their lives. Some need to work for financial reasons. Others want to work for personal reasons—to learn, to grow, to be part of a community, to do meaningful things. Work offers many of the essentials of vital aging, including identity, structure, personal fulfillment, and a reason to get up in the morning.

But today's new elders want to work on their own terms. So the challenge for the organizations of the future will be to find new ways to connect with these people before they "take the package," and offer them a "new package." Creative organizations will need to rewrite the rules of engagement beyond retirement. They will need to create work arrangements that make *staying* more attractive than *leaving*.

Business philosopher Charles Handy declared that the very word *retirement* should be banned because "retirement is death." I agree! Face it: we're going to live longer and be far more productive in the second half of our lives than our parents were.

The second half of life, however, is a territory with no maps. Until the late twentieth century, there was no concept of retirement and beyond because there wasn't enough time between midlife and dying. In 1900, the average life expectancy was around forty-seven years. This differed little from human experience throughout the ages. Today, the average life span in the United States is around eighty years! For most of human history, people died around what we call midlife. We are the first humans to venture into retirement and beyond, in large numbers.

RETIREMENT ISN'T WHAT IT USED TO BE

Retirement isn't what it used to be, so the successful organization of the future will have to take a different point of view on age and the mature worker.

In my executive coaching practice, I have heard over and over, "What's next?" and "I want to work beyond retirement, but what can I do?"

Retirement offers a critical yet confusing choice to grow or die! Why do so many retirees get sick or die shortly after retiring? Why do so many marriages go through so much disruption, or end altogether? Why is the suicide rate in the United States highest among white males over the age of sixty-five? Retirement without a purpose is an invitation to an early demise.

Retirement mirrors the paradox of life itself. It offers us simultaneously the opportunity to grow whole as we grow old. The work of growing whole, in fact, is essential to our health and longevity beyond retirement. Continuing to learn and grow promises us the vitality essential to staying alive. And work could be the perfect school for vitality beyond retirement.

Normal retirement is not normal. The longevity revolution is giving many people pause to reconsider what is normal about retirement. Over the past fifty years, retirement has been viewed as an ending—the end of working—and the beginning of a lifelong vacation. Today, however, retirement is viewed by many as a beginning—an empty canvas, a blank page, a hunk of clay to be shaped in new, creative ways. The new normal—beyond retirement—demands a new purpose for retiring.

Working on Purpose

Over the past several years, I have designed and led (and taught others to lead) a program titled Working on Purpose. People from all walks of life between the ages of forty and eighty engage in a reflective daylong experience that provides the framework and the tools to make and sustain change at midlife and beyond. The goal is to help people devise a guidance system beyond retirement—into a new territory without maps.

The second half of life often means a longer life, but buried inside this quantitative change is the possibility of a qualitative one—the evolution of a different view of life from the one that got us to midlife in the first place. The new viewpoint involves redefining the purpose of retirement.

For people moving into this new territory, an external guidance system often loses its potency in favor of an internally directed one. E. B. White captured the essence of this idea when he wrote, "I arise in the morning torn between a desire to save the world and a desire to savor the world. This makes it hard to plan the day." With all due respect to Mr. White, this integrated viewpoint makes it *easier* to plan the day. Choosing to both save and savor life opens the possibility for more authenticity, wholeheartedness, and propensity for true joy beyond retirement.

Many people who attend the Working on Purpose seminar are surprised to learn that just because they are grown-ups doesn't mean they are finished growing. But they must make a choice. Qualitative change beyond retirement isn't inevitable. The first half of life requires building a life structure; the second half is about freedom. Many people contemplating the "What's next?" question are wondering whether they can be themselves and do what they want and still make a living. Of course, some people simply don't think much about what they will do in the second half of their lives; instead, they simply plan to extend the first half of their lives. But increasingly, for many, the first-half structure no longer works. They find themselves feeling uneasy. They struggle with not being able to decide, "What's next?"—the drain of indecision. They need help, and successful organizations of the future will offer them that help through programs like Working on Purpose.

Many people see the end and feel a deep need to live life now, in the present moment. Sometimes they are in real pain. The questions I hear reflect both the hunger and the fear that come with facing what's beyond retirement. "Is this all there is?" "Why don't I feel the passion I once did?" "Will the second half just be a repeat?" Sometimes major events, such as deaths, illness, divorce, financial failures, job loss, or other family issues, trigger the uneasiness. For those who get guidance to squarely face the years beyond retirement, exploring the new questions can lead to the revelation that they do have choices. And the new choices can be exhilarating! They have discovered that the period of life beyond retirement can be about far more than the continuation of their first half—that it can be about the awakening of their finest and wisest selves.

ORGANIZATIONS OF THE FUTURE WILL HELP RE-CREATE RETIREMENT

Many organizations are beginning to recognize that it is in their self-interest, as well as enlightened policy, to emphasize retention and recruitment of the age fifty-plus worker. The value of these employees will become increasingly apparent as the workforce ages in the years ahead. For example, by the year 2010, more than 40% of the registered nurse workforce will be over the age of fifty. This has profound implications for the health care system overall as well as for individual nurses who face a myriad of decisions to make regarding the second half of their lives.

The annual AARP Best Employers for Workers Over 50 awards are dominated by health care companies, followed by financial services and educational institutions. Many in these fields recognize the advantages that older workers bring to their organizations. Consistent winners include a broad range of employers, including these, to name just a few:

- Scripps Health (San Diego)
- Deere and Company (Moline, Illinois)
- Massachusetts Institute of Technology (Cambridge)
- The Principal Financial Group (Des Moines, Iowa)
- Pitney Bowes (Stamford, Connecticut)
- Whirlpool Corporation (Benton Harbor, Michigan)
- Volkswagen of America, Inc. (Auburn Hills, Michigan)

The following are the top five criteria most important in the AARP Best Employers selection process:

1. Employee development opportunities
2. Health benefits for employees and retirees
3. Age of the employer's workforce
4. Alternative work arrangements and time off
5. Retirement benefits and pensions

And the top advantages of mature workers (based on a nationwide AARP survey of human resource managers) included their experience, reliability, knowledge, loyalty, and stability.

AARP also awards the annual Bernard E. Nash Award for Innovation. This award is given to three AARP Best Employers with exemplary practices in recruitment, flexible work options, and rehiring of retirees. Examples of past winners include the following:

- First Horizon National Corporation (for its flexible work options)
- Pepco Holdings, Inc. (for its retiree work opportunities)
- Carondelet Health Network (for recruitment)

As the population ages, the organizations of the future will no longer be able to rely on a large pool of young workers. Hiring mature workers seems like a natural solution: they will be better educated, they will have a lifetime of experience, and they will be better suited to a job market that has become more flexible, mobile, and much less physically demanding.

The wave of baby boomers entering retirement age threatens to create such a void in the workforce that even state governments are shaping policies and programs to keep older workers working. It is even on the radar screen of the National Governor's Association to study ways to keep mature workers in the workforce, including as volunteers or part-time workers.

The longevity revolution might turn out to be something good for individuals and organizations across the country. Here are just a few examples:

- Arizona launched a Mature Workforce Initiative and a Web site (www.azmatureworkers.com) that will provide online listings of paid and volunteer work. The program also highlights businesses that are perceived to be "mature worker friendly."
- Maryland passed the Baby Boomers Initiative Act.
- New York has a Mature Worker Task Force.
- Massachusetts has a Coalition on Vital Aging.

FINDING NEW PURPOSE FOR THE SECOND HALF OF LIFE

Many mature workers today are envisioning what kind of life they want at sixty, seventy, eighty, and beyond. What will be the defining purpose of their day? Instead of narrowing their horizons as they age, they want to widen them. Instead of withdrawing from active life, they want to push out their boundaries. They realize that they have more time, and no time to waste. They are choosing what's worth doing with their most precious currency—their time.

Many, of course, need to work in the second half to survive, but there are others in less financial need who simply want to do meaningful work. Both want a clear answer to the question, "What will make me want to get out of bed in the morning?"

Purpose is the answer to that question. Purpose is the operating system beyond retirement. It is on our hard drives. We are born for a reason, and that reason doesn't disappear at some particular age. But we must install new software in the second half of our lives. We must discover a new reason for getting up in the morning.

Most religious and spiritual traditions support the notion that there is a purpose, a reason each of us is on the planet. It's the spiritual sense that each of our lives matters. Somehow each of us fits into the larger patterns of life from cradle to grave. Purpose does not cease calling forth our talents at age sixty, seventy, eighty, and beyond.

We sense this in wise leaders in our organizations. We observe the energetic power of purpose in new elders like Jimmy and Rosalyn Carter. Jimmy Carter won the Nobel Peace Prize twenty years after losing the White House. New elders like the Carters share a powerful intention to work on purpose in the second half of life—to do work that is at once meaningful to themselves and at the same time of value to the organizations, communities, or world at large they care about.

In 1900, there were thirteen million people in the United States over the age of forty-five. Now there are nearly one hundred million. The organizations of the future will employ many new elders who are engaged in a whole new experiment in working beyond retirement.

CHAPTER ELEVEN

THE BEST HOPE FOR ORGANIZATIONS OF THE FUTURE

A Functioning Society

Ira A. Jackson

Ira A. Jackson is dean and professor of management at the Peter F. Drucker and Masatoshi Ito Graduate School of Management at Claremont Graduate University in Claremont, California, where he is also a board member of the Drucker Institute. Previously he was director of the Center for Business and Government and associate dean of the John F. Kennedy School of Government at Harvard, executive vice president of BankBoston, and Massachusetts Commissioner of Revenue. With Jane Nelson, Jackson is the author of Profits with Principles: Seven Strategies for Delivering Value with Values *(Doubleday).*

Peter Drucker rarely predicted the future. He thought it more prudent to capture the future that is already here but not yet fully understood by others: "I look out the window and see what is visible, but not yet seen." If he were here to look around today, he might well tell us what leading-edge organizations are doing in ways seen and unseen. So let's take a tour of emergent organizations with Peter Drucker at our side and ask, What would he think they tell us about where we are?

New Organizations with New Attitudes Toward Creating, Connecting, and Giving Back

We can only imagine what Drucker might say about organizations of the future already around us today. Some, like Google and Teach For America, have already enriched the lives of millions. Others, like Al Qaeda, have introduced the world to tremendous new evils. And there are some, like MySpace and the UN Global Compact, that are full of promise but whose potential we don't yet know.

Drucker might have observed that Google, which encourages employees to devote a day a week to doing something outside their job description, represents a new paradigm. Theirs is a knowledge-based business where human creativity is the most precious resource and where loyalty is equated with fulfillment and freedom with innovation. I think Peter would have been delighted and would have seen in Google a company that is creative, knowledge and innovation driven, and socially conscious. He would have seen a business that constantly reinvents itself, yet is organized more as a lattice and a network than a hierarchy. Google is less an adaptation, migration, or iteration of organizations from some other era than a truly new form of organization for a new reality. (Not coincidentally, Eric Schmidt, Google's CEO, says, "At Google, we think business guru Peter Drucker well understood how to manage the new breed of 'knowledge workers.' After all, Drucker invented the term in 1959.")

Peter might have seen in MySpace, YouTube, Craigslist, and eBay fluid new forms of organization that reflect society's need for flexibility, immediacy, community, and connections that traditional organizations and business simply don't provide. Again, I think Peter would have been pleased with the fusion of technology and changing lifestyles, where novel forms of organizational adaptation meet new social and economic needs and norms.

He would have applauded Teach For America's success in unleashing the idealism of some of the best and the brightest, luring them to inner-city classrooms rather than to Wall Street. Teach For America, founded in 1990, has attracted seventeen thousand recent college graduates and professionals who commit to teaching for two years in urban and rural public schools in low-income communities, where they have reached out and touched some 2.5 million students. CityYear and Jumpstart are other examples of idealism put into practice—exciting new social initiatives started by college and university students, run with entrepreneurial savvy and in partnership with business and government, leveraging the skills of young people to give back and help out with intractable problems usually associated with young people. CityYear, the granddaddy of the three, is now twenty years old; it operates in eighteen cities and has nine thousand alumni who have given a year and collectively more than fifteen million hours of disciplined community service in exchange for a minimal stipend and a tuition scholarship. Jumpstart, with an incredible 20% annual growth rate, has plans to engage five thousand college students reaching out to twenty thousand preschool children primarily in Head Start programs by 2011. In Teach For America, CityYear, Jumpstart, and so many other new forms of social innovation, Drucker would have seen the flowering of a new age and new wave of social entrepreneurship—something arguably not seen in America in more than a century.

Looking at the opposite end of the spectrum, Drucker might have warned us that Al Qaeda is yet another creative adaptation of a new organizational form, a stateless terrorist network of amazing ingenuity and dastardly ambition that suggests yet another form that organizations will mutate and migrate to in the future—as they are already. (Presciently, he warned about terrorism, the suitcase-size nuclear bomb, and the urgent need for new forms of international cooperation as far back as 1973.)

He might have offered a curious nod to the UN Global Compact that bridges businesses, governments, and NGOs in a voluntary network pledged to advance human, labor, and environmental rights and to fight corruption. And he might have seen in this unusual and creative alliance the emergence of a new and needed form of transnational organization to address issues too complex for governments alone to solve and too intractable for any one sector to tackle by itself. We haven't witnessed anything as organizationally original on the international scene perhaps since Bretton Woods more than sixty years ago. Peter saw the need for stronger and smarter government, not less government, to handle transnational issues.

A NEW SENSE OF SOCIAL RESPONSIBILITY

I think Drucker would have smiled at the proliferation of new versions of old institutions and the revival of some old practices at new institutions—and he would have seen these developments as suggestive that, in some ways, we are rushing headlong back to the future. That durable old standby, the most enduring secular institution in our society, the university, is finally reinventing itself with enormous rapidity, developing linkages with business and government, creating new transdisciplinary initiatives, going global, and repricing its products and finding new methods of distribution for radically different markets.

Drucker would have delighted, I think, in much of this organizational improvisation. He would have taken great satisfaction in seeing business taking on a needed sense of social responsibility. He might have said, "What took you so long!" to university presidents. He would have been excited to learn that the largest student group at the Harvard Business School today is not the venture capital or investment banking association, but the social entrepreneurship club. This would have been especially welcome to Peter because he almost gave up on business and looked to the social sector and perhaps this new fourth sector, the combination of social mission with sustainable profitability, to provide community and to solve some of society's most daunting challenges.

I think he would have been elated to see millions of young people, whatever their political orientation, suddenly energized by the U.S. presidential race, connecting with each other in new ways, and re-igniting a sense of responsibility and engagement and idealism that America hasn't experienced in forty years.

Many of us in the academy focus on the internal processes of organizations and their behaviors. We have scholars here at the Drucker School, for instance, such as Craig Pearce, who are researching, writing about, and teaching new concepts of distributed and shared leadership. Others, like Jean Lipman-Blumen, have identified what makes "hot groups" work, and have written about toxic leaders and their intoxicated followers. Mihaly Csikszentmihalyi has been writing about "flow" and how to release organizational creativity in ways that parallel the peak performance of great athletes and artists. Charles and Liz Handy were here at the Drucker School and Drucker Institute this year and developed a novel course titled the Odyssey, which explores values and ambitions through an inner journey of discovery. Drawing on all the disciplines—from art and architecture to biology and psychology—the Handys used photographs, artifacts, and narrative to help students unlock the inner passions and beauty of individuals and their organizations.

Peter would have loved these lines of inquiry and the creative search for new ways to build more effective organizations. He would have seen in Lipman-Blumen's work somber reflections of his own concern about charismatic leadership and the perils of totalitarianism that he first wrote about after fleeing his native Austria in 1933. I think he would have seen in Pearce's work manifestations of his own belief that innovation and creativity are the inexhaustible and renewable fuel of the knowledge economy, and that only through new and better ways of connecting, respecting, and engaging knowledge workers can a firm's innovative productivity be fully realized. He would have marveled at Csikszentmihalyi's use of psychology and neurology, because Peter saw management as a liberal art that linked disciplines, cut across boundaries, and integrated insights from various perspectives in a coherent vision and operating philosophy. And he would have beamed at Charles and Liz's photomontage of student introspection and visions of the future; after all Peter arrived here at Claremont thirty-five years ago initially to study and teach not about management but about Japanese art.

My own work, and that of others such as David Cooperrider (at the Center for Business as an Agent of Social Change at Case Western Reserve University) and Jane Nelson (director of the Corporate Social Responsibility Program at Harvard), has shifted from the processes of the firm to its *purpose*, from techniques to *principles*, from structure to *design*. I'm not certain how Peter would have regarded this work, but I sense that he would have been both thrilled by some of the new trends and skeptical that we yet have a firm grasp on exactly what it is we are describing. For instance, my gut feeling is that he would have applauded the notion of triple-bottom-line accounting (to measure not only economic but also environmental and social results); after all, Peter basically predicted the concept of a balanced scorecard.

Peter was perhaps the first to identify that a company's social impact is as important as its financial contribution. In his waning days, he spoke as a modern-day Jeremiah about how we were not yet adequately counting or accounting for the destruction we are doing to the environment. Peter would have commended organizations that now incorporate critical assessments of social and environmental impacts. He also would have cautioned that we not let a fad or trend overcome the need to base our understanding on analysis of performance and not just intent. He would have been rigorous, perhaps ruthless, in calling for a much more empirical approach—and he would have been very pleased to see solid work being done on new accounting schemes and values-based accounting and analysis, along the lines of what James Wallace is pursuing here at the school named in honor of Peter Drucker himself. Drucker always looked at the organization from the outside in, and social responsibility—including social responsibility for wealth creation—was at the heart of managerial responsibility.

HUGE GROWTH IN THE SOCIAL SECTOR AND NONPROFIT ORGANIZATIONS

One trend in society and in organizations in particular that I think would have most intrigued and most encouraged Drucker is the explosion of creativity and new organization in the social sector. NGOs have grown by some 50% in the United States in the last ten years alone, from a million to more than 1.5 million nonprofit institutions. More important, Brazil and other emerging powers have witnessed a similar flowering and proliferation of social experimentation through voluntary and nonprofit action. Drucker would have said "Amen!" He firmly believed that there cannot be a healthy economy in a sick society. He felt that it is in the nonprofit social sector that we can rediscover our sense of community and achieve the legitimacy that has always been the glue of American society, as de Tocqueville observed almost two hundred years ago. And Drucker would have continued to push for more effective management in the social sector as he did just in the last two decades of his life.

Last year, I delivered the keynote address at a meeting of the Peter F. Drucker Academy in Beijing. The organizers didn't want a lecture on the latest on global supply chain management or international trade trends, but, rather, a talk about the importance of social entrepreneurship and what successful capitalists in China can and should do to foster more social innovation by building partnerships with NGOs, training social risk takers, and leveraging corporate philanthropy for societal transformation. How Drucker would have smiled to know that a convening of fabulously successful managers of growing businesses in China were focusing on the importance of civil society, not just economic growth—and in his name!

MORE CORPORATIONS ARE "DOING GOOD WHILE DOING WELL"

Another trend in society and organizations that would have intrigued and encouraged Drucker is what folks at Procter & Gamble call "corporate social opportunity." This is the trend to create new organizations or to re-create existing organizations deliberately to do good while also doing well, to meet pressing social needs while also opening new markets, creating new products, and eventually creating new value. In an interview with David Cooperrider, Peter said, "I wrote about it many years ago . . . that every single social and global issue of our day is a business opportunity in disguise—just waiting for the innovation, the pragmatism, and the strategic capacity of great companies to aim higher."

Drucker was often years if not decades ahead of the rest of us, and his decades-old vision of corporate social opportunity is only now coming of age. He planted the seeds of this turn at General Electric when he counseled Jack Welch to have GE focus on being number one in only four or five lines of business (which was pretty sound advice, given that GE emerged as the single most successful firm in the world by market cap while Jack focused on implanting that simple strategy). I can only imagine how pleased Peter would be to see that Jeff Immelt, Jack's successor, has built on that solid foundation to now pursue a new focus, cutting across all its businesses, of finding opportunity in the global climate crisis by driving GE's future growth through "ecomagination."

Drucker would have been similarly proud of his disciple A. G. Lafley at P&G, who is pioneering new products, some in conjunction with the Centers for Disease Control and Prevention and with international NGOs, which combine P&G's capacity for innovation with the needs of desperately poor people for basic nutrition and sanitary products, such as antibacterial soap and basic water purification. In these and other instances, we aren't witnessing so much the invention of new organizations as the adaptation of existing organizations to focus on new markets in new ways—new markets that are, to use C. K. Prahalad's helpful imagery, at the bottom of the pyramid. P&G and GE and many others are turning developing countries, inner cities, and other previously marginalized markets into fertile soil and beta sites for product innovation and corporate reinvention. This isn't corporate social responsibility; it's reengineering the basic DNA of the firm to take on and create new customers (and make a profit) by addressing and solving some of the world's most intractable problems. These organizations are creating value with values.

FAILURES IN TAKING CARE OF COMMUNITY, PEOPLE, VALUES: A RESPONSIBILITY GAP

Despite the encouraging trends and organizations creating hope for the future, there is a third, countervailing, trend that I think Peter would be most alarmed by. Too many of our organizations are failing to be good stewards of their resources, their communities, their people, and their values. As a result, much of society is unhealthy.

Consider just a few examples of how far we have deviated from a responsible path, and how far and fast we need to engage in midcourse correction before it is too late:

- According to the World Bank, $1 trillion in bribes change hands each year.
- One in ten citizens in the world paid a bribe to receive a basic service last year.
- 31%: that's the amount of time employees waste each year on the job in the private sector due to poor planning and mismanagement.
- $4,100: that's the cost per employee of theft and fraud in the workplace.

- 56%: that's the proportion of MBA students who admit to cheating on exams; these are the same young people we are training to be future effective managers and ethical leaders.
- 82%: that's the proportion of existing managers and business leaders who admit to cheating on the golf course, where so many business transactions occur.
- 257: that's the number of firms actively under investigation by the SEC or the FBI or the Justice Department or that are conducting internal reviews for backdating stock options—a practice akin to betting on the ponies after they have left the gate.
- 24,000: that's the number of people who die each day from hunger or malnutrition—at a time when we have adequate supplies to feed everyone in the world.
- $9 trillion: that's the size of our accumulated federal deficit, which has been rising exponentially over the past two decades. The Government Accountability Office forecasts that by 2040, we will be able to pay for nothing more than Social Security and interest on the debt.
- 1.2 million: that's the number of high school kids who drop out of school each year—relegating them to a life of menial labor at a time of labor shortages in our knowledge economy.
- Five hours: that's how long it takes the average CEO of a major firm in America to earn as much as the average employee at his or her firm earns in a year.

A great distance has opened up between the obligations of our organizations—to be effective managers and ethical leaders—and their actions. This distance—this chasm, this gulf—is the Responsibility Gap. This is the gap between what we know and what we do; between what we have and how we deliver what we have; between what we were given and what we leave behind; between what we know is right and what we actually produce, which is frequently wrong and harmful. I believe that Drucker would have been concerned, even alarmed about this Responsibility Gap.

Remember: Drucker saw society not as something that organizations *belong to*, but rather as something that organizations *make*. He was concerned that organizations in all sectors of society—public, private, and philanthropic—operate responsibly. For Drucker, responsibility meant combining effective management (doing things right) and ethical leadership (doing the right thing). Drucker was haunted by the specter of Nazi Germany and the failure of organizations to work effectively and honestly, which ushered in the rise of totalitarianism in the twentieth century. He would be concerned today, as he was when he last wrote and spoke in 2005, that the most important organization of all—our society—is increasingly dysfunctional and too often acts irresponsibly.

Drucker called himself a social ecologist, one concerned with the man-made environment and systems, the way a natural ecologist is concerned with the biological environment and natural systems. If he were alive today, I think he might have seen the Responsibility Gap as the moral equivalent of global warming. Unless we improve our environmental stewardship and reduce our carbon footprint, the earth stands to perish. Unless our organizations become more effective and ethical, society stands to perish.

Back to the Future: It's About Responsibility, Stupid!

So I conclude, regretfully, on a subdued note. The organization most desperately in need of improvement and reinvention is not a firm or a collection of NGOs or even our government. It is the larger organization of society itself that now beckons. We are now at what Pete Peterson, the senior chairman of the Blackstone Group and former U.S. Secretary of Commerce, calls "the make or break point in American history." Organizations in each sector and across sectors must work in closer collaboration, in better harmony and purpose and balance to get the entire equation—of more responsible management and leadership—right for all for the future.

The Puritans traveled west in 1620 with visions of a city on a hill, a beacon to all mankind. Talk about an organization for the future, or a big audacious goal! They espoused the notion of stewardship—that they would leave things better than they found them—and we are their heirs. We are the heirs of ancient Greece and the Athenian oath, whereby citizens pledged not only to obey the law but to leave things better than they found them, more beautiful, and with greater opportunity for others to come. And we are heirs of the Navajo, who say that we don't inherit the land from our parents—we borrow it from our children.

If Drucker were alive today, he might remind us that the first obligation of any organization should be *primum non nocere*—above all, do no harm. (And oh, how he would have railed against the greed that propelled the subprime lending meltdown, and how avoidable he would have thought it might have been if, first, lenders and bankers and regulators had stopped to think through the predictable consequences of loaning to poor people at predatory rates in the middle of a classic bubble in the housing market.)

Maybe in thinking about the future of organizations, it is back to the future. Back as far as the Hippocratic oath and requiring such a commitment from every manager and every leader: first, do not knowingly do anything that might be harmful or hurtful or destructive. And only then would we move on to other, more virtuous aspects of management and leadership—such as acknowledging that management is first and foremost about people, that values matter, that effectiveness is a higher standard than brilliance, that learning from each other and for a lifetime matters, and that we are all in this together.

Here in Claremont, Peter Drucker's home for over three decades and the perch from which Drucker issued his clarion call, we have created a new organization to answer that call. The Drucker Institute, based at Claremont Graduate School and closely affiliated with the Drucker School of Management, is stimulating ethical leadership and effective management across all sectors of society by taking Drucker's principles and practices well beyond Claremont, to new audiences in new ways. We have transformed Drucker's archives into an active memorial, much the way the Institute of Politics at Harvard has transformed John F. Kennedy's legacy into an active memorial to public service. Through the patient and skillful updating by Joe Maciariello, we are making Drucker's thirty-nine books and hundreds of articles available in condensed curricular form for audiences ranging from corporate CEOs to high school students in Estonia. We are linking scholars with doers and engaging them in a new global network of Drucker Societies, now numbering twelve, and spanning from New York City to Vienna, from Buenos Aires to Beijing. We are planting the seeds of a global, grassroots movement that rallies concerned individuals and organizations to close the Responsibility Gap. We are helping create organizations that are both effectively managed and ethically led. And we are building partnerships to bring a balance between sectors through the convergence of market efficiency, social equity, and moral legitimacy.

Whatever form organizations take in the future, we know that in a world that has acted so irresponsibly and unethically, organizations will require better management and leadership. That's perhaps the only sure antidote to growing inequality and injustice and floundering democracies in so many lands. We are now at the tipping point as a society. If we want to leave to our children a healthy society, one that offers growth and security, meaning and freedom, opportunity and fairness, then the organization we most urgently need to repair is society itself. We need to create what Drucker called a functioning society: one that is well managed, well led, and respectful of the need for innovation and strength and accountability in each of its sectors, public, private, and philanthropic. That organization—the functioning society—is what Drucker saw as the best hope for our future.

CHAPTER TWELVE

REFRAMING ETHICS, SPIRIT, AND SOUL

Lee G. Bolman and Terrence E. Deal

Lee G. Bolman holds the Marion Bloch Missouri Chair in Leadership at the Bloch School of Business and Public Administration, University of Missouri-Kansas City. Bolman's interests lie in the intersection of leadership and organizations, and he has published numerous articles, chapters, and cases, and is coauthor with Terrence E. Deal of numerous books on leadership and organizations. Bolman has been a consultant to corporations, public agencies, universities, and public schools in the United States, Asia, Europe, and Latin America.

Terrence E. Deal is a retired professor who has taught at Stanford, Harvard, Vanderbilt, and the University of Southern California. Deal has been a police officer, public school teacher, high school principal, district officer administrator, and university professor. His primary research interests are in organization symbolism and change. He is the author of thirty books, including the best-seller Corporate Cultures *(with A. A. Kennedy) and* Shaping School Culture *(with K. Peterson).*

What shall an organization profit if it should gain the world but lose its soul?[1]

For Starbucks chairman Howard Schultz, the answer is "not a lot," which is why he raised exactly that question in a memo to everyone in his company in 2007.

In the case of Enron, the answer was evidently "nothing at all"; the company eventually lost both its soul and the world it hoped to gain when its financial maneuvers inflated revenue and hid debt, the off-balance-sheet shenanigans came home to roost, and the company imploded. At the heart of this tragedy, the company lost track of what it was or stood for.

Enron's story is far from unique. Over the years, corporate flameouts have recurred around the world. What can managers and organizations do about this abysmal state of moral lapse? We believe that ethics must reside in soul, a sense of bedrock character that harbors core beliefs and values. In this chapter, we discuss why soul is important and how it sustains spiritual conviction and ethical behavior. We then present a variegated picture of leadership ethics.

SOUL AND SPIRIT IN ORGANIZATIONS

What Enron lacked becomes obvious if we compare it to the pharmaceutical giant Merck, one of America's most successful firms. Merck states its core purpose as preserving and improving human life, above making a profit. A noble sentiment, but is it reflected in key decisions and everyday behavior? Mostly yes, though Merck has sustained legitimate criticism in recent years for being slow to acknowledge health risks with some of its best-selling drugs, such as Vioxx.[2] But Merck can also point to a number of instances of its selling a drug at a loss or giving it away to fulfill the company's core value of putting patients first.

In one well-known example, Merck had to decide whether to develop and distribute a drug for river blindness, an affliction of poor people in many third-world countries. From a cost-benefit viewpoint, the choice was clear: the drug had little chance of making money. For bottom-line-driven companies, such a decision would be a no-brainer. Yet Merck, true to its emphasis on health, developed the drug and then gave it away. The company's commitment to its values made the decision easy, the CEO said afterward.

In contrast, "the woods were filled with smart people at Enron, but there were really no wise people, or people who could say 'this is enough.'"[3] Some of us have such strong ethical convictions that it matters little where we work, but many of us are more shilly-shally, attuned to cues and expectations from our colleagues at work about what to do and not to do. Enron lost track of its redeeming moral purpose, and it failed to provide ethical guardrails for its employees. Some went to jail, and many others suffered damage to careers and self-worth.

Many dispute the notion that organizations possess soul, but there is growing evidence that spirituality is a critical element in long-run success. A dictionary definition of soul uses such terms as "animating force," "immaterial essence," and "spiritual nature." For an organization, group, or family, soul can also be viewed as a resolute sense of character, a deep confidence about who we are, what we care about, and what we deeply believe in. Merck had it. Enron did not. Starbucks is concerned about losing it.

Why should an organization—a company, a school, or a public agency—be concerned about soul? Many organizations and most management writers either scoff at or ignore the matter. For example, some management strategists attributed the enormous success of Southwest Airlines to its strategic prowess,[4] but founder Herb Kelleher offered a very different explanation for what makes Southwest work, one that features people, humor, love, and soul: "Simply put, Kelleher 'cherishes and respects' his employees, and his 'love' is returned in what he calls 'a spontaneous, voluntary overflowing of emotion.'"[5] But Kelleher's attitude is only part of the Southwest success story. Soul, the heart of the "Southwest spirit," is shared throughout the company. Kelleher claimed that the most important group in the company was the "Culture Committee," a seventy-person cross section of employees established to perpetuate the company's values and spirit. There were plenty of skeptics, but even after Kelleher turned over the reins to hand-picked successors in 2001, Southwest's growth and profitability continued to top its industry year after year.

A growing number of successful leaders embrace a philosophy much like Kelleher's. Ben Cohen, cofounder of the ice cream company Ben & Jerry's Homemade, observes, "When you give love, you receive love. I maintain that there is a spiritual dimension to business just as there is to the lives of individuals."[6] And Howard Schultz of Starbucks echoes Cohen's sentiments in his emphasis on culture and heart. Moreover, evidence suggests that tapping a deeper level of human energy pays off: *Built to Last* describes how corporations that have succeeded over the long haul had a core ideology emphasizing "more than profits" and offering "guidance and inspiration to people inside the company."[7]

Soul and ethics are inextricably intertwined. Recent decades have regularly produced highly public scandals of major corporations engaging in unethical, if not illegal, conduct. It happened in the 1980s, a decade of remarkable greed and corruption in business. It happened again with the spate of scandals in 2001 and 2002, as well as in the subprime mortgage mess of 2007–2008. Efforts to do something about the ethical void in management have ebbed and flowed as dishonor comes and goes.

One proposed remedy is to place more emphasis on ethics in professional training programs. A second has sparked a flurry of corporate ethics statements. A third has pushed for stronger legal and regulatory muscle, such as the Foreign Corrupt Practices Act, forbidding U.S. corporations from bribing foreign officials to get or retain business, and "SOX"—the Sarbanes-Oxley Act of 2002[8]—which mandated a variety of measures to combat fraud and increase corporate transparency.

These are important initiatives, but they only skim the surface. Robert C. Solomon calls for a deeper "Aristotelian ethic": "There is too little sense of business as itself enjoyable (the main virtue of the "game" metaphor), that business is not a matter of vulgar self-interest but of vital community interest, that the virtues on which one prides oneself in personal life are essentially the same as those essential to good business—honesty, dependability, courage, loyalty, integrity. . . . The point is to view one's life as a whole and not separate the personal and the public or professional, or duty and pleasure."[9]

Solomon chose the term *Aristotelian* because it makes no pretensions of imparting the latest cutting-edge theory or technique of management. Rather, he reminds us of a perspective and debate reaching back to ancient times. The central motive is not to commission a new wave of experts and seminars or to kick off one more downsizing bloodbath. "It is to emphasize the importance of continuity and stability, clearness of vision and constancy of purpose, corporate loyalty and individual integrity."[10] Solomon reminds us that ethics and soul are essential for living a good life as well as for managing a fulfilling organization.

We've identified four frames that carry implications for creating ethical communities and for reviving the moral responsibilities of leadership. Exhibit 12.1 summarizes our view, and the rest of this chapter explains each of the frames in more detail.

EXHIBIT 12.1.   REFRAMING ETHICS.

Frame	Metaphor	Organizational Ethic	Leadership Contribution
Structural	Factory	Excellence	Authorship
Human resource	Extended family	Caring	Love
Political	Jungle	Justice	Power
Symbolic	Temple	Faith	Significance

THE FACTORY: EXCELLENCE AND AUTHORSHIP

One of our oldest images of organizations is that of factories engaged in a production process. Raw materials (steel, peanuts, or five-year-olds) come in the door and leave as finished products (refrigerators, peanut butter, or educated graduates). The ethical imperative of the factory is *excellence:* ensuring that work is done as effectively and efficiently as possible to produce high-quality yields. Since the publication of Tom Peters and Bob Waterman's famous book, almost everyone has been searching for excellence, though flawed products and mediocre services keep reminding us that the hunt does not always bring home the quarry.

One source of disappointment is that excellence requires more than pious sermons from top management; it demands commitment and autonomy at all levels of an enterprise. How do leaders foster such dedication? As we've said before, "Leading is giving. Leadership is an ethic, a gift of oneself."[11] Critical for creating and maintaining excellence is the gift of authorship:

> Giving authorship provides space within boundaries. In an orchestra, musicians develop individual parts within the parameters of a musical score and the interpretative challenges posed by the conductor. Authorship turns the pyramid on its side. Leaders increase their influence and build more productive organizations. Workers experience the satisfactions of creativity, craftsmanship, and a job well done. Gone is the traditional adversarial relationship in which superiors try to increase control while subordinates resist them at every turn. Trusting people to solve problems generates

higher levels of motivation and better solutions. The leader's responsibility is to create conditions that promote authorship. Individuals need to see their work as meaningful and worthwhile, to feel personally accountable for the consequences of their efforts, and to get feedback that lets them know the results.[12]

Southwest Airlines offers a compelling example of authorship. Its associates are encouraged to be themselves, have fun, and above all use their sense of humor. Only on Southwest are you likely to hear required FAA safety briefings sung to the music of a popular song or delivered as a stand-up comedy routine. ("Those of you who wish to smoke will please file out to our lounge on the wing, where you can enjoy our feature film, *Gone with the Wind*.") Too frivolous for something as serious as a safety announcement? Just the opposite: it's a way to get passengers to pay attention to a message they usually ignore. Surely, it's also a way for flight attendants to have fun and feel creative rather than being mechanically scripted by routine.

THE FAMILY: CARING AND LOVE

Caring—one person's compassion and concern for another—is both the primary purpose and the ethical glue that holds a family together. Parents care for children, and, eventually, children care for their parents. A compassionate family or community requires servant-leaders concerned with the needs and wishes of members and stakeholders. This creates a challenging obligation for leaders to understand and to provide stewardship of the collective well-being. The gift of the servant-leader is love.

Love is largely absent from most modern corporations. Most managers would never use the word in any context more profound than their feelings about food, family, films, or games. They shy away from love's deeper meanings, fearing both its power and its risks. Caring begins with knowing; it requires listening, understanding, and accepting. It progresses through a deepening sense of appreciation, respect, and ultimately love. Love is a willingness to reach out and open one's heart. An open heart is vulnerable. Confronting vulnerability allows us to drop our mask, meet heart to heart, and be present for one another. We experience a sense of unity and delight in those voluntary, human exchanges that mold "the soul of community."[13]

They talk openly about love at Southwest Airlines. As president Colleen Barrett reminisced, "Love is a word that isn't used often in Corporate America, but we used it at Southwest from the beginning." The word love is woven into the culture. They fly out of Love Field in Dallas; their symbol on the New York Stock Exchange is LUV; the employee newsletter is called *Luv Lines;* and their twentieth-anniversary slogan was "Twenty Years of Loving You."[14] They hold an annual "Heroes of the Heart" ceremony to honor members of the Southwest family who have gone above and beyond even Southwest's high call of duty. There are, of course, ups and downs in any family, and the airline industry certainly experiences both. Through life's peaks and valleys, love holds people—both employees and passengers—together in a caring community.

For Levi Strauss, the issue of caring came to a head in trying to apply the company's ethical principles (honesty, fairness, respect for others, compassion, promise keeping, and integrity) to the thorny dilemmas of working with foreign subcontractors. How should the company balance concern for domestic employees with concern for overseas workers? Even if pay and working conditions at foreign subcontractors are below those in the United States, are inferior jobs better than *no* jobs? A task force set to work to collect data and formulate guidelines for ethical practice.

Ultimately, the company wound up making some tough decisions. It became the first American clothing company to develop a set of standards for working conditions in overseas plants. It pulled out of China for five years beginning in 1993 because of human rights abuses, despite the huge market potential there. In a factory in Bangladesh employing underage children, Levi's arranged for the children to go back to school while the contractor continued to pay their salaries.[15]

THE JUNGLE: JUSTICE AND POWER

We turn now to a third image: the organization as jungle. Woody Allen captured the competitive, predator-prey imagery succinctly: "The lion and the calf shall lie down together, but the calf won't get much sleep."[16] As the metaphor suggests, the jungle is a politically charged environment of conflict and pursuit of self-interest. Politics and politicians are routinely viewed as objects of scorn—often for good reason. Their behavior tends to prompt the question: Is there any ethical consideration associated with political action?

We believe there is: the commitment to justice. In a world of competing interests and scarce resources, people are continually compelled to make trade-offs. No one can give everyone everything they want, but it is possible to honor a value of fairness in making decisions about who gets what. Solomon sees justice as the ultimate virtue in corporations, because fairness—the perception that employees, customers, and investors are all getting their due—is the glue that holds things together.[17]

Justice is never easy to define, and disagreement about its application is inevitable. The key gift that leaders can offer in pursuit of justice is to share power. People with a voice in key decisions are far more likely to feel a sense of fairness than those with none. Leaders who hoard power produce powerless organizations. People stripped of power look for ways to fight back: sabotage, passive resistance, withdrawal, or angry militancy.

Giving power liberates energy for more productive use. If people have a sense of efficacy and an ability to influence their world, they are more likely to direct their energy and intelligence toward making a contribution, rather than making trouble. The gift of power enrolls people in working toward a common cause. It also creates difficult choice points. If leaders clutch power too tightly, they activate old patterns of antagonism. But if they cave in and say yes to everything, they put an organization's mission at risk.

During the Reagan administration, House Speaker "Tip" O'Neil was a constant thorn in the side of the president, but they carved out a mutually just agreement: they would fight ferociously for their independent interests but stay civil and find fairness wherever possible. Their rule: "After six o'clock, we're friends, whatever divisiveness the political battle has produced during working hours." Both men gave each other the gift of power.[18]

Power and authorship are related; autonomy, space, and freedom are important in both. Still, there is an important distinction between the two. Artists, authors, and craftspeople can experience authorship even working alone. In contrast, power is meaningful only in relation to others. It is the capacity to wield influence and get things to happen on a broader scale. Authorship without power is isolating and splintering; power without authorship can be dysfunctional and oppressive.

The gift of power is important at multiple levels. As individuals, people want power to control their immediate work environment and the factors that impinge on them directly. Many traditional workplaces still suffocate their employees with time clocks, rigid rules, and authoritarian bosses. A global challenge at the group level is responding to ethnic, racial, and gender diversity. Dominant groups typically don't see the problems of others: "Systems are most often designed by dominant group members to meet their own needs. It is then difficult to see the ways in which our institutions and structures systematically exclude others who are not 'like us.' It is hard to…question what we have always taken for granted and [it is] painful to confront [our] personal complicity in maintaining the status quo. Privilege enables us to remain unaware of institutional and social forces and their impact."[19]

Therefore, justice requires that leaders systematically enhance the power of subdominant groups, in the following ways:

- Ensuring access to decision making
- Creating internal advocacy groups
- Building diversity into information and incentive systems
- Strengthening career opportunities[20]

All this happens only with a rock-solid commitment from top management, which was the only condition that one researcher found to be universal in organizations that led in responding to diversity.[21]

Justice also has important implications for the increasingly urgent question of "sustainability": How long can a production or business process last before it collapses as a result of the resource depletion or environmental damage it produces? Decisions about sustainability inevitably involve trade-offs among the interests of constituencies that differ in role, place, and time. How do we balance our company's profitability against damage to the environment, or current interests against those of future generations? Organizations with a commitment to justice will take these questions seriously and look for ways to engage and empower diverse stakeholders in making choices.

THE TEMPLE: FAITH AND SIGNIFICANCE

An organization, like a temple, can be seen as a hallowed place, an expression of human aspirations, a monument to faith in human possibility. A temple is a gathering place for a community of people with shared traditions, values, and beliefs. Members of a community may be diverse in many ways (age, background, economic status, personal interests), but they are tied together by shared faith and bonded by a sanctified spiritual covenant.

In work organizations, faith is strengthened if individuals feel that the organization is characterized by excellence, caring, and justice. Above all, people must believe that the organization is doing something worth doing—a calling that adds something of value to the world. Significance is partly about the work itself, but even more about how the work is embraced. This point is made by an old story about three stonemasons giving an account of their work. The first said he was "cutting stone." The second said that he was "building a cathedral." The third said simply that he was "serving God."

Temples need spiritual leaders. This does not mean promoting religion or a particular theology; rather, it means bringing a genuine concern for the human spirit. The dictionary defines spirit as "the intelligent or immaterial part of man," "the animating or vital principle in living things," and "the moral nature of humanity."

Spiritual leaders help people find meaning and faith in work and help them answer fundamental questions that have confronted humans of every time and place:

- Who am I as an individual?
- Who are we as a people?
- What is the purpose of my life, of our collective existence?
- What ethical principles should we follow?
- What legacy will we leave?

Spiritual leaders offer the gift of significance, rooted in confidence that the work is precious, that devotion and loyalty to a beloved institution can offer hard-to-emulate intangible rewards. Work is exhilarating and joyful at its best; arduous, frustrating, and exhausting in less happy moments. Many adults embark on their careers with enthusiasm, confidence, and a desire to make a contribution. Some never lose that spark, but many do. They become frustrated with sterile or toxic working conditions and discouraged by how hard it is to make a difference, or even to know if they have made one. The gift of significance helps people sustain their faith rather than burn out and retire from a meaningless job.

Significance is built through the use of many expressive and symbolic forms: rituals, ceremonies, stories, and music. An organization without a rich symbolic life grows empty and barren. The magic of special occasions is vital in building significance into collective life. Moments of ecstasy are parentheses that mark life's major passages. Without ritual and ceremony, transition remains incomplete, a clutter of comings and goings; "life becomes an endless set of Wednesdays."[22]

When ritual and ceremony are authentic and attuned, they fire the imagination, evoke insight, and touch the heart. Ceremony weaves past, present, and future into life's ongoing tapestry. Ritual helps us face and comprehend life's everyday shocks, triumphs, and mysteries. Both help us experience the unseen web of significance that ties a community together. When inauthentic, such occasions become meaningless, repetitive, and alienating—wasting our time, disconnecting us from work, and splintering us from one another: "Community must become more than just gathering the troops, telling the stories, and remembering things past. Community must also be rooted in values that do not fail, values that go beyond the self-aggrandizement of human leaders."[23]

Stories give flesh to shared values and sacred beliefs. Everyday life in organizations brings many heartwarming moments and dramatic encounters. Transformed into stories, these events fill an organization's treasure chest with lore and legend. Told and retold, they draw people together and connect them with the significance of their work.

Music captures and expresses life's deeper meaning. When people sing or dance together, they bond to one another and experience emotional connections otherwise hard to express. The late Harry Quadracci, CEO of the printing company Quadgraphics, convened employees once a year for an annual gathering. A management chorus sang the year's themes. Quadracci himself voiced the company philosophy in a solo serenade.

Max De Pree, famed both as both a business leader and an author of elegant books on leadership, is clear about the role of faith in business: "Being faithful is more important than being successful. Corporations can and should have a redemptive purpose. We need to weigh the pragmatic in the clarifying light of the moral. We must understand that reaching our potential is more important than reaching our goals."[24]

Spiritual leaders have the responsibility of sustaining and encouraging faith in themselves and in recalling others to the faith when they have wandered from it or lost it.

CONCLUSION

Ethics ultimately must be rooted in soul: an organization's commitment to its deeply rooted identity, beliefs, and values. Each of the frames we have discussed offers a perspective on the ethical responsibilities of organizations and the moral authority of leaders. Every organization needs to evolve for itself a profound sense of its own ethical and spiritual core. The frames offer spiritual guidelines for the quest.

Signs are everywhere that institutions in many developed nations suffer from a crisis of meaning and moral authority. Rapid change, high mobility, globalization, and racial and ethnic conflict tear at the fabric of community. The most important responsibility of managers is not to answer every question or get every decision right. Though they cannot escape their responsibility to track budgets, motivate people, respond to political pressures, and attend to culture, they serve a deeper, more powerful, and more enduring role if they are models and catalysts for such values as excellence, caring, justice, and faith.

Endnotes
1. The question paraphrases Matthew 16:26: "For what is a man profited, if he shall gain the whole world, and lose his own soul?" (King James version).
2. Fielder, J. H. "The Vioxx Debacle Revisited." *Engineering in Medicine and Biology Magazine, IEEE*, 2005, *26*(4), 106–109.
3. John Olson, cited in Eichenwald, K. "Audacious Climb to Success Ended in a Dizzying Plunge." *New York Times*, January 13, 2002, pp. 1, 26–27.

4. Hamel, G., and Prahalad, C. K. *Competing for the Future*. Boston: Harvard Business School Press, 1996; Treacy, M., and Wiersema, F. *The Discipline of Market Leaders*. New York: Basic Books, 1997.
5. Farkas, C. M., and De Backer, P. *Maximum Leadership: The World's Leading CEOs Share Their Five Strategies for Success*. New York: Henry Holt, 1996, p. 87.
6. Levering, R., and Moskowitz, M. *The 100 Best Companies to Work for in America*. New York: Plume, 1993, p. 47.
7. Collins, J. C., and Porras, J. I. *Built to Last: Successful Habits of Visionary Companies*. New York: HarperBusiness, 1994, pp. 48, 88.
8. Officially, the Public Company Accounting Reform and Investor Protection Act of 2002.
9. Solomon, R. C. *Ethics and Excellence: Cooperation and Integrity in Business*. Oxford, Engl.: Oxford University Press, 1993, p. 105.
10. Solomon, 1993, p. 104.
11. Bolman, L. G., and Deal, T. E. *Leading with Soul: An Uncommon Journey of Spirit*. 2nd. ed. San Francisco: Jossey-Bass, 2001, p. 106.
12. Bolman and Deal, 2001, pp. 111–112.
13. Whitmyer, C. *In the Company of Others*. New York: Putnam, 1993, p. 81.
14. Levering and Moskowitz, 1993.
15. Waterman, R. H., Jr. *What America Does Right: Learning from Companies That Put People First*. New York: Norton, 1994.
16. Allen, W. *Without Feathers*. Cambridge, Mass.: Ballantine, 1986, p. 28.
17. Solomon, 1993, p. 231.
18. Neuman, J. "Former President Reagan Dies at 93." *Los Angeles Times*, June 6, 2004, p. 1.
19. Gallos, J. V., Ramsey, V. J., and Associates. *Teaching Diversity: Listening to the Soul, Speaking from the Heart*. San Francisco: Jossey-Bass, 1997, p. 215.
20. Cox, T., Jr. *Cultural Diversity in Organizations: Theory, Research, and Practice*. San Francisco: Berrett-Koehler, 1994; Gallos, Ramsey, and Associates, 1997; Morrison, A. M. *The New Leaders: Guidelines on Leadership Diversity in America*. San Francisco: Jossey-Bass, 1992.
21. Morrison, 1992.
22. Campbell, D. "If I'm in Charge, Why Is Everyone Laughing?" Paper presented at the Center for Creative Leadership, Greensboro, N.C., 1983, p. 5.
23. Griffin, E. *The Reflective Executive: A Spirituality of Business and Enterprise*. New York: Crossroad, 1993, p. 178.
24. De Pree, M. *Leadership Is an Art*. New York: Dell, 1989, p. 69.

CHAPTER THIRTEEN

ENVIRONMENT DRIVES BEHAVIOR AND EXPECTATIONS

Bill Strickland with Regina Cronin

Bill Strickland is the president and CEO of Manchester Bidwell Corporation and its subsidiaries, Manchester Craftsmen's Guild and Bidwell Training Center. The facilities include a 40,000-square-foot production greenhouse, where students cultivate orchids for wholesale distribution; a 70,000-square-foot medical technology complex that has exceeded $8 million in value; and a 62,000-square-foot facility as a mortgage-free asset. The facilities also include a music and lecture hall; library; art studios and labs; dining and meeting rooms; and state-of-the-art, award-winning audio and video recording studios. Strickland has affiliates in three major U.S. cities and is currently cultivating collaborative partnerships in ten other domestic and international cities. Throughout his distinguished career, he has been honored with numerous prestigious awards for his contributions to the arts and the community, including the MacArthur Fellowship for leadership and ingenuity in the arts.

Regina Cronin is a freelance writer who has been a public school teacher in Japan on the JET Programme and worked in the financial services sector. She holds a BA in Japanese and a BS in finance from the University of Maryland and an MA in international relations specializing in Japan from the Paul H. Nitze School of Advanced International Studies (SAIS) of the Johns Hopkins University. Cronin has been a longtime friend of the MBC family.

The organization that I built in 1968 has evolved into a nationally recognized center for vocational and arts education for the economically dislocated and underserved. Today it is known as Manchester

Bidwell Corporation (MBC). It began with very modest roots during the riots and civil disturbances of the mid- and late 1960s. I remain a native of the Manchester community where our center is located in Pittsburgh, Pennsylvania.

The organization of the future—particularly in the fields of education, community economic development, and social service—must bring an alternative value proposition to seemingly insurmountable problems in these fields. Countless millions of dollars have been spent over the years to rehabilitate large-scale public school systems and job training centers, with limited success. These failed attempts were caused in part by the inability of some organizations to adopt cultures that emphasize *individual participation, creativity*, and *responsiveness*. Also, many of these organizations would benefit by embracing a values-based organizational culture that views the future as one of *hope* and *promise*. These organizations need to engage challenges, retain inherent flexibility, and view human beings as assets and not as liabilities.

Organizations that embrace this values-based strategy are the ones that are best adapted to be part of the complex global economy that moves across languages, geography, religious affiliations, and political differences. The organization of the future must create a new universal enterprise language based on culture and enlightened work environments. These organizations need a cultural system that is nimble and based on nonbureaucratic organizational structures that focus on the needs of the customers and not exclusively on the needs of the company itself.

The philosophy that my small administrative staff adopted early on was to redefine the way we looked at poverty and to bring innovative solutions to the problems of the inner city. We have held the belief that all people, regardless of background and social circumstances, are entitled to be valued as assets and not liabilities. So many organizations have drifted away from this view. Given a fair chance, people will respond to hope and high expectations if offered on a consistent and systematic basis. We knew that our organization needed to move away from the pervasive "poverty program" approach. Our organization has provided people who have a complex set of problems with a way to fight the "charity" label in order to view themselves as a group joined in an effort to find and realize a life free of guilt and apology and full of promise and purpose. The principle revealed through the establishment of our center is that if you want to involve yourself in the life of people who have been given up on, you need to look like the *solution* and not the problem. Our center has produced decades of success stories, each encapsulating eloquent testimony to the power that hope instills.

Over the years, I have come to know a set of beliefs, ideas, and values in association with the work we do at our center. We had no blueprint for success other than following our innovative approach and letting visible success confirm our path forward. Consider for a moment the hundreds of millions of dollars that have been spent and perhaps lost on poverty programs, inner-city economic strategies, and subsidized housing programs of one type or another. Many of these programs were created with very high expectations and hopeful ideas, but they failed in part due to their method of execution and their lack of a leadership strategy that measured itself on performance goals and verifiable achievement. In contrast to that approach, success on this front should be based on realized *gains in the community*, not on whether the poverty program is long-standing or consistently receiving grant funds.

In fact, in many respects, the best organizations that I have encountered working in this unique space are those that routinely measure the success of their organization by gains in the community in which they have decided to focus. These organizations span a variety of sectors. For example, Southwest Airlines has high responsiveness to its employee needs. Starbucks develops innovative ideas and an environmental setting that is devoted to the promotion of community. The online commerce giant eBay focuses on the consumer experience and promotes a consumer-friendly approach. The value proposition for our organization is the success within the organization and among the clients with whom we work so that people make it out of poverty and move well beyond the need for programming in their lives.

FINDING A WAY OUT OF POVERTY

As I developed personally and professionally, I came to know these ideas, values, and beliefs that are pivotal in the work we do at our center, but when I started out in this world, I faced the same set of conditions that surround our student body today. My early academic experience provided limited possibility, and by the time I reached high school, I found myself unable to compete in a rigorous academic situation. My luck changed through what can only be described as both persistence and being in the right place at the right time.

One day in my junior year, I happened upon the art room at the very time that the art teacher—Mr. Frank Ross—was creating a large ceramic bowl. This moment in time was both magical and riveting in its glamour. I had never come across any experience in my life that affected me so profoundly. I also noted a deep sense of life and human possibility in that art room. I asked Mr. Ross right then if he would teach me that craft. He agreed, and for the remaining two years of high school, I exclusively focused on ceramics and on English literature taught by an English teacher who doubled as a jazz musician on the side.

I experienced firsthand how the arts can and often do provide transformative pathways to open the mind to different ways of assessing reality and discovering yet unexplored feelings. For people who may find their path forward blocked or unclear, the expressive process opened through the arts has facilitated the creation of brilliant insights and principles throughout history. For people whose dreams are crushed or never allowed to develop at all, being able to participate in dance, painting, music, poetry, photography, or drawing allows them to connect with fundamental feelings common to us all and unleash creative energy previously stifled.

CHANGING THE FUTURE OF VOCATIONAL EDUCATION

Upon graduating from the University of Pittsburgh in 1972, I took over a floundering vocational program called Bidwell Training Center (BTC), which at the time had completely lost its way. The center was in an abandoned warehouse with boarded-up windows, doors hanging on one hinge each, a malfunctioning heating system, and classrooms full of dilapidated furniture. The broken-down structure matched the broken culture inside. This place was supposed to be a federally backed vocational training center, but it had spiraled out of control, leaving hopelessness in its wake and a management team with pockets lined with money that should have been invested in the client base. It was a culture of failure. My first official act was to paint the entire building, establish work schedules, and insist on the total participation of the one-hundred-person staff. From our earliest days forward, I applied a combination of the principles of empathy, innovation, and high expectations enveloped in a healthy environment that began to remind people that they indeed mattered to the world at large. We used BTC as a laboratory of sorts to test these ideas.

A perceptible shift began to occur. Over time, the ideas of self-respect, pride, and taking oneself seriously began to take hold among our clients. At that time, our target client base was Pittsburgh's out-of-work steel workers, ex-convicts, and adults in transition. Through this experience, I learned the first principle for organizations of the future: that even though you may find yourself in an impossible situation, there is no excuse for dismissing it as an insurmountable challenge without question or examination. In fact, the very act of pushing back may be the first step toward freeing yourself from the bondage of seemingly impossible circumstances. Changing the way you feel and sense reality can be an act of redemption in and of itself. The act of painting our building and establishing schedules was one small step toward creating our future culture of excellence and quality.

REDEFINING AT-RISK STUDENTS AS ASSETS, NOT LIABILITIES

The Manchester Craftsmen's Guild (MCG), which I had founded in 1968, was created on an entirely different basis than Bidwell. While a college freshman, I was committed to replicating the transformative power of the arts for young people that I myself had experienced in high school. From its inception, MCG incorporated views on excellence and values-based education. The old row house we adopted as our original MCG home was extensively renovated and had state-of-the-art equipment, an experienced arts faculty, and courses offered at no cost to the students. In our early years, our staff was limited to only six people, but we provided our after-school clay arts program for over a hundred students on a weekly basis. We would go on to expand our program offerings, hire the best and brightest artists in the community, and partner with the Pittsburgh Public School System, and today we share art with more than five hundred students each week. MCG's focus, then and now, is on students who are at risk of not graduating from high school who have been given up on as hopeless. These children live in environments that are steeped in violence, leaving little room for them to dream of a better life.

I felt strongly that the best way to symbolize change was to be the change in real life. Environment drives behavior. This concept represents my second strong belief for organizations of the future. Environment is fundamental to a person's well-being, whether the environment is found in a community-based arts program, a college or university, a bank, or a global computer operations entity. People respond, as all living things do, to their customary and familiar environment. If you build a bland and uninteresting space that dulls the senses, the work product will follow in the same vein. In contrast, if you create beautiful spaces as we did, you immediately establish an entirely different way of presenting ideas to people (in our case, children) who were previously accustomed to failure and mediocrity. Our facility was calm, inviting, and emotionally safe.

Over the many years of operation since 1968, we have never experienced a fight, a drug incident, or any racial turmoil. This record has remained intact for forty years. Our experience demonstrates that a small financial investment in a good, clean, and well-articulated space generates an improved educational environment and dramatically lowers maintenance costs because of the absence of vandalism and property destruction. This is a lesson that designers of public schools should take to heart, instead of building large green edifices that have metal detectors, bars on the windows, and surveillance cameras. I believe that the organization that invests in its people by way of well-articulated locations that are modern, thoughtful, and life affirming will realize large gains in company morale, productivity, and goodwill.

For example, Steelcase, the global office furniture manufacturer, is one of our corporate partners that exemplifies this environmental philosophy in its workspaces. Organizations such as Bayer, the University of Pittsburgh Medical Center, and the regional grocery chain Giant Eagle also are organizations that demonstrate this essential philosophy. Organizations succeed when they have consciously created a work environment and organized a philosophy that is compatible with the best aspects of the human experience.

HELPING THE MOST DISADVANTAGED IN OUR SOCIETY

We have applied these principles to our development of MBC, which encompasses Bidwell Training Center (BTC) and Manchester Craftsmen's Guild (MCG). Through the incorporation of MBC in 1986, the organization has continued to respond to the needs of some of the most challenged among us, such as former drug offenders, ex-convicts, mothers on welfare, and at-risk inner-city children, through the BTC adult vocational training programs and the MCG art programs for young people. We have applied our experience gained over more than twenty years of trial and error and expanded the scope of our program offerings.

When it became time in the mid-1980s to construct new MBC facilities to respond to future challenges, I summoned all my beliefs, values, energy, and corporate contacts to build the center of the future. The way in which we approached the development of our new center in many ways embodied the very message of this chapter—that is, that values, empathy, environment, innovation, and expectations are fundamental to an organization's success. It is my belief that organizations that embrace this concept will carry us forward in the future.

In the case of our MBC building project, we hired a student of Frank Lloyd Wright to design and construct a facility that symbolized a culture of hope and promise. Our new center, which opened its doors in 1986, is a 62,000-square-foot arts and career training center, and it was so well received that the future Pittsburgh airport incorporated a number of key architectural and design elements proven to be successful in our building. MBC comprises classrooms, workshops, gallery spaces, studio space, and a 350-seat auditorium. We provide training in fields as varied as gourmet food preparation; chemical, office, and medical technologies; and education arts programming in ceramics, photography, and digital imaging to more than five hundred MCG students each year, and a total of more than fifteen thousand students so far in academia and vocational training over the past twenty-two years.

I remain convinced that many of our subsequent training and arts programs, as well as all the artistic and human achievements we have realized, were outgrowths of our community's willingness to invest substantially in a school—and workplace—of the future.

These days, when you visit our facilities in Pittsburgh, as people now do from all over the world, the hallways are flooded with sunlight, everywhere your eye turns there is something beautiful looking back at you, and our music hall contains state-of-the-art recording and audio technology. We have hosted jazz greats from all over the world—far too numerous to name them all, but a few include the late Dizzy Gillespie, McCoy Tyner, Wynton Marsalis, Herbie Hancock, Joe Williams, and Dakota Staton. Our recording label has been the recipient of five Grammy nominations and four awards for the work of the Count Basie Orchestra, Paquito D'Rivera, and Nancy Wilson. Our gourmet food training program trains unemployed people for well-paying permanent employment in the food-service industry with such organizations as Marriott, Holiday Inn, and regional Pittsburgh fine dining establishments like the Duquesne Club and the Rivers Club. This program also provides a gourmet lunch for our students, many of whom are unable to afford good, nutritious, and balanced meals each day. Our arts program includes ceramics, photography, drawing, and state-of-the-art digital imaging. Each year, more than 85% of our graduating high school seniors enter college or some other form of higher education.

In the most recent years, we have expanded our facilities in new directions. We added a 40,000-square-foot greenhouse, which provides market-ready orchids for the retail industry. The original concept was to provide a first-rate horticultural training experience for underemployed and unemployed inner-city residents. It has achieved quite a bit more: we have placed a significant number of individuals in the horticultural and floral industry who most likely would never have had a chance at life with greater possibility. We also added a retail office complex, which is fully leased. This office complex resides next door to our center in an area that was considered unleasable ten years ago. It has also stimulated peripheral new investment opportunities for area businesses.

Our experience is evidence that doing things the right way pays enormous dividends later. We established early on in our organization that we would have beauty, ambiance, food, music, orchids, modern furnishings, a bright and educated faculty, and a culture that constantly strives for the best it can do. In doing so, we have created an environment that builds on itself. Excellence is contagious once it gets going. It has been a notable accomplishment for an organization like MBC to have achieved these results in a community long considered to have among the highest of crime rates.

Our experience should also drive home the point that if the principles of fairness, excellence, beauty, and life affirmation can be achieved in a location like the north side of Pittsburgh, why not apply them to any and all companies regardless of purpose, product, or location? People are fundamentally people, regardless of their origins. I believe people would favorably respond to companies that invest time, money, and material in their well-being.

OTHER CITIES IN THE UNITED STATES AND AROUND THE WORLD ARE ADAPTING OUR MODEL

In part because of our organization's accomplishments and diversity of purpose, MBC has raised awareness levels about people once considered liabilities who are becoming assets in their communities around the United States. Subsequently, cities and civic leaders have begun to raise the question of whether the idea of Manchester Bidwell should be replicated in their communities. After some initial inquiries, it was determined that a trial replication model would be established in San Francisco. After some initial starts and stops, the Bayview Center for Arts and Technology (BAYCAT) began in 2001 as a distillation of the best practices of MBC in Pittsburgh.

In order to best meet the needs of the San Francisco community, we did not replicate the vocational and arts programs directly from Pittsburgh; rather, we adapted programs to fit the San Francisco community, not the Pittsburgh community. Instead of crafting a "franchise" of the model, we provided high-level consultation, faculty training, and organizational guidance when needed. BAYCAT adopted MBC's lessons learned regarding the physical plan of the building, the need to have high-quality equipment and amenities, and the attention that needs to be paid to the overall environment.

BAYCAT put in place a responsive and interactive program and a faculty that created a nonbureaucratic atmosphere. It also has a functioning board with representatives from a cross section of corporate and civic leadership. BAYCAT has proved to be a great success and works with more than 250 students annually on a sustained basis in film, design, and Web design.

The lessons learned from the BAYCAT experience played directly into the strategy used in the next two replication sites in Cincinnati (Cincinnati Arts and Technology Center, CATC) and Grand Rapids (West Michigan Center for Arts and Technology, WMCAT). These two centers have adopted small and efficient boards of directors, and they have created superior training facilities that are well designed, well equipped, and staffed with a responsive and innovative faculty. In response to local needs, each center has identified unique training areas in the arts and in vocational education. The centers work with an average of three hundred individuals each year on a consistent basis. Graduation and employment results have been impressive and suggest bright futures for each of these replication sites.

In addition, MBC has established the National Center for Arts and Technology (NCAT) as a subsidiary organization. NCAT has become the vehicle for replicating the model and for going to scale nationally and, someday, internationally. Formal planning processes have been created in the following cities thus far:

- New Haven, Connecticut
- Cleveland, Ohio
- Columbus, Ohio
- Philadelphia, Pennsylvania
- New Orleans, Louisiana

On the international stage, early conversations have started in Israel, Japan, Ireland, Brazil, and Costa Rica with regard to adopting the MBC model of vocational and arts education for disadvantaged and dislocated workers in these countries.

How Other Organizations of the Future Can Learn from What We Do

MBC offers the following principles for future organizations that wish to replicate the MBC model:

1. Use the core MBC program as a guide, not a template.
2. Assist, rather than direct, the effort of your local leaders to organize and articulate their own program goals and aspirations.
3. Insist on superior facilities, faculty, board, and administration of your programs.
4. Work diligently to establish a culture of innovation and enterprise.
5. Document and celebrate organizational goals and accomplishments on a routine basis, as these become guides to future successes.
6. Continually evaluate whether your program goals and aspirations are on target relative to your initial projections, and be prepared to immediately adjust strategy and goals once you've determined your focus.

These six principles have proven to be successful values for all the organizations involved, and they are based in part on the successful replication completed in the three cities outside of Pittsburgh.

Conclusion

The organization of the future must establish itself as one that elevates its employees to the level of assets and creates an environment of constant interaction between managers and employees in conjunction with an established protocol that constantly strives for excellence and ongoing improvement. It is an organization that focuses its attention on the future rather than dwelling on the past. It concerns itself with more than the financial bottom line. It defines itself as part of the global community and steps up to all the risks and responsibilities associated with executing on those values.

Through these organizations, we will begin to see the ushering in of perhaps a more humane and globally responsive system that views human beings as assets—more alike than unalike, talented, and celebrated. The system that we continue to build at MBC in Pittsburgh may hold valuable lessons for many organizations as we all examine the part we play in the future.

DESIGNING THE ORGANIZATION OF THE FUTURE

Part Three focuses on organization design, from a wide variety of perspectives: how employees work, how organizations are structured, how they need to be built to change, and how they *can* change (even if they're a hundred years old). In addition, this section offers insight into the particular needs of nonprofit organizations and educational institutions.

Leader development consultants Christopher Gergen and Gregg Vanourek kick off this part of the book by focusing on employees: they describe five significant shifts in employment; what organizations need to do differently to recruit, develop, and retain talented workers; and three trends that are changing the way people work.

Organization design expert Jay R. Galbraith shows how organizations need to change the way they're structured to accommodate an increasingly global business world. He contrasts the traditional two-dimensional structure, where businesses and functions report to the office of the CEO, with a "multidimensional" multinational structure, and shows how two blue-chip companies—Procter & Gamble and IBM—have adopted this model successfully.

Management professors Edward E. Lawler III and Christopher G. Worley focus on the need for organizations to be more agile, flexible, and innovative—in other words, to be able to adapt and change. Unfortunately, successful change efforts are few and far between, so this chapter describes how organizations need to be *built* to change, and leaders need to "create organizations that *love* changing." This chapter offers ideas on how to do exactly that.

Kathy Cloninger is the CEO of the Girl Scouts of the USA, and her chapter describes the challenges she faced trying to breathe new life into this hundred-year-old organization and make it viable in a very different world from the one it faced when it was founded. Those problems pertained to declining membership, internal struggles regarding the structure of the organization, a lack of focus, and the need for new strategy and "gap teams" to bridge the old with the new. The lessons she learned and the changes she made are relevant to any long-standing company, organization, association, or institution: read and learn!

Roxanne Spillett is the CEO of the Boys & Girls Clubs of America; in her chapter, she describes three challenges facing *all* nonprofits. One is finding the next generation of leaders (and offering compensation and other incentives to attract them). Another is finding funding in creative new ways (such as partnering with corporate giants). And the third is coordinating the organization's strategy and resources—a 360° approach—with other organizations to provide education, housing, and other services needed by the communities each organization serves.

Finally, Darlyne Bailey, who is dean of education and human development at the University of Minnesota, offers her thoughts on how the *college* of the future needs to change in order to prepare its graduating students for meaningful work in for-profit or nonprofit organizations.

CHAPTER FOURTEEN

DYNAMIC ORGANIZATIONS FOR AN ENTREPRENEURIAL AGE

Christopher Gergen and Gregg Vanourek

Christopher Gergen is a founding partner of New Mountain Ventures, an entrepreneurial leadership development company that serves clients nationwide. Gergen is also the cofounder and chairman of SMARTHINKING, an online tutoring company that has served more than two hundred thousand students; he is also a visiting lecturer and director of the Entrepreneurial Leadership Initiative in the Hart Leadership Program at Duke University.

Gregg Vanourek is also a founding partner of New Mountain Ventures. Previously, he ran Vanourek Consulting Solutions and served as senior vice president of school development for K12 Inc. (NYSE: LRN), a national online education company, and vice president for programs at the Thomas B. Fordham Foundation, a national education foundation where he also helped launch a scholarship program for underserved youth. Gergen and Vanourek are coauthors of Life Entrepreneurs: Ordinary People Creating Extraordinary Lives *(San Francisco: Jossey-Bass, 2008).*

Entrepreneurship is a defining feature of the early twenty-first century—and is certain to be an influential force in the organization of the future—but most people's thinking about entrepreneurship is now obsolete. They typically think about entrepreneurship solely in the business context (what we call "version 1.0" of entrepreneurship). But in recent years, the phenomenon of social entrepreneurship (what we call "version 2.0") exploded onto the scene, transforming the nonprofit sector and reflecting new societal values and priorities.

Today, there is a new phenomenon emerging with implications equally large: what we call *life entrepreneurship* (or "version 3.0" of entrepreneurship). With life entrepreneurship, people—especially rising generations of leaders—aren't merely embracing the entrepreneurial principles of opportunity recognition, innovation, risk, and ownership for dynamic enterprise creation or social transformation; rather, they are integrating these principles into their entire lives. Drawing from interviews with fifty-five leading entrepreneurs worldwide, we got the first deep look at this emerging cadre of social change agents. These life entrepreneurs are harbingers of changing times, signaling important shifts in the way rising generations are leading and living—and in the way tomorrow's organizations will be structured and led.

In this chapter, we identify five socioeconomic shifts—already well under way—that are bound to leave their mark on the organization of the future. Our frame is the individual—the talented knowledge worker, free agent, or self-starter who represents the spoils in what has been called the "war for talent." We also identify three newly emerging overarching trends that carry the potential to utterly transform the organization of the future.

SOCIOECONOMIC SHIFTS

In its landmark study of almost thirteen thousand executives in 120 large U.S. companies across a wide range of industries, McKinsey & Company at the turn of the millennium sounded the alarm bell that there was a "war for talent."[1] Meanwhile, executives and researchers were beginning to link talent and organizational performance. Today, forward-thinking organizations the world over are recognizing the critical importance of talent and are investing in bold initiatives to attract, develop, and retain the best and brightest. This war for talent is being waged within a context of five important socioeconomic shifts that are bound to influence the nature of tomorrow's organizations.

• • •

1.   **The increasing prevalence of "knowledge workers" is changing the nature of our workplaces.** The rise of knowledge workers

that Peter Drucker identified in the 1960s has gained momentum in the wake of the Internet boom, profoundly affecting our economy and the balance of power between employers and employees. In the 1930s, information workers were an estimated one-third of the workforce. Today, estimates put them at between two-thirds and four-fifths of the workforce.[2] Furthermore, the performance differential between a talented knowledge worker and an unexceptional one is significant, fueling demand for the most talented performers.

2. Dramatic increases in job mobility and corresponding decreases in organizational loyalty are altering the dynamics of career paths and employment trends. According to the Bureau of Labor Statistics, the median tenure for employed wage and salary workers is just four years, and 23% of them have been with their current employer for one year or less. As Harvard-based strategist and author Rosabeth Moss Kanter has pointed out, the trend is toward weaker attachments to organizations and stronger attachments to projects and teams.

3. Workers are experiencing the "flattening" of the global economy. This flattening brings with it a propensity for outsourcing, offshoring, and other disruptive competitive practices. In this environment, there is increasing commoditization of certain services. This, in turn, challenges organizations to give their talent room to collaborate, experiment, and innovate across boundaries.

4. We are on the cusp of a tectonic demographic shift. As the demand for skilled knowledge workers is increasing, the supply of foot soldiers is shrinking. In the United States, eight thousand to ten thousand baby boomers (born 1946 to 1964) turn sixty every day. By 2010, the number of what are called "prime age workers"—those between the ages of thirty-five and forty-five, from whom organizations draw most of their midlevel managers—will *decrease* by 10%. As boomers retire, this puts a double bind on the talent markets. According to one recent estimate, for every two experienced workers leaving the workforce, only one (relatively inexperienced) worker joins it.[3]

5. We are seeing a boom in entrepreneurship and related phenomena of "intrapreneurship," self-employment, and free agency. For evidence, we need only look to the darlings of today's economy: the founders of Google, YouTube, Facebook, Skype, MySpace, and others. It has been said that generations are shaped by defining moments—from World War II, the Vietnam War, and the countercultural movements of the 1960s in the United States to the Cultural Revolution in China, the fall of the Berlin Wall in Europe, and the antiapartheid movement in South Africa. Today's rising generations have come of age during the entrepreneurship era and are beginning to shape the future through their disruptive organizations and innovations. Think social networking, streaming media, open source collaboration, renewable energy, microlending, file sharing, bioengineering, nanotechnology, and more.

"At any given time," according to Carl Schramm, president of the Ewing Marion Kauffman Foundation (a leading foundation focused on entrepreneurship and education), "15% of the [U.S.] population is running their own companies. . . . These entrepreneurs, people who now create more than half the new jobs in America, are defining the new economy not just here but around the world. . . . We now live in the most entrepreneurial time in history."[4] Further, consider the following statistics:

- Nearly half a million new businesses are created each month in the United States.
- The rate of new firm creation currently exceeds the rate of new household creation and that of new births.
- More than one-third of U.S. households include someone who has founded, tried to start, or helped fund a small business.[5]

THE TALENT BATTLE FRONT

Recognizing these changes and their implications, forward-thinking organizations are making talent management a top priority—focusing on talent attraction, development, retention, and measurement (described in more detail in the next sections of this chapter). The best organizations weave all of this together into a dynamic entrepreneurial leadership culture in their organizations, with exceptional results. This has been called a "talent mindset—the passionate belief that to achieve your aspirations for the business, you must have great talent."[6]

Adopting a talent mind-set, organizations of the future are making the following changes:

- All managers in an organization—starting with the CEO—are held accountable for strengthening their talent pool (as opposed to the human resources department being solely responsible for people management).
- Leaders shape the entire company, even its strategy, to appeal to talented people (as opposed to focusing solely on pay and benefits).
- Development is fueled through stretch jobs, coaching, entrepreneurial team projects, and mentoring (as opposed to relying on traditional training programs).
- Leaders invest differentially in A, B, and C players (versus treating everyone in the same way).[7]

Attracting Talent

Starting with a talent mind-set, organizations of the future will need fresh ways to attract talent. As such approaches as on-campus recruiting, signing bonuses, multifaceted compensation packages, and the use of executive search firms become commonplace, organizations are being forced to dig deeper to attract talent. Tomorrow's organizations will have to appeal to the heartstrings and values of their recruits, some even "segmenting" their workforce and offering what have been called "employee value propositions" to their charges—a clear message to potential recruits and new hires about the unique values of the organization and what it is like to work there. Perhaps the organization of the future will spend as much time and money on research and analytics to understand its own workforce as it does on its customers.

Of course, a primary talent attractor in an organization (or sector) is the prevalence of talent already there. Talent begets talent, and so it is with mediocrity. Once an organization earns a reputation for rewarding excellence and rejecting mediocrity, it can become a magnet for top performers.

For example, consider Google, which has been able to nab the crème de la crème of the tech world, including an award-winning physician, an Internet pioneer, and top executives and engineers from Microsoft, Apple, eBay, and Amazon.[8] The company's hiring process has been called "grueling." One of Google's core principles is that "Great just isn't good enough." It values not only intelligence and aptitude but nonconformity as well, with preference given to recruits with unconventional experiences and worldviews. Each year, the company hands out multimillion-dollar "Founders' Awards" to honor teams that have made extraordinary contributions to the company.[9] Together, these approaches have sealed the company's reputation as "the place to work" for today's tech-savvy creative class.

Developing Talent

Once talented people are on board, they must be developed. In the organization of the future, training and development programs will be mission-critical. Leadership development, knowledge sharing, cross-functional teamwork, creativity, and network creation will be leading strategic priorities.

For example, Trilogy Software, a high-growth technology company based in Austin, Texas, provides an inkling of what's to come with its three-month "boot camp" for new employees:

- In the first month, teams of twenty participate in fast-paced creative exercises coached by an experienced executive (a "section leader").
- In the second month, Trilogy forms smaller "breakthrough teams" and charges them with developing new product and service ideas, creating business models, building prototypes, and developing marketing plans.
- In the third month, the company fosters personal initiative, allowing employees to continue working in breakthrough teams or to find a company sponsor to support a new project they will lead.
- At the end of the boot camp, each employee receives a comprehensive performance evaluation, including rigorous feedback from colleagues, section leaders, and senior management.

The results are impressive: more than $100 million in new business has been generated as the result of the recruits' projects. The company also credits the program with intangible benefits, such as enhanced camaraderie and motivation among new recruits and better insight into their strengths, weaknesses, and developmental needs.[10]

Google also allows engineers to devote 20% of their time—essentially a day a week—to any project they choose. This policy has the twin benefit of letting talented people push their limits while also creating a robust pipeline of innovative products and services. Many high-profile products have origins in the 20% rule, including Google News, Gmail, Orkut, Google Sky, and Google Grants. Other companies that use some version of this approach include 3M, Intuit, and Linden Lab, the company behind the hugely popular Second Life (a form of virtual shared experience now being used in two hundred countries worldwide).[11]

Retaining Talent

Of course, the organization of the future must also set its sights on talent retention. Unfortunately, there is no magic formula for maximizing retention. In the organization of the future, flextime, telecommuting, job sharing, and sabbaticals will be even more widespread, and they will help with retention. But much of what keeps people in jobs has to do with best practices in leadership, governance, and organizational alignment and culture, including progressive talent development and empowerment practices.

For example, when Internet advertising firm DoubleClick was started in 1996, the founders invested in all the dot-com accoutrements, including an espresso bar in the lobby and free salsa lessons for employees. Most important, though, is the opportunity the company provides all employees to shape their own careers. Employees are encouraged to switch jobs internally, learn new skills, and take risks. Workers are given a high degree of autonomy and accountability, with performance-based bonuses. According to CEO Kevin Ryan, "I judge my people on two people leadership questions: are the people in their group happy working for them? And do they bring in great people? If managers cannot help us attract and retain the best people, they are not doing a good job."[12] This approach has served DoubleClick well. In the wake of the dot-com crash in 2000, the company did not lose any of its top hundred people even after its stock price dropped 80%, helping it rebound and position itself for a $3.1 billion acquisition bid by Google in 2007.

EMERGING TRENDS

Now that we have explored the implications of five current socio-economic shifts and how they are affecting organizations and their talent dynamics, we turn our attention to three emerging trends that will shape not only the organization of the future but also our communities, social frameworks, and life priorities.

UNTETHERING

The first emerging trend is what we call *untethering*—in which people, teams, and organizations are breaking away from traditional institutions and structures while coalescing into increasingly "virtual" configurations and connections, shedding the ties that have conventionally bound them.

Untethering at Work

We are catching glimpses of this in the shift from people working in highly structured, full-service corporations to dynamic "free agents" and specialized providers of products and services. People are untethering from traditional careers and opting instead for discrete sets of work activities and periodic professional reinventions.

Today, people are shunning centralized work centers and gravitating toward flexible, "virtual" productivity in a range of unlikely places. Work is becoming unhitched from the standard workweek of nine to five, Monday through Friday. Instead, it is being blown out into "bursts of time" that are based on productivity and outputs, not time and inputs.

For example, consider the dynamic start-up company called the Savvy Source for Parents, an information hub and network for parents looking for quality early childhood education options. Its founder, Stacey Boyd, built a "virtual" company comprising a hundred part-time working moms across the country, with all employees and contractors working from home. Together, they created a Web-based guide to nearly all the preschools in the United States and are now expanding into providing consumer ratings for camps, educational games, learning activities, and more. According to Boyd, "I would say 95% of our work is done in the morning before the kids wake up, in the afternoon when they take naps, and at night when they go to bed. . . . Everything gets done faster and better. It's extraordinary."[13]

We also see this in the increasing prevalence of what has been called the "boundaryless" organization, with more permeability and flexibility between vertical and horizontal organizational silos, not to mention connections with external stakeholders and bridges across geographic divides. For example, 42% of Procter & Gamble's products have an externally sourced component, thanks to the company's "Connect + Design" program, which allows outside developers to get their concepts and designs into the consumer giant's product pipeline.[14] Organizations that adjust to this untethered mode will thrive; others will founder.

Untethering in Schools

In education, we are increasingly moving away from "one size fits all" large schools and beginning to embrace smaller learning communities focused on individual learning needs. People are learning on their own time in their own ways, and entrepreneurs are creating new learning environments to meet this demand. We see this with the rise of "virtual" schools (in which students can study anytime and anywhere assisted by online instruction and tutoring) as well as courses and learning modules catering to discrete and disparate needs and interests. We are "unpacking" the traditional schooling environment through innovative instructional practices and multimedia technology so that learning is no longer associated with rows of children facing a blackboard. In the best classrooms, student learning is becoming more individualized—identifying students' strengths and weaknesses, catering to their learning interests and skills, and allowing each student to develop skill sets that will help them navigate a future of dynamic change and uncertainty.

Untethering in Our Communities

We are also untethering from local neighborhoods as the focal point of our social lives; today, those physical communities are now being supplemented by distributed networks based on shared values and interests. This is being facilitated by technology and increased mobility. We see this in emerging connections among what have been called the "cultural creatives" and in networks of free agents. Further, many in the rising generations are drifting away from affiliations with organized religion and its traditions and institutions and gravitating to more personalized approaches to the divine, from yoga and meditation to encountering spirituality in nature.

• • •

The result of all this untethering will be a growing number of lives and careers that are more free-flowing and uniquely designed by each person, no longer tied to traditional notions. Tomorrow's organizations must adapt or be left behind.

AUTHENTICITY

The second emerging trend is *authenticity*. Rising generations are tired of losing themselves in busyness and putting in ungodly hours at workplaces that define them by the narrow confines of a job description instead of recognizing their humanity, distinctive gifts, and interest in community contribution. The organization of the future will become a surrogate community for many people.

People are looking for workplaces that value them as individuals, with their unique ideas, talents, skills, and interests. For example, a recent study in the United Kingdom revealed the following changes:

- Nearly nine out of ten young people are seeking careers that will add purpose to their lives as well as fulfill their potential at work.
- Among these individuals, 59% feel that their current job doesn't fulfill these wider life ambitions.
- Half of them feel that their employers do not care about them as individuals.[15]

A telling harbinger of what is to come is Clif Bar & Co., a leading producer of organic nutrition bars. Its leaders developed "five aspirations" for the company, centered on sustaining its brands, business, people, community, and planet. Clif Bar offers flex time, sabbaticals and a wellness program, including an in-house gym, four full-time trainers and more than thirty fitness classes per week—during working hours. An employee band holds weekly jam sessions in the company theater. Clif Bar also offers financial incentives for energy-efficient home improvements, bicycle commuting, alternative transportation, and the purchase of a hybrid or biodiesel vehicle.[16] The result of such initiatives is that Clif Bar has become a hot place to work in the Bay Area, contributing to its strong growth as a company.

Today there is a hunger for work infused with purpose. For the organization of the future, engaging workers with a higher purpose—including involvement with the community, a cause, or both—will be a competitive advantage. Organizations that don't capture the hearts, minds, and souls of their workforces will struggle over the long haul. Employees will explicitly value the "psychic income" of their jobs as well as the monetary income. Today's companies that point the way on this front include Herman Miller, Ben & Jerry's, Timberland, the Body Shop, Starbucks, and Chipotle (the "fast-casual" gourmet burrito chain, now the largest restaurant seller of naturally raised meat in the world).

The rise of social entrepreneurship, in which people are creating dynamic nonprofit enterprises focused on innovative social transformation, is a leading indicator of this trend. These principles are also appearing in the consumer choices people are making, as they use them to send signals about their concerns and values.

Finally, with regard to where they want to live, people are increasingly basing their choices on their values and priorities. We can be confident that the workforce of tomorrow will insist on living in places that resonate with their values, interests, and needs. These are most likely to be places that attract "cultural creatives," free agents, and entrepreneurs by investing in infrastructure— such as mass transit, bike lanes, free wi-fi, abundant cultural and learning opportunities, and communal work and social spaces— that reflects emerging sensibilities and values.

INTEGRATION

The third emerging trend destined to alter the organization of the future is *integration*—a restoration of coherence and congruence in our lives. Rising generations are eager to address the unhealthy disconnect that arises from compartmentalizing our work and personal lives. People work with a different blend of motivations today: less of an emphasis on income and security and more on learning, challenge, fun, fulfillment, and service. This means looking for work that provides opportunities to contribute value and pay the bills while also allowing for robust outside pursuits, including time for family, health and wellness, adventure, travel, enjoyment, learning, and spirituality.

Even today, we are beginning to witness major changes in societal values and perceptions of work. This shows up in two ways. First, there is a louder call for "work-life balance" among rising generations. As shown in Exhibit 14.1, younger generations have different priorities when it comes to work and family. Second, new generations of leaders also appear to be more inclined to seek work of significance and impact, as reflected in increasing interest in "socially responsible business" and the "triple bottom line" of people, profits, and planet.

Integration can also be seen in the blurring of our sectors. For example, consider the following organizations, which are applying for-profit principles and practices to nonprofit organizations

Exhibit 14.1. Relative Priority of Work and Family Across Generations.

Emphasis	Gen Y (under 23) n = 250 (%)	Gen X (23–37) n = 855 (%)	Boomer (38–57) n = 404 (%)	Mature (58+) n = 276 (%)
Work centric (work higher priority than family)	13	13	22	12
Dual centric (work and family equal priority)	37	35	37	54
Family centric (family higher priority than work)	50	52	41	34

Source: Adapted from Families and Work Institute, *Generations and Gender in the Work Place*, Issue Brief (Newton, Mass.: American Business Collaboration, 2004). Note that it's possible for members of Generations X and Y to "age into" new values.

via "venture philanthropy" and other innovative social enterprise models:

- Share Our Strength—an innovative nonprofit dedicated to eradicating childhood hunger
- New Profit—a fund designed to empower social entrepreneurs with targeted resources
- NewSchools Venture Fund—an organization that supports education entrepreneurs and start-up or early-stage organizations with strategic investments and management assistance

Likewise, companies like Hanna Andersson (a Swedish-inspired quality children's clothing company) and Bright Horizons Family Solutions (the world's leading provider of employer-sponsored child care) are systematic about measuring and maximizing their positive community impact through charitable donations, mutually beneficial community partnerships, volunteer work, and more. We have also seen the emergence of what are being called "for-benefit" companies (or "B corporations") that have access to the capital markets while also making their employees, their community, or the environment a high priority in their mission.

It is these types of organizations that are likely to develop a competitive advantage when it comes to attracting and retaining emerging leaders who factor their values and lifestyles heavily into their career equations. We believe this enlightened approach to the war for talent will, in turn, translate directly into growth and prosperity for organizations of the future.

Conclusion

These three nascent trends—untethering, authenticity, and integration—are worth watching as we seek to evolve our organizations, our communities, and our lives with the times. The fact that we are now in a period of profound transformation, including significant economic, technological, demographic, and social shifts, presents major opportunities for the organization of the future. It is now up to us to grasp the changes engulfing us and rise to the occasion with inspired solutions worthy of our entrepreneurial age.

Endnotes

1. Ed Michaels, Helen Handfield-Jones, and Beth Axelrod, *The War for Talent* (Boston: Harvard Business Press, 2001), p. xxii. See also Charles Fishman, "The War for Talent," *Fast Company*, July 1998, p. 104; Elizabeth Chambers, Mark Foulon, Helen Handfield-Jones, Steven Hankin, and Edward Michaels III, "The War for Talent," *McKinsey Quarterly*, Aug. 1998; Elizabeth Axelrod, Helen Handfield-Jones, and Timothy Walsh, "The War for Talent, Part Two," *McKinsey Quarterly*, May 2001; and Matthew Guthridge, Asmus Komm, and Emily Lawson, "Making Talent a Strategic Priority," *McKinsey Quarterly*, Jan. 2008.

2. Vivek Agrawal, James Manyika, and John Richard, "Matching People and Jobs," *McKinsey Quarterly*, 2003 Special Edition. See also Allan Schweyer, "An Internal War for Talent," *Inc.*, Apr. 1, 2005, www.inc.com/resources/recruiting/articles/20050401/talentwars. html.

3. Carolyn Martin and Bruce Tulgan, *Executive Summary: Managing the Generation Mix 2007* (New Haven, Conn.: Rainmakerthinking, 2006), pp. 3, 25.

4. Carl Schramm, *The Entrepreneurial Imperative: How America's Economic Miracle Will Reshape the World (and Change Your Life)* (New York: HarperCollins, 2006), pp. 11, 49, 78.

5. Robert Fairlie, *Kauffman Index of Entrepreneurial Activity, 1996–2006* (Kansas City, Mo.: Ewing Marion Kauffman Foundation), p. 1; *The Entrepreneur Next Door: Characteristics of Individuals Starting Companies in America: An Executive Summary of the Panel Study of Entrepreneurial Dynamics 2002* (Kansas City, Mo.: Ewing Marion Kauffman Foundation), p. 14. Michael Selz, "Survey Finds 37% of Households Involved in Small-Business Arena," *Wall Street Journal*, Dec. 13, 1996.

6. Michaels et al., *The War for Talent*, p. 11.

7. McKinsey Web site: www.mckinsey.com.

8. Elinor Mills, "Who's Who of Google Hires," CNET News, Feb. 27, 2006.

9. Gary Hamel, "Management a la Google," *Wall Street Journal*, Apr. 26, 2006.

10. Tamara Erickson and Lynda Gratton, "What It Means to Work Here," *Harvard Business Review*, Mar. 1, 2007.

11. Hamel, "Management a la Google"; "A Conversation with Scott Cook," *Inc.*, Sept. 2007, p. 214.

12. Michaels et al., *The War for Talent*, p. 42.

13. Authors' interview with Stacey Boyd. See Christopher Gergen and Gregg Vanourek, *Life Entrepreneurs: Ordinary People Creating Extraordinary Lives* (San Francisco: Jossey-Bass, 2008).

14. Mark Borden et al., "The World's 50 Most Innovative Companies," *Fast Company*, Mar. 2008, p. 96.

15. Study cited by Kate Fox, *Coming of Age in the eBay Generation* (England: Social Issues Research Centre, 2005), p. 5.

16. Authors' interview with Gary Erickson, with additional information provided by a company spokesperson. See also Gary Erickson with Lois Lorentzen, *Raising the Bar: Integrity and Passion in Life and Business* (San Francisco: Jossey-Bass, 2004).

CHAPTER FIFTEEN

MULTIDIMENSIONAL, MULTINATIONAL ORGANIZATIONS OF THE FUTURE

Jay R. Galbraith

Dr. Jay R. Galbraith is an internationally recognized expert on organization design. Currently, he is an affiliated research scientist at the Center for Effective Organizations at the University of Southern California, and professor emeritus at the International Institute for Management Development in Lausanne, Switzerland. He is also the president and founder of Galbraith Management Consultants, an international consulting firm that specializes in solving organization design challenges across corporate, business unit, and international levels. With more than forty years of research and practical applications, Galbraith has a breadth of experience that enables him to see problems from a unique perspective. He is the creator of the widely used Star Model™ and other tools and is regularly sought after for his expert opinion by the media, including BusinessWeek, *the* Wall Street Journal, Fortune, *the* Economist, *and the* Financial Times. *For more information, please visit www.jaygalbraith.com.*

It seemed to me as I was thinking about my chapter for this book that a better title might have been *Organizations of the Future*. The reason is that there is a rich landscape of organizations that are emerging and reemerging. For example, Tom Malone suggests that the fastest-growing type of company is the one- and two-person shop that makes its money on the Web.[1] About 150,000 entrepreneurs make their living on e-Bay while advertising for free on MySpace and YouTube. The top-performing mutual funds and hedge funds have twenty-five or fewer employees. They do not need size. And if they need scale, they can buy computing power and storage capacity from Amazon and Microsoft. But if Amazon, Microsoft, and IBM are to provide scale, then *they* need to be large. And what kind of organization will these large companies use to execute their global strategies? It is that type of organization, which I call the multidimensional multinational, that I want to describe as an organization of the future.

In the following sections of this chapter, I describe the forces that are shaping these multidimensional organizations:

1. The first is *growth,* which drives simple functional organizations to adopt three-dimensional matrix designs consisting of functions, business units, and geographies.
2. The second shaper is the *fragmentation of the business environment.* The marketing function alone is dealing first with proliferating market segments. Then, to reach these segments, companies introduce multiple products that are customized to various degrees and distributed through multiple channels. Multiple types of media are also needed to reach these multiple segments. When the business environment proliferates, our organizations proliferate with new departments to manage the new segments, channels, products, and media.

Following the discussion of forces are descriptions of a couple of multidimensional multinationals: Procter & Gamble and IBM. P&G describes itself as a "four-pillar organization." The four pillars are structures for customers, geographies, global business units, and functions. IBM employs at least six dimensions. It has the same four as P&G, plus channels, solutions, and some others. These companies represent the cutting edge of complex designs. They are employing an organization of the future for the rest of us.

The last section speculates about a question that the IBM case raises: In the future, how much more complex can these organizations get? Is there a limit to the complexity that a company's leadership can manage? This is the question for the organizations of the future.

THE TRADITIONAL MULTIBUSINESS MULTINATIONAL ORGANIZATION

The forces driving the traditional multibusiness multinational are the growth strategies needed to win investor support. The City of London and Wall Street have growth expectations for companies. If the Street identifies your company as a no- or slow-growth company, your stock trades like a bond at a low price-to-earnings ratio. But if your company wants to create wealth for your shareholders, it has to grow. Then the stock trades at a premium price-to-earnings ratio depending on the market's growth expectations.

But the growth opportunities in your core business in your home market eventually become limited. And then Wall Street wants to know what you are going to do for an encore. Traders ask, "Where are your new growth opportunities?" Most companies expand internationally. That is, they take their core business from their home country and set up operations in host countries. They become a multinational.

The process repeats when growth in the core business slows on a global scale. Wall Street and the City ask the same question again. This time, your company diversifies: it expands into businesses adjacent to your core business. For example, Dell Computer expands into printers, small storage devices, low-end routers, and computer services. It has become simply Dell, a multibusiness multinational.

The organization follows on directly from the growth strategy. The process has been well documented.[2] When a business—any business—starts up, it is a single business in a single country. It always starts as a functional organization; that is, reporting to the CEO are the functions: product or service development, operations, sales, marketing, finance, legal, and human resources. This form of organization was adopted by Dell, Costco, Amazon, Microsoft, Countrywide Mortgage, and so on. If you are a single business, you organize around a functional structure. And if you can grow and remain a single business in a single country, you should retain the functional structure. Size is not a factor.

What is a factor is the *growth strategy*. When growth in the core business slows, the company usually diversifies into related businesses. It transforms itself from a single-business, single-profit-center company into a multibusiness, multiple-profit-center organization. The structure is usually referred to as a divisional or strategic business unit structure. That is, reporting to the CEO are the business units, each of which is a single business, single-profit-center functional organization. Also reporting to the CEO are the usual corporate functions, such as finance, legal, and human resources. When the businesses are related, reporting to the CEO are also corporate staff functions for marketing, operations, R&D, and so on. This is a two-dimensional structure in which businesses and functions report in to the office of the CEO.

The three-dimensional structure results when the growth strategy leads the multibusiness company to expand internationally. Initially, the company adds a new division—that is, an international division—to its portfolio of business divisions. But when the division's revenues exceed 20 to 25% of the company's total revenue, the international division is split into regions. These regions report in to the company leadership, making the structure a three-dimensional one. Reporting to the offices of the CEO are business units, regions, and functions. The company becomes a multibusiness multinational.

An example of a three-dimensional structure is shown in Exhibit 15.1, depicting the general structure of a multibusiness multinational. The structure is flexible because the distribution of power and authority can vary, depending on strategy, from a business-dominant model to a geography-dominant model.

For example, global electronics giant Philips has a diverse portfolio of businesses and invests approximately 6% of sales in R&D. These strategic factors favor global businesses and weaker countries. Philips follows the business-dominant model. In contrast, Nestlé has a portfolio of food and beverage businesses and invests only about 0.5% of sales in R&D. These strategic factors favor strong countries and regions and weaker businesses. Nestlé follows the geography-dominant model. Various other combinations are also possible.

In the 1970s, the three-dimensional organization shown in Exhibit 15.1 was the organization of the future. And indeed it was implemented in many multibusiness multinationals in the 1980s and 1990s. But it was also during this time that the mass market began to fragment into segments. And along with that segment fragmentation came the fragmentation of mass merchants and

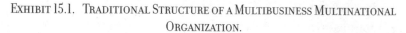

EXHIBIT 15.1. TRADITIONAL STRUCTURE OF A MULTIBUSINESS MULTINATIONAL ORGANIZATION.

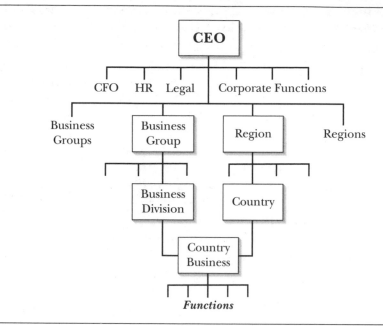

the mass media. Growth strategies now required large companies to master the proliferation of products, segments, channels, and media as well as businesses and countries.

A DIFFERENT STRUCTURE: THE MULTIDIMENSIONAL ORGANIZATION

The fragmentation of the business environment began in the 1990s. This fragmentation was aided, in part, by the rise of the Internet. Other contributing factors were the globalization of the customer and the rise of the buying power of the large customer. These large, globally present customers began to demand special treatment from multibusiness multinational companies. For starters, they did not want forty sales forces calling on them from different businesses in different countries from the same supplier. In response, companies created global account teams. These were teams of salespeople from the multiple businesses and multiple countries in which the company served the large customer. But many of these customers wanted more than a single interface.

So Wal-Mart approached P&G about a supply chain partnership. And IBM's customers no longer wanted to buy stand-alone products. They wanted IBM to deliver a complete solution for applications, such as customer relationship management (CRM). The customer teams at P&G and IBM became multifunction, multibusiness, and multicountry teams. These customer teams became virtual customer business units. Let's take a closer look at P&G and IBM.

Procter & Gamble's Four-Pillar Organization

In the late 1980s in the United States, P&G and Wal-Mart began a partnership. Wal-Mart was the first national retailer to centralize its buying. P&G created an eighty-person team that was located with Wal-Mart in Arkansas. This team was multifunctional and multibusiness. It worked directly with an equivalent team from Wal-Mart to create a supply chain partnership. The partnership was regarded as a success on both sides. P&G then extended the team approach to K-Mart, Target, and eventually to all large U.S. retailers.

When Wal-Mart expanded outside the United States, P&G expanded the customer team to become multicountry as well. From this experience, P&G extended its customer team concept to other global retailers, including Carrefour, Tesco, and Metro. P&G also reorganized into what it calls Organization 2005, shown in Exhibit 15.2. The organization has a customer-facing front-end structure, called the market development organization (MDO), that focuses on regions and global customers. The MDOs contain the geographic and customer pillars. The back end is focused on products, which are the responsibility of the global business units (GBUs). This is the business pillar. The fourth pillar is the functions, which also have global responsibility. The functions are matrixed across the GBUs, the customer teams, and the MDOs. In addition to the functions, the MDOs have matrix relationships with people from the customer teams and the GBUs. P&G is truly a four-dimensional organization.

In P&G's 2004 annual report, the CEO explained the reasons for the company's recent success. One reason was P&G's strategy, in which it exited low-growth, low-margin food businesses and

EXHIBIT 15.2. P&G's FOUR-PILLAR ORGANIZATIONAL STRUCTURE.

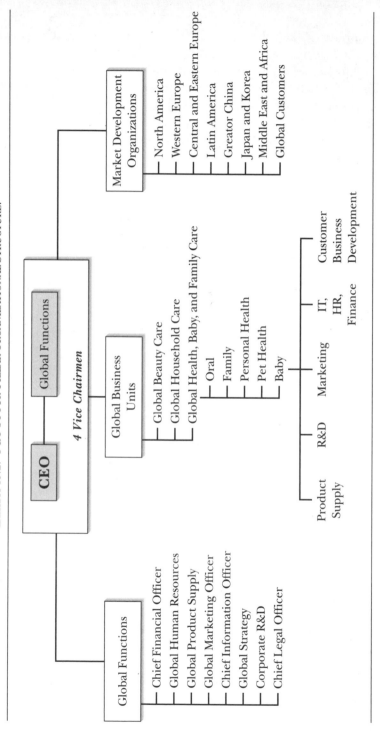

invested instead in high-growth, high-margin health and beauty care businesses. But he also singled out Organization 2005. He said that a reason for P&G's success was "a unique organization structure that creates advantage."[3] Then in 2005, P&G's competitor, Unilever, paid P&G the ultimate compliment: Unilever reorganized its global operations into an almost identical organization structure. So P&G's four-pillar structure may very well be the organization of the future for other consumer packaged-goods companies.

IBM's Six-Dimensional Structure

IBM, like P&G, was a multibusiness multinational in the 1990s. Like P&G, IBM got requests from its global customers for a single interface. IBM also got requests to integrate all the different kinds of IT products that were being offered by hardware and software vendors. Customers found that a client server did not work except with lots of systems integration work from Accenture or EDS. They asked IBM to put these systems and applications together for them. IBM had all the hardware, software, and services under one roof. So in the mid- to late 1990s, IBM reorganized into the same type of front-back structure shown in the P&G example. The IBM structure is shown in Exhibit 15.3.

IBM has a three-dimensional front-end structure. Like P&G, it has a matrix of regions and global customers. IBM's customers are gathered into industry segments. A major difference is these industry segment organizations: these are not just sales and marketing units. Instead, they have IT experts from the industry and software people dedicated to particular customers. Financial services even has its own R&D unit dedicated to insurance industry applications. The R&D facility is located in La Hulpe, Belgium, and is funded by IBM and a consortium of the insurance companies. A primary purpose of R&D is to find ways to take the legacy systems of insurance companies and get them to function over the Internet. So these segment organizations are multifunction, multiproduct units. The customer account teams are located in the regions. In the Americas, there are teams for Citigroup, Royal Bank of Canada, and JP Morgan. In EMEA (Europe, Middle East, and Africa), there are teams for Barclays, Deutsche Bank, Allianz, AXA, and so on.

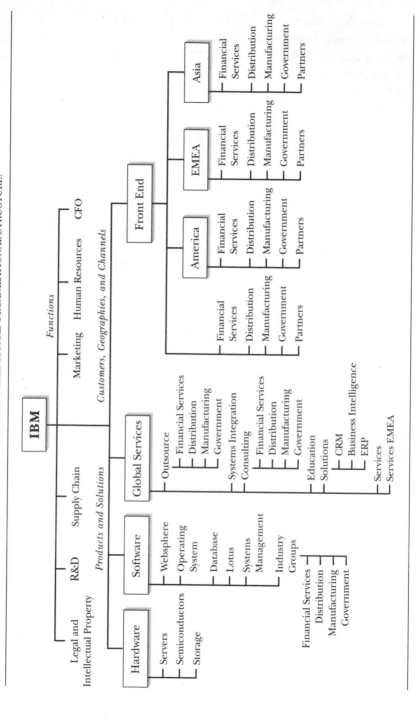

EXHIBIT 15.3. IBM'S SIX-DIMENSIONAL ORGANIZATIONAL STRUCTURE.

Another difference shown in the IBM structure is the partners unit. These are channel partners who sell IBM products and solutions. Originally, IBM sold directly to customers only through its own sales force. But today it can sell directly to customers through its own sales force, call centers (usually referred to as inside sales), and Web sites. It can also sell indirectly through the sales forces of any and all of the following:

- Independent software vendors (ISVs), such as SAP
- Systems integrators (SIs), such as Cap Gemini
- Value-added resellers (VARs), such as Reynolds and Reynolds (which takes IBM products, adds software, and resells the products to auto dealers)
- Original equipment manufacturers (OEMs), such as Philips Medical Systems (which puts IBM computers in digital X-ray machines, which it then sells under its own brand)
- eBay resellers (whether IBM likes this or not)

The computer industry is a good example of channel proliferation. Usually the IT vendors want to be present in all these channels, so in the channel organization are units for ISVs, SIs, VARs, and OEMs. The front end of IBM's structure therefore consists of three dimensions: geographies, customer segments, and channels.

The back end consists of global business units for hardware and software products and services. These products and services are combined into solutions for customers. If the solution is unique to an industry, the responsibility rests with the industry segments in the front end. If a solution is generic and applicable across industry groups, the responsibility rests with global services. CRM is an example. So the back end is responsible for solutions and products.

Finally, there are the corporate functions that report in to the CEO. Like those at P&G, these functions are matrixed across the businesses, the regions, and the customer segments. The functions, businesses, solutions, segments, channels, and regions make IBM a six-dimensional organization. Structures as complex as IBM's usually prompt readers to ask, "How do these organizations work? How do people get anything done?" The key is through the use of management processes.

USING THE STAR MODEL TO ALIGN KEY ELEMENTS IN ANY ORGANIZATION

Any organization, whether it is complex or not, consists of the elements shown in the Star Model in Exhibit 15.4. These elements are structure, processes, reward systems, and people practices. To have an effective organization, a company needs to have all these elements aligned with each other and with the strategy. When a company follows a complex growth strategy, that strategy leads to multidimensional structures, as described in the previous sections of this chapter. In turn, the company needs information and accounting processes so that it can keep score on each dimension. When appropriate, profits are computed for businesses, countries, customer segments, and channels. This accounting information is fed into the planning and budgeting process. The planning process then becomes the key process for aligning the company around shared goals.

The planning process serves its usual purpose of setting goals and targets to guide efforts over the time horizon. But in a multidimensional organization, planning also serves to align the goals

EXHIBIT 15.4. THE STAR MODEL™: ALIGNING THE KEY ELEMENTS IN ANY ORGANIZATION.

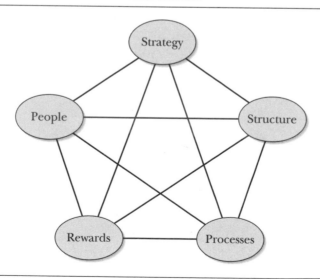

of the various dimensions to produce a one-company plan. If every dimension pursues its own goals—which might work at cross purposes with other dimensions—chaos will result. Therefore, it is the leadership's task to design a planning process that results in alignment. For example, Exhibit 15.5 shows a spreadsheet for a multibusiness multinational.

Each cell in Exhibit 15.5 represents the goals for a business unit within a country. The planning process is to produce an agreement between the country manager and the business unit manager. When they achieve agreement, alignment results, and the country and the business unit have the same shared goal. Often, of course, agreement is not reached. The two managers and their teams negotiate and solve problems until they do achieve an agreement. Often these negotiations are organized for the whole company.

For example, Canon has summit meetings where the leadership gathers for a week in Tokyo. During this time, the printer business and European region gather in one meeting room to reach agreement, and facilitators are often present from strategic planning. Meanwhile, the camera business and the North America region are meeting in another room.

EXHIBIT 15.5. PLANNING MODEL FOR MULTIBUSINESS MULTINATIONALS: ALIGNING TARGETS AND PRIORITIES.

Countries

Shared goals: Revenue Growth P&Ls		**Shared goals:** Revenue Growth P&Ls		
	Shared goals: Revenue Growth P&Ls		**Shared goals:** Revenue Growth P&Ls	**Business Units**
Shared goals: Revenue Growth P&Ls				

It is not a good idea to fail to reach an agreement. Giving each other more information, getting others' ideas, and using facilitators all help in this process. At the end of the week, Canon managers complete the spreadsheet, and the goals are aligned until the next planning period.

The planning process is therefore the key process. It is the conflict resolution process. It is the vehicle through which the leadership exercises its influence. Multidimensional companies are continually inventing new mechanisms, such as Canon's summit meetings, to manage the conversations between managers from the various dimensions.

The reward systems follow from the numbers on the spreadsheet. The shared goals are the performance metrics for the country and business managers. But like many companies today, managers have to do more than make their numbers. Performance is not only *what* you did but *how* you did it. Are you easy to work with? Do you share ideas, work on customer relationships, develop and recruit talent, and contribute to the intellectual property of the firm? Today's performance management is a subjective process by which to achieve a full and fair evaluation of performance. The leaders in performance management are the professional services firms, such as Goldman Sachs, McKinsey, and Latham Watkins. People are measured and rewarded for working for the good of the firm.

The people side is managed so that the organization attracts, recruits, hires, develops, and promotes the right talent. Command-and-control types are weeded out. People who want to be autonomous and run their own show are discouraged from joining. The rule is that you "hire hard and manage easy." Again, the professional services companies show the way: they recruit as hard as they develop new business, but in the end, they get people who fit the organization and thrive in multidimensional structures.

The organizations of the successful firms result in a complete and aligned Star Model. The strategies, structures, information systems, and planning processes are all multidimensional. The reward system is based on full and fair evaluations. The people are the right people who will thrive in complex organizations. It is easy to see why so few companies have mastered and will master these complex organizations of the future.

The Multidimensional Organization of the Future

If this book were being written in 1920, the multibusiness, multifunction, two-dimensional structure would have been the organization of the future. And it was. If it were 1970, the three-dimensional multibusiness multinational would have been the organization of the future. Today I am predicting that, just as P&G has become a four-dimensional structure and IBM has become a six-dimensional structure, the four-, five-, and six-dimensional structures will be adopted by more firms. They will be adopted by firms following a growth strategy and adapting to the fragmenting environments.

But is there a limit to the complexity? Already, middle managers at IBM are throwing up their hands and saying "Isn't this enough?" But just when I think that IBM cannot get more complex, it adds another dimension. It now has a manager in the software business who is responsible for "pervasive computing." That is a concept for a future when microprocessors are embedded everywhere. Sometimes this concept of the future is called "ubiquitous computing." And this manager has companywide responsibility for developing a plan for products, services, and solutions for implementing this concept in the future. IBM just keeps going, like the Energizer Bunny.

My guess is that we have not seen the end. Maybe it will be IBM or Microsoft or Google, but one of them will find ways to use technology to capture the efforts of people who thrive in these organizations of the future.

Endnotes

1. Malone, T., *The Future of Work*. Harvard Business School Press, Boston, Mass. 2004.
2. Chandler, A. *Strategy and Structure*. MIT Press, Cambridge, 1962; Stopford, J., and Wells, L. *Managing the Multinational Enterprise*. Longmans, London, 1972.
3. *Procter & Gamble Annual Report*. 2004, p. 7.

CHAPTER SIXTEEN

DESIGNING ORGANIZATIONS THAT ARE BUILT TO CHANGE

Edward E. Lawler III and Christopher G. Worley

Edward E. Lawler III is director of the Center for Effective Organizations at the University of Southern California (USC) and Distinguished Professor of Management and Organization in the USC Marshall School of Business. Named one of the country's leading management experts by BusinessWeek *magazine, he is the author or coauthor of more than forty books, including* Treat People Right!, Built to Change, *and* Talent.

Christopher G. Worley is a research scientist at USC's Center for Effective Organizations in the Marshall School of Business. He is also an associate professor of management and former director of the MSOD program at Pepperdine University. Dr. Worley is coauthor of Built to Change, Integrated Strategic Change, *and* Organization Development and Change, *the leading textbook on organization development.*

For decades, the predominant logic of organizational effectiveness has been that an organization's fit with its environment, its execution, and its predictability are the keys to its success. However, as the rate of change continues to increase, we need to look at organizational effectiveness very differently. More and more executives are correctly calling for greater agility, flexibility, and innovation from their companies. Indeed, one would think that the ability of organizations to adapt and change, not to mention the number of successful change efforts, should be high. But they are not.

Like many others, we have been intrigued by why organizational change efforts so often fail. Our analysis has led us to some interesting conclusions, the most salient of which is the importance given to *stability*. Largely ignored in the calls for more agility is the fact that organizations still are designed to seek sustainable competitive advantages through stability and execution. Apparently, buried deep in the managerial psyche (and bolstered by decades of theory and practice) is the assumption that stability is not only desirable but attainable.

However, we believe that the only way to ensure that organizations will be able to change is to *build* them to change, to create organizations that *love* changing.[1] Therefore, after we briefly explore the stability assumption, we propose a set of principles to guide the design of an organization that changes *all the time*.

THE STABILITY ASSUMPTION

We believe that some (maybe even most) large-scale strategic change projects are doomed to failure from the beginning. The type and amount of change that is being attempted is beyond the ability of most organizations to implement successfully.

Admittedly, some organizations have made amazing transformations. For example, Nokia has become a successful global electronics company, even though its roots were in a different technology and a local market. Similarly, Intel completely shifted its technical core from memory to microprocessors.

But the reality is that most large-scale change efforts in established organizations fail to meet expectations because nearly all models of organization design, effectiveness, and change assume stability is desirable. Let's look briefly at each of these three factors.

STABILITY AND DESIGN

Most organization design and management models were born in an age when environments were stable or at least predictable. They created organizations that were characterized by rules, regulations, and systems that limited experimentation, controlled variation, and rewarded consistent performance. When the environment was changing slowly or predictably, these were fine models.

But the pace and uncertainty of change, brought on by globalization, technological innovation, and political change, strongly argue for a new model. What is needed is a model of organizing that is built on a different assumption, one which assumes that organizations need to change all the time and that change is the normal state of affairs.

STABILITY AND EFFECTIVENESS

Stability is a strong driver in organization design because of its expected link to effectiveness. Stability and its progeny, "sustainable competitive advantage" and "alignment," are believed to be key drivers of performance. Leveraging a competitive advantage requires commitments that focus attention, resources, and investment to the exclusion of alternatives. In other words, effectiveness results when organizations finely hone their operations to perform in a particular way. This leads to large investments in operating technologies, structures, and ways of doing things. If such commitments are successful, they lead to a period of high performance and a considerable amount of positive reinforcement. Financial markets reward stable competitive advantages and predictable streams of earnings.

Typically, a commitment to alignment is a commitment to stability. To get the high performance they want, organizations put in place practices they see as a good fit, without considering whether they can be changed and whether they will support change. That is the great irony: by aligning themselves to achieve high performance *today*, organizations often make it difficult to change so that they can have high performance *tomorrow*.

STABILITY AND CHANGE MANAGEMENT

In another irony, the traditional approaches to change management reinforce the assumption of stability. The overwhelming change logic for decades has been a model of unfreezing, changing, and refreezing.[2] "Unfreezing" implies that some form of equilibrium exists that needs to be disrupted. Once organizations implement changes that move them to a new and desired future state, they are supposed to "refreeze," which involves institutionalizing the change and returning to a period of stability. The idea of unfreezing and refreezing is widely accepted because it supports traditional views of how organizations can be effective—that is, by being stable and predictable and by executing effectively. The fallacy in this approach is that it suggests that change will end or at least be episodic, when in fact in today's world, it is continuous.

The Built-to-Change Approach

So what does an organization that is built to change look like? The atomic image in Exhibit 16.1 captures our thinking, and suggests that three core processes—strategizing, creating value, and designing (described in the next three sections of this chapter)— are in constant motion, spinning around a core nucleus of identity. Thus, almost everything in a built-to-change organization (b2change for short) is changing. Understanding and coordinating what is changing—and what is not—is the key to effectiveness in a b2change organization.

EXHIBIT 16.1. THE BUILT-TO-CHANGE MODEL.

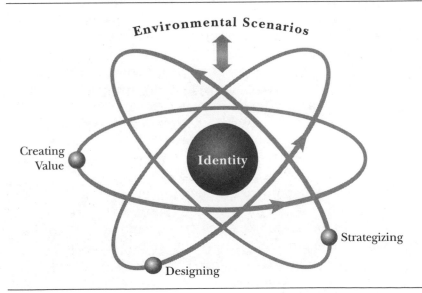

STRATEGIZING: CRAFTING A SERIES OF MOMENTARY ADVANTAGES

Strategizing describes how an organization achieves and maintains "proximity"—that is, how close an organization's outputs are to the demands of its environment. As the environment shifts and changes, the organization's responses must shift and change to drive effectiveness.

Thus, instead of pursuing a single sustainable advantage, a b2change organization seeks a *series* of momentary advantages that can create and maintain proximity. Momentary advantages have a "hit-and-run" or "entry-and-exit" logic—similar to the way HP approached its small instruments business in the 1970s and how Southwest Airlines uses a point-to-point system (instead of the traditional hub-and-spoke route system) so that it can easily enter and exit those city pairs that offer the best return at the time.

Bringing an organization into proximity with environmental demands and defining a series of momentary advantages involve the relationship among the environment, strategic intent, and organizational performance. To achieve and maintain proximity, b2change organizations first must develop a sense of the future. Rather than scheduling static annual reviews of the environment, organization members—not just senior managers—need to observe and report on trends and to identify competitive opportunities. They need to think constantly about potential alternative futures and create a variety of short- and long-term scenarios.[3] This is just what the U.S. Secret Service does to protect the president. As we will see in the designing process, b2change organizations are capable of developing scenarios when their members are in close contact with the external environment and, as a result, are able to identify key trends.

To achieve and maintain proximity, b2change organizations must define strategy in a new way. Success within a range of possible futures requires b2change organizations to seek a *robust* strategy that will succeed under a variety of conditions and yet be flexible enough to adjust to those conditions. A robust strategy is created by tinkering with the tension between strategic intent and identity.

Strategic intent provides the flexibility and describes the organization's breadth of products and services, the aggressiveness with which it pursues advantages, and the product and services that distinguish its offerings from those of competitors. Thus, for any temporary set of product or service features, an organization can have a broad or narrow product line and can be relatively aggressive or passive in its approach. These elements can be changed quickly. Strategic intent also includes a road map for how offerings will be orchestrated over time in response to environmental changes and in concert with an organization's capabilities and design.

Identity is what keeps the organization from being whip-sawed by environmental demands for change in strategic intent. Identity—a combination of both culture and image—is a central concept in the b2change approach because it is the most stable element.[4] Like an individual's personality, an organization's identity is a defining characteristic that does not change, except perhaps slowly or as the result of a major jolt.

Organizations that are built to change have a clear sense of who they are and what they stand for. When organizations know their identity, they are less likely to propose adjustments to their strategic intent that will not be supported by the organization's culture or that are not in line with its brand image. When new ideas bubble up that honor identity, they are easily supported and implemented. For example, when Harvey Golub became CEO of American Express in 1993, he spent a lot of time developing future leaders in the organization by asking them, "Does that strategy sound like 'American Express'?" He was teaching his managers to leverage the power of identity and propose strategies that would be understood, at a gut level, by the people who would have to implement them.

CREATING VALUE: LEVERAGING LEARNING

Creating value is concerned with how competencies and capabilities support the organization's strategic intent and how those capabilities evolve over time. The key to b2change thinking is the integration of competencies and capabilities with learning. Instead of "What do we do well?" a b2change firm asks the following questions:

- "What do we need to learn?"
- "How do our capabilities need to evolve?"
- "What new capabilities do we need to develop?"
- "What do we need to do better so that we can add value in the future?"

The strategizing and creating value processes have one important characteristic in common: they are both driven by worry—even paranoia—about what the future will bring.

For example, Google constantly thinks about how to refine and extend its basic search algorithms in both subtle and grand ways. Simple extensions of its advantage include moving into scholarly Web sites and published articles; grand schemes include how to substitute search algorithms into operating systems. Similarly, Starbucks has redefined the basic coffee-drinking experience advantage into a social advantage by creating stores where you download music and conduct business. As part of their process, Google and Starbucks are asking how their competencies and capabilities can be refined and reconfigured to redefine their products and add new ones.

The hit-and-run economic logic of the strategizing process requires b2change firms to be as effective in executing the current strategy and capabilities as they are in thinking about how and what they will need to change to be effective in the future. A b2change firm must constantly balance and trade off resource allocations for *present* performance against investments that will create *future performance capabilities.*

DESIGNING: IMPLEMENTING STRATEGIC INTENT

Designing is concerned with how the organization's features (for example, structure, processes, people, rewards) are orchestrated over time to support each other and the organization's strategic intent, identity, and capabilities.[5] To support a dynamic alignment among these features, each one needs to be changeable, flexible, and agile because they will be changing all the time. The designing process must support the idea that the implementation and reimplementation of a strategy is a continuous process.

Many traditional organization design practices have no place in a b2change organization. For example:

- *Job descriptions* are emblematic of stability and as a result are a poor fit with b2change thinking. Ignoring for the moment that job descriptions can be changed (when was the last time *your* organization updated its job descriptions?), why go to the trouble of specifying job responsibilities and repeatedly telling employees that their latest assignment comes under "other duties as assigned"? Instead of telling employees what their jobs are, b2change organizations encourage people to find out what needs to be done. In lieu of job descriptions, frequent goal-setting reviews help establish what individuals and teams are expected to accomplish in the near future.

- *Rewards based on seniority or tenure* are stifling to change: they do little but reward people for growing old.
- *Annual budgets* are a poor fit because they are usually outdated by the end of their existence. Why should spending patterns change every time the earth revolves around the sun?

What does have a place in b2change organizations is organization design and management practices that support change and an organization's strategic intent. The specifics will vary somewhat from organization to organization because strategic intents vary, but it is possible to identify what they should be in most b2change organizations.

Talent Management

When hiring people, b2change organizations seek individuals who are quick learners and like change. That's why companies like Southwest Airlines, Nike, and W.L. Gore and Associates specifically look for people with initiative and the right attitude, including the desire for professional growth. B2change companies need to have an employment contract which states that change is to be expected and that support for change is a condition of long-term employment.[6]

Of course, people should be made aware of the b2change employment deal before they're hired, so that they can make an informed decision about whether they want to work in such an environment. Once they join, training should be a normal, ongoing process, focused on the skills and knowledge necessary to support change and other organizational capabilities, and aimed at the competencies that will help the company add value both now and in the future.

Reward System

Pay and other rewards that are based on seniority stifle change. They do little but reward people for surviving.[7] In contrast, b2change organizations utilize a variety of reward practices, including bonuses, stock, and "person-based pay," that encourage both current performance and change.

Bonus systems can be particularly effective motivators during periods of change; they establish a clear line of sight between results and rewards. For example:

- Individual plans that offer relatively large bonuses can provide powerful incentives for employees and alter their individual behaviors when a new element of strategic intent calls for it.
- Group and business unit bonuses can be very helpful in focusing team performance and creating a shared need for change.
- One-time bonuses can be awarded for the completion of a strategic change effort. For example, members of a new-product development team can be given bonuses when the product ships or reaches a sales goal.

Broad-based stock ownership can be an incentive for change because everyone is rewarded for performance improvement. It is superior to a stock program that includes only senior managers. Under those conditions, employees can't be faulted for thinking, "Why should I listen to calls for change that only benefit those at the top?"

Finally, companies should consider shifting the basis of pay from the job (and seniority) to the individual (and what he or she can do). In work environments that call for changing task assignments, paying the person—as opposed to paying the job—is a much more effective approach, particularly when it comes to retaining the right people. After all, people have a market value; jobs do not. People can change companies for higher pay; jobs cannot.

Perhaps the most important benefit of person-based pay is the effect it has on organizational culture and on employees' motivation to change. Instead of rewarding people for expanding their jobs or for moving up the hierarchy, the organization recognizes them for increasing their skills and for developing themselves. This reinforces a culture that values growth and personal development; the result is a highly talented workforce that is receptive to change. Those characteristics are particularly valuable when an organization needs to improve its competencies and capabilities, because the company can adjust its reward system to encourage individuals to develop the necessary skills.

The implementation of a person-based pay system must start with a clear model of the competencies required to meet current customer and environmental demands, as well as a notion of the kinds of skills and knowledge that employees will need in the future. This information can guide professional development activities that are tied to the reward system. One indirect effect of person-based pay is a decreased emphasis on hierarchy, because individuals don't need to be promoted to receive a significant raise. Instead, they can develop a new expertise. Among the positive results of that change are fewer individuals jostling for promotions merely because they want higher salaries.

Organization Structure

B2change organizations must be in close touch with the market and other environmental demands in order to continually define and redefine a series of short-term competitive advantages. To achieve that high level of external awareness, all employees—not just senior managers—must observe and report on market trends and identify competitive opportunities. They need to think constantly about potential alternative futures, creating a variety of short- and long-term scenarios. Thus, instead of scheduling static annual reviews of the environment, b2change companies must adopt a strategy development process that continuously monitors the environment.

The key design principle here is to maximize the "surface area" of the organization by connecting as many employees as possible with the external environment.[8] Structures that accomplish this sharpen the external focus of its members; bring in critical information about trends, opportunities, and issues; and prevent people from becoming ossified in their roles. Thus as many employees as possible should have contact with regulators, suppliers, the local community, watchdog groups, and, most important, customers. B2change firms are anxious about being caught off-guard, so they place everyone close to customers and the environment. That way, when the time comes to alter the direction of the organization, everyone moves together based on a common understanding and felt need for the change.

A variety of companies, including IBM, Nokia, the proactive disease management company Healthways, and diversified technology manufacturer Lord Corporation, have increased their surface area by adopting front-back, process-based, or network structures that increase the centrality of customer and other external demands.[9] These multidimensional structures continually ask employees to consider the interests of customers and other outsiders in the decision-making process. For example, at Healthways, each core process—understanding the market, developing new businesses, building solutions, or delivering value— must balance *current* demands for efficiency with *future* market needs. Although each process within the organization might have a slightly different focus, successful execution requires the application and coordination of each function in service of customer requirements and corporate objectives.

Network structures consist of individual organizations (or units within a company) that have been pulled together to exploit specific opportunities. An integrating organization coordinates the activities of the different entities, much as a studio assembles and coordinates the work of actors, screenwriters, camera crews, and other groups necessary to create a movie.

Opportunity networks, such as those deployed by Li and Fung Ltd. (a Hong Kong–based consumer products trading company) are particularly effective for enabling an organization to think global but act local. As the integrator, Li and Fung has an overall perspective that is decidedly global, constantly monitoring trends in fashion accessories, toys, sporting equipment, and other goods, while each entity in the company's network concentrates on what it does best (for example, developing a local marketing campaign for a particular product line). In general, a network structure leads to organizations with large surface areas because of all the alliance relationships that managers and employees must address.

Other companies have maximized their surface area by deploying multiple independent business units, outsourcing, and matrix relationships. For instance, Berkshire Hathaway, with its wide range of autonomous business units, faces multiple markets and can adjust its corporate portfolio relatively easily without the angst and grief associated with traditional downsizings and resizings of integrated divisions. Similarly, W.L. Gore's small, interrelated divisions ensure that each unit is maximally exposed to its relevant market. Internal matrix relationships can also increase an organization's surface area because, when employees from different functions or programs interact, they often must deal with a variety of alternative market perspectives.

Information and Decision Processes

Instead of relying on annual budgets to control costs, b2change companies deploy profit centers and activity-based costing. Whenever possible, a P&L should govern each business unit. To ensure good decision making, information needs to be transparent and up-to-date, indicating the current condition of the organization's capabilities and providing a clear view of how the company is performing relative to its competitors and its strategy.

Performance-based information systems are a particularly effective way to motivate and empower employees in a b2change organization because such systems facilitate moving decision making to wherever decisions can best be made and implemented.[10] A good example is mySiebel, a personalized information system created by Siebel Systems before its acquisition by Oracle. Each employee could log on to mySiebel and gain access to corporate, market, and competitor information; data on current projects; and quarterly objectives for any individual in the organization (including Tom Siebel, the CEO). This widely available information allowed everyone throughout the organization to make customer-related decisions with the most up-to-the-minute data available, and it helped people align their individual behaviors with corporate objectives. The system thus facilitated the goal-setting, performance review, and reward processes.

Leaders

Executives in b2change organizations need to practice shared leadership—what Mark Hurd, the CEO of Hewlett-Packard, has described as "leadership as a team sport." Viewing CEOs as captains at the helm of a big ship setting direction and ordering people around is the wrong metaphor. It might be appropriate for traditional hierarchical organizations, but it does not fit a b2change organization.[11] A better analogy is to think of the corporation as a community of people spread over miles of hills, fields, and forests. To get everyone moving in a new direction, competent leaders need to be dispersed across the countryside, all connected by a shared sense of identity and purpose.

Shared leadership has four advantages:

1. It effectively substitutes for hierarchy. Spreading knowledge and power across many people allows the organization to process information and respond to it quickly without requiring a tremendous amount of top-down direction.
2. A shared approach builds a large cadre of leadership talent. By involving everyone in strategizing, creating value, and other activities typically performed mainly by senior execs, a company can develop leadership and management skills throughout the organization.
3. Multiple leaders at all levels who understand the external environment and the internal capabilities of the organization often see important trends that call for corporate change before senior management does.
4. Most important, shared leadership supports more effective change management. In any change effort, there is typically more to do than a single leader or a few leaders can handle. Shared leadership helps solve that problem. Also, change efforts that are led by a single hero leader are fragile entities; if that individual falters or leaves, the change effort stalls. With shared leadership, competent others are always available to keep the momentum going.

To develop a shared leadership capability, a company has to implement a program for leadership development that involves many employees and not just a few "stars." It also needs to share strategy information and business results with managers at all levels. Finally, it needs to obtain continual input from employees to develop and evolve its business strategy.

THE BUILT-TO-CHANGE ORGANIZATION

Exhibit 16.2 compares and summarizes the characteristics of traditional firms with the features of a b2change organization. They are different in many ways. B2change organizations

Exhibit 16.2. Comparison of Traditional and Built-to-Change
Organizations.

Traditional Firms	Built-to-Change Firms
Strategy	**Strategizing**
• Environmental scans and industry structure	• Possible alternative future scenarios
• Sustainable competitive advantage	• A series of temporary advantages
• Culture as a constraint to change	• Identity as an enabler of change
Competence and Capability	**Creating and Adding Value**
• What can we do well?	• What do we need to learn?
Design	**Designing**
• Structures with jobs and hierarchy	• Structures with maximum external surface area
• Information silos	• Information transparency
• Rational decision making	• Improvisation
• Leaders as heroes	• Leadership as a team sport
• Rewards for jobs, seniority	• Rewarding skill, performance

challenge the assumption of stability that drives traditional models of organization design, effectiveness, and change. Anchored by the organization's identity, the processes of strategizing, creating value, and designing constantly adjust to maintain proximity with a changing environment and drive a series of temporary advantages. The b2change organization may not always outperform traditional firms in the short term or in all situations. But there are many reasons to believe that over the long term, under conditions of rapid change, b2change organizations will outperform all others.

Endnotes

1. E. Lawler and C. Worley, *Built to Change* (San Francisco: Jossey-Bass, 2006).
2. T. Cummings and C. Worley, *Organization Development and Change, 8th Ed.* (Mason, OH: Southwestern College Publishing, 2005).
3. Scenarios have a solid history of success and many practical tools, so it is surprising how few organizations use them. For an overview

of scenarios, see P. Schwartz, *The Art of the Long View* (New York: Doubleday, 1991), and P. Schoemaker, "Scenario Planning: A Tool for Strategic Thinking," *Sloan Management Review*, 1995, *36*, 25–41.

4. For a sound introduction to and treatment of the identity concept, see M. J. Hatch and M. Schultz, "The Dynamics of Organizational Identity," *Human Relations*, 2002, *55*, 989–1019.

5. E. Lawler and C. Worley, *Built to Change* (San Francisco: Jossey-Bass, 2006).

6. E. Lawler, *Talent* (San Francisco: Jossey-Bass, 2008).

7. E. Lawler, *Rewarding Excellence* (San Francisco: Jossey-Bass, 2000).

8. E. Lawler and C. Worley, *Built to Change* (San Francisco: Jossey-Bass, 2006).

9. Our colleague Jay Galbraith has been a prolific writer on the subject of organization design at the business, corporate, and global levels. See J. Galbraith, *Designing Organizations: An Executive Briefing on Strategy, Structure, and Process* (San Francisco: Jossey-Bass, 2002); and *Designing the Global Corporation* (San Francisco: Jossey-Bass, 2000).

10. E. Lawler, *Talent*, 2008.

11. The classic studies on leadership include the Ohio State University studies and the Michigan studies. For the former, see R. M. Stogdill and A. E. Coons (eds.), *Leader Behavior: Its Description and Measurement* (Columbus: Bureau of Business Research, The Ohio State University, 1957); for the latter, see R. Likert, *New Patterns of Management* (New York: McGraw-Hill, 1961).

CHAPTER SEVENTEEN

REFOUNDING A MOVEMENT
Preparing a One-Hundred-Year-Old Organization for the Future

Kathy Cloninger

Kathy Cloninger is the CEO of Girl Scouts of the USA (GSUSA) and is a recognized expert on and advocate for girls' and women's issues. On her arrival at Girl Scout headquarters in late 2003, Cloninger launched a sweeping transformation of the entire Girl Scout movement, refocusing it on developing girls' leadership capabilities and implementing a new strategic business plan affecting every major area of organizational activity: programs, volunteerism, brand, funding, and structure and governance. A native of Dallas, Texas, Cloninger got her start as a Girl Scout in her mother's troop. Her twenty-five years in Girl Scouting include service as CEO with Girl Scout councils in Tennessee, Texas, and Colorado; as national management consultant for GSUSA; and as a participant in task groups strategizing on girls' well-being. Cloninger holds an MS in counseling and business management from East Texas State University. Her mentor is Frances Hesselbein, former CEO of Girl Scouts of the USA.

For the last few years, we've been transforming the Girl Scouts, a nonprofit organization nearly one hundred years old. In the process, we've learned a good deal about what it takes for an organization to be successful in today's world. Our experience has convinced us that an organization of the future—any organization that wants to have a future—must

- Have a clear vision of itself and its mission
- Be driven by strategy

- Have the courage to face facts
- Have the courage to change
- Be committed to open communication
- Be able to continue changing as needed
- Have the strength and stamina to see it through to the end

This chapter shows how the Girl Scouts have relied on these characteristics as guideposts on the path to making very deep organizational changes.

Before I get into that, though, I want to touch on a couple of other fundamental aspects of success. One of them is leadership. Rather than being primarily a matter of power and control (which is the traditional model), it seems to me that leadership today is above all a matter of *values:* a leader must understand and articulate what the organization stands for and what it wants to be, and the leader must also embody those values in his or her actions.

Another critical success factor is culture, which in some ways is very closely tied to leadership: the CEO is the organization's cultural leader. In an organization (as in society at large), culture comprises a set of underlying assumptions, a system of values based on those assumptions, and a system of behaviors based on the values. Organizations maintain their culture the same way a society does: by rewarding some behaviors and punishing others.

CULTURE VERSUS STRATEGY: CULTURE WILL WIN EVERY TIME

Culture becomes a major issue when an organization needs to change its strategy, because executing a strategy is also a matter of behaviors. Because behavior is so ingrained (and often unconscious), any time strategy and culture compete, culture wins. Changing the strategy may—in fact, probably will—require you to change the culture. For example, at Girl Scouts, some of the cultural changes we've had to make (and are still in the process of making) include these:

- A shift from avoidance of change to *risk taking*
- A shift from consensus to *individual accountability*
- A shift from knowledge hoarding to *open communication*

Making these types of change is slow and difficult, but essential. At the same time, some values and behaviors are so fundamental to an organization that they cannot and should not be changed. At the Girl Scouts, one of these values is *inclusiveness*. Our founder had a vision of a movement that would reach out to *all* girls. We are the stewards of that vision, and our stewardship involves making sure that our movement reflects the diversity of the culture around us. Our behavior is harmonious with this strategy: some 50% of our national board members are drawn from diverse racial and ethnic backgrounds, as is the staff at GSUSA, from entry-level staff positions to the senior leadership team.

How Our Organization Has Evolved— and the Challenges We Faced

The Girl Scouts of the USA was founded in 1912 in Savannah, Georgia, by Juliette Gordon Low. The founder was a remarkable woman who was in many ways years ahead of her time. From the beginning, she emphasized the development of self-reliance, leadership, a sense of adventure, and a vision of girls not only as homemakers but in nontraditional roles in the arts and sciences and in business—eight years before women even had the vote, and decades before women were represented in significant numbers in professions other than teaching, nursing, and domestic service.

Moreover, she succeeded in doing this in a way that was not only *not* perceived as a threat by the general public but actually embraced by it. Girl Scouting struck a chord both with girls and with their parents, and the new organization grew rapidly: by the early 1930s, it had some three hundred thousand girl members and had become an American institution. Membership swelled with the baby-boom generation and hit its peak from the late 1950s through the 1960s.

Declining Membership and Internal Structural Struggles

Energy and focus tend to ebb and flow in a large organization as it ages, and by the mid-1970s, the Girl Scouts had become somewhat tradition bound. Fortunately, it underwent a rejuvenation under

Frances Hesselbein, who served as CEO from 1976 to 1990, after which—for a variety of reasons—momentum slowed once again.

By 2003, a continuing decline in girl membership and adult volunteers had become a source of concern. Meanwhile, difficulties had arisen in the relationship between the headquarters organization in New York and the national network of federated councils that actually deliver services (troop meetings, camping trips, the cookie program, and so on) to the Girl Scouts themselves.

A LACK OF FOCUS

In addition to declining membership and structural problems, Girl Scouting suffered from a lack of focus. Over the years, the organization had fragmented its mission to the point that no one could say with any clarity what the Girl Scouts was for and what it did. This unclarity was exacerbated by the fact that each of the 315 local councils that existed in 2004 was free to pick and choose among the various messages and programs and present its own mixture as the essence of what Girl Scouting "was."

The position of CEO of GSUSA at this time was open. The organization, which has historically tended to look for well-known executives from the outside for this post, had searched for some time without finding anyone on whom the national search committee could agree. The search organization broadened its reach to inside candidates; I was a Girl Scout council CEO in Nashville at the time, and I was approached about the job. After some hesitation (I asked to have my name taken out of consideration once, and was approached again some months later), I accepted and took office in November 2003, making me the second national CEO in the organization's history to come to the position from being CEO of one of our local Girl Scout councils. The first was Frances Hesselbein.

I was aware, as were others, that the organization needed to undergo some changes. There was no looming crisis—GSUSA was stable financially and in a position to remain so for some time, and the decline in girl members and adult volunteers, though inexorable, was slow. However, it seemed clear that the pattern of gentle decline we were witnessing could, if left untended, steepen and become a death spiral. I decided that we would do whatever we had to do to prevent that.

A CLEAR VISION OF OUR MISSION FOR THE FUTURE

Very early in my tenure as CEO, I read a book by Willie Pietersen, a management expert and former CEO who is now on the faculty of the Columbia University Business School. *Reinventing Strategy* expands on concepts laid out by Jim Collins in *Good to Great* (which was also very helpful to us, as was a subsequent supporting volume, *Good to Great and the Social Sectors*). Stimulated by Willie's ideas, I was convinced that we needed to rethink our core strategy, and I was equally convinced that the rethinking needed to emerge from the entire organization.

Therefore, we assembled a twenty-six-member strategy team, drawn from people throughout the Girl Scout movement, from senior leadership to people in quite junior positions, and from headquarters personnel to council staff to volunteers. This group began working to define our core mission: What can we be best in the world at? Jim Collins refers to this process as "finding your hedgehog," a reference to an ancient Greek maxim ("The fox knows many things, but the hedgehog knows one big thing") as used by Isaiah Berlin in his famous essay on Tolstoy's theory of history.

We wanted a source of expert advice and guidance, and were fortunate to be able to engage Willie Pietersen himself, who had been a CEO in the corporate sector and had not at that time applied his masterful strategic learning process in the not-for-profit sector. Working with Willie, the strategy team conducted a detailed situation analysis: we looked at the market we served, our competitors, socioeconomic trends affecting us, alternative revenue models, and the realities of our own organization.

THE COURAGE TO FACE FACTS

This process uncovered a number of brutal truths. In addition to declining membership, declining volunteerism, lack of a focused mission, and an unwieldy (and somewhat fractious) organizational structure, we faced a crisis of relevance. Not only did Girl Scouting have a dated, "uncool" image, particularly among eleven- to eighteen-year-olds, but it was culturally alien to many American girls in the target age group, particularly among the rapidly growing Hispanic demographic sector. These girls—who were first-, second-, or third-generation immigrants—did not have mothers or grandmothers or aunts who had been exposed to Girl Scouting when they were young. Therefore, we were starting from scratch with them, and it was apparent that we were neither used to having to explain who we were nor very good at it. Nor were we accustomed to such fierce competition: girls today have many more activities available and many more demands on their time than they did even twenty years ago.

In addition to these largely exterior challenges, there were some interior challenges to be dealt with as well:

- We were heavily dependent on internal funding in the form of membership dues, training programs, and materials (books, uniforms, badges, and other paraphernalia).
- Because our organizational structure was bureaucratic and heavily consensus based, decision making was a very slow process.
- What decisions we did make were constricted by a tradition-bound, risk-averse, internally focused culture.

From this situation analysis, two key conclusions emerged:

1. We needed a differentiated and relevant core purpose that would provide a compelling benefit to girls and would also enable us to attract external funding.
2. We needed a simpler, faster governance and decision-making process.

By this time, it had become apparent, not only to me but to the board, senior GSUSA staff, and many of the CEOs and board chairs of the councils, that incremental changes to the existing organization would not accomplish our objectives. *What was needed was a full-scale transformation.*

DRIVEN BY A NEW STRATEGY

We began by trapping a hedgehog: all right, then, what was it the Girl Scouts could be best in the world at? The answer was, and is, that we could be best at *developing and fostering the capacity for leadership in girls.*

This is not new, by any means; as I noted earlier, from the very beginning, Girl Scouting has encouraged leadership and self-reliance. (And, apparently, to good effect. Although historically only about 10% of American girls have participated, approximately 80% of women business executives, 69% of the women currently serving in the U.S. Senate, and 65% of the women serving in the House of Representatives are former Girl Scouts!)

Hedgehog in hand, we developed a vision for the organization:

GIRL SCOUTING IS THE PREMIER LEADERSHIP EXPERIENCE IN THE UNITED STATES FOR GIRLS.

And we developed a mission statement:

BUILDING GIRLS OF COURAGE, CONFIDENCE, AND CHARACTER WHO MAKE THE WORLD A BETTER PLACE

CONFRONTING OUR PROBLEMS

We then revisited the brutal truths we had uncovered. We suffered from problems in all the following areas:

- *Program offerings:* these were weak; we had too many, and they were too diffuse—everything from aerospace to origami.
- *Volunteerism:* as noted, this was declining, at least partly because our model of volunteer service was incompatible with the schedules many women live with, and because our internal bureaucracy made it something of an ordeal to become a volunteer in the first place.
- *Brand:* it was dowdy and unclear.
- *Funding:* we were too dependent on internal sources.
- *Organizational structure:* it was overcomplicated, cumbersome, and slow.

DEVELOPING SOLUTIONS

We turned this catalog of weaknesses inside out and used it as the basis for a set of strategic priorities:

- *Program:* we would develop a consistent, unified leadership experience relevant to the lives of girls today and based on measurable and testable outcomes.

- *Volunteerism:* we would revamp the system to make it easier to join, more flexible in terms of the required time commitment, and a genuine opportunity to learn.
- *Brand:* we would develop a contemporary, attractive brand that inspires girls to join.
- *Funding:* we would clarify our identity and mission to prospective donors, take a more active role in fundraising, and work to make girls a national philanthropic priority.
- *Governance:* we would restructure our organization to make it decisive, agile, and market driven.

ESTABLISHING "GAP TEAMS" TO BRIDGE THE OLD AND NEW

As a first step toward turning our strategic priorities into a full-blown plan of action, we appointed "gap teams" to find ways to close the gap between where we were (the brutal truths) and where we wanted to be (the strategic priorities). There were six of these teams, one for each of the five strategic priorities and an additional team focused on the organizational culture. As with the original strategy team, the gap teams were drawn from a broad cross section of the organization.

The gap team's recommendation on organizational structure and governance was that we "create an efficient and effective organizational structure and democratic governance system that achieves decisiveness, speed of action, and optimum use of resources." These were precisely the qualities we would need to achieve our goals in any of the other areas, so it was obvious that this component of the core business strategy would have to be made a top priority.

RESTRUCTURING THE ORGANIZATION

Organizationally, the Girl Scouts is what is known as a federated nonprofit. The national organization, GSUSA, provides overall direction, materials, programs, some degree of fundraising coordination, and certain administrative services to the councils. In turn, the councils—a network of more or less freestanding 501(c)(3) nonprofit corporations—deliver services and programs to the Girl Scouts themselves. The councils recruit girls, organize troops and activities, maintain community relations, and carry out their own fundraising activities. They manage their own budgets, and they acquire and manage property: it is the individual councils, not GSUSA, who own the campgrounds, lodges, and other recreational facilities associated with Girl Scouting. Many of the councils are old and well established; in addition to relative legal and financial autonomy, they have their own history and traditions, and they are accustomed to governing themselves.

THE COURAGE TO CHANGE

In its charter—the legal framework defining its relationship with GSUSA—each council is assigned a certain geographic area in which it is to serve as the exclusive provider of the materials and services of the Girl Scouts. From time to time, it has been necessary to adjust these territories and, in the process, increase or decrease the total number of councils.

In 2004, at the time the series of decisions I have been describing took place, there were a total of 315 Girl Scout councils in the United States. There was wide disparity in size and effectiveness among the councils. In terms of number of girls served, they ranged from a low of 735 to a high of 62,000; the largest 20% served 50% of the total number of girls in Girl Scouting, and the smallest 20% served 5%. In terms of annual budget, they ranged from $250,000 to $10 million. Nearly one hundred councils—some 30% of the total—had 2004 operating budgets of less than $1 million, which meant they were unable to maintain an adequate infrastructure or sufficient professional staff.

After considering all the available options, the structure and governance gap team recommended the creation, through a series of mergers, of a smaller total of "high capacity" councils, each of which would have the funding, the connections, and the scale to achieve its purposes and make effective use of the movement's resources.

REDRAWING THE MAP

We created a set of criteria for evaluating council capacity, based on resources, funding base, regional identification, population diversity, anticipated population growth, alignment with transportation patterns, respect for natural geographic boundaries, and presence of significant media markets. To these we added some minimum size requirements: to be considered a high-capacity Girl Scout council, an area needed to have a minimum of one hundred thousand girls ages five to seventeen residing in it, have at least $15 billion in total household income, and, in most cases (there are occasional exceptions in areas like the High Plains), have to contain at least one city of fifty thousand or more residents.

With the aid of a team of demographers, we drew up a map based on these criteria and laid it over our existing council structure. Of the 312 existing councils (3 had been absorbed in interim mergers), 29 met the capacity criteria and did not need to be merged. The remaining 283 would be realigned into 80 larger councils, for an eventual overall total of 109.

I want to jump ahead of the story a bit to note that this series of mergers (known in the Girl Scout movement as the council realignment process) is on schedule and moving toward a successful conclusion. The federated structure of the Girl Scouts is fairly common among nonprofit organizations, and virtually all federated nonprofits of comparable size and age are facing the same problems we did. Because successful restructuring in this sector and on this scale is quite rare, I have been asked by heads of other organizations, some of them significantly larger than GSUSA, how we have managed to accomplish it.

OPEN COMMUNICATION IS CRITICAL DURING A RESTRUCTURING

An important part of the answer to the question, How did we do it? is *communication*. The process I've described was not concocted in New York and imposed as a fait accompli on the councils; instead, council leadership has been involved every step of the way. GSUSA worked in partnership with the councils to prioritize the criteria and jurisdictional boundaries before the demographers created the resource map. Once it was created, we held a national work session with council CEOs and board chairs. Also, ten council groups representing thirty-seven existing councils volunteered to take the plunge and become "early adopters."

This part of the process lasted from fall 2005 to July 2006. In August 2006, when every leader of every council had had a chance to weigh in on the subject and we had our thirty-seven early adopters, the national board approved the new map and set a deadline of October 2009 for completion of the process. Since then, the councils have received a regular *Realignment News* bulletin from GSUSA. There are periodic national conference calls among the chair of the national board, the CEOs of the councils, and myself, and there continue to be national meetings with all stakeholders.

Seeing Things Through to the End

As you can see, this was and is a carefully planned, systematic, widely (relentlessly, some have said) discussed, open, and—as far as humanly possible—democratic process. All the study and research we did before embarking on it pointed to its necessity, and the results we have seen in the first eighteen months have done nothing but validate our decision.

For all that, it has not been easy for me, for GSUSA, or for the councils. Change is wrenching and can be quite painful, and some of this has hurt. Overall personnel shrinkage has been less than 20%, as most of the staff from the smaller merged councils have found positions in the larger realigned councils. However, I have seen a few close colleagues lose their jobs. In addition to employment, of course, decades-old traditions have been upended. There has been resistance, there have been hard feelings, and, in one case, there has been legal action. All of this will pass, and it pales in comparison to the good coming out of the process, but it is real, and it is one of the challenges an organization of the future—and its leadership—must face head-on. To be successful as an organization, you must have the courage not only to change but also to see change through to the end.

During all this, of course, we have also been pressing ahead with our other strategic priorities. Most of these initiatives are either in a much less developed stage or more idiosyncratically "Girl Scout–centric" or both, so I will simply touch on a few highlights.

Reaffirming Our Role in Society

As I mentioned earlier in this chapter, our core mission is developing the girl leaders of today who will be the women leaders of tomorrow. We regard this as urgent, and we believe that there need to be far more women leaders—of business, of the arts and sciences, and of government—than there are now. We believe this both because women are seriously underrepresented in the ranks of our nation's leaders and because the entire model of leadership as it is generally practiced needs to be revised by the increased presence of what are generally thought of as "female" characteristics, among them openness, inclusion, and a preference for consensus building over hierarchical command and control.

At the Girl Scouts, we also believe that it is our responsibility to take the lead in this effort, because there simply is no other organization of remotely comparable size, experience, and resources devoted to developing leadership in girls. To enable us to do better at what we do, we are in the process of replacing the rather diffuse catalogue of programs and activities I mentioned with what we are calling the Girl Scouts New Leadership Experience. It has been designed in consultation with a board of experts in education and childhood development and is intended to produce specific, measurable outcomes related to girls' self-confidence, their ability to interact and collaborate, and their ability to use their leadership and organizational skills to have an impact on the society around them.

All of this, needless to say, has to be transparent to the girls— if it isn't fun and doesn't feel like fun, they won't do it—as well as easy to manage for the volunteers who will actually be working with the program and the girls. We will roll this program out over a period of about three years, testing and changing it as we go, to make certain that it does what we intend it to do. All I can report at this point is that it has the approval of two important audiences: the educators and childhood development specialists with whom we have consulted, and the girls who have seen it thus far.

Success in the other areas will flow pretty naturally from the two we have been discussing. With restructuring completed and a testable, verifiable program executing our core mission in place, reestablishing our brand, increasing volunteerism, and expanding fundraising should be a great deal easier.

MAKING CHANGE A CONSTANT

In summer 2005, we restructured the GSUSA headquarters organization, which resulted in a reduction from five hundred to four hundred employees. The resulting organization is still in a state of becoming, as is its administrative mission. We do not know yet what the exact relationship will be between GSUSA headquarters and a network of strong, professionally run realigned councils that have just been through a testing self-examination process. We know they will be (to a degree perhaps unprecedented in Girl Scouting) clearheaded and focused about their own powers and sense of mission, and that they will have high expectations of us.

Exactly how we will meet those expectations—with what people and administrative structure and in what relationship vis-à-vis the realigned councils—is a question still in the process of being answered. As with many of the questions raised by the transformation process, there almost certainly is no final answer. Being what we need to be for the councils, for girl welfare and leadership, and for the two million or so actual girls participating in Girl Scouting at any given moment will require a continual restructuring and cultural transformation of GSUSA.

That brings me to what may be the fundamental challenge for an organization of the future: *adaptability*. To succeed over time, an organization must somehow institutionalize the ability to change, yet in the process continue to be itself. There is no sure recipe for that, but it seems to me absolutely essential, and I believe the key to it is *strategic learning*—to observe change, learn from it, and use what you learn as the basis of an evolving strategy. In the hope that our learning at the Girl Scouts might serve as guideposts toward this kind of permanent adaptability, I want to close with three lessons from our experience of the past few years:

- It is possible to make enormous changes without compromising an organization's soul. We have stayed steadfast in our commitment to diversity and to the other core beliefs that underlie our business strategy.
- Organizational restructuring is a slow, methodical process, and we are nowhere near finished, which I suppose is a way of

saying that you need to move quickly and deliberately at the same time.

- Although there is an absolute need for commitment and resolve, there is no absolute certainty. If you're leading this kind of change, you can gather information and advice until you're 99.999% sure you're doing the right thing, but you'll never get to 100%. All you can do is think it through the best you can, make your decision, and jump.

CHAPTER EIGHTEEN

THREE CHALLENGES FACING NONPROFITS OF THE FUTURE
People, Funding, and Strategy

Roxanne Spillett

As president and CEO of Boys & Girls Clubs of America (BGCA), Roxanne Spillett heads one of the nation's leading youth development organizations, one with a primary focus on young people from challenging circumstances. Spillett has led BGCA through a period of dramatic growth, with particular emphasis on children in areas of greatest need, including public housing and Native American lands. One of her most noteworthy achievements is a partnership with the Department of Defense to charter Boys & Girls Clubs on more than 470 U.S. military bases worldwide. Her career spans thirty years in Boys & Girls Club work. Spillett and BGCA were cited by Newsweek *in 2006 as "15 People Who Make America Great," part of the magazine's annual Giving Back Awards. In 2005, President George W. Bush appointed Ms. Spillett to the President's Council on Service and Civic Participation. In addition, she teaches MBA candidates at the University of Notre Dame about nonprofit board management.*

To contemplate the future, consider the past. For example, consider the Cathedral of Notre Dame: it is a remarkable structure, made even more so because the people who envisioned it knew they would never see it finished, never attend a service there. Nor would their children, grandchildren, or great-grandchildren. It took nearly two hundred years to complete the original Notre

Dame, and the cathedral has been changed and improved on many times since. Leaders of the project passed into history, but their mission was carried on. So was their faith in the future. That's what belief in mission is all about.

Like Notre Dame, the mission of nonprofits is a continual work in progress, rarely ever completed—the star on the horizon. Yet the need for continual preparation is always with us. After thirty years with a nonprofit organization that recently celebrated its centennial, I have come to appreciate that fact. And although much is written about *corporate* leadership and management—past, present, and future—less attention is given to nonprofits, particularly in terms of the future. Yet the need to focus on the future of this sector has never been greater.

According to the IRS, there are more than one million nonprofit organizations in the United States. According to Lester Salamon, professor and author of the first book to document the scale of the U.S. nonprofit sector, almost ten million people— 7.2% of the U.S. economy—are employed in 501(c)(3) organizations. Salamon observed "that paid employment alone in nonprofit organizations is three times that in agriculture, twice that in wholesale trade, and nearly 50% greater than that in construction and finance, insurance, and real estate."

This is the sector that cares for our children and our aging parents, helps the poor and disadvantaged, takes care of the sick and the dying, improves neighborhoods, and preserves culture. Yet this is also the sector with the most limited resources and infrastructure and, accordingly, some of the greatest leadership and management challenges.

Three emerging and very real challenges will be increasingly apparent in the years ahead and must be addressed by the nonprofit organization of the future:

1. Workforce issues—especially the retirement of baby boomers and the shortage of talent to take their place
2. The need for "creative capitalism" and corporate engagement to help solve social problems and strengthen nonprofits
3. The need for even greater collaboration and consolidation if the nonprofit sector is to be more effective, eliminate redundancies, and put more money behind mission

In three words: people, funding, strategy. Let's look at each of these in more detail.

People: Finding the Next Generation of Leaders

The success of the nonprofit sector lies at all levels with its people, which includes

- Those who work directly to implement the mission and its plan
- The leaders who guide them
- The board volunteers who—through governance, generative thinking, and financial support—oversee and support the mission and its implementation

Although people are important at all levels, I have learned that the need for the right leadership and judgment *at the top* of an organization is key to the right leadership and judgment throughout that organization. At no level is a talent shortage more acute and potentially damaging than at the leadership level.

In a recent white paper, Tom Tierney, cofounder of the Bridgespan Group (which provides management consulting services to nonprofits), analyzed the need for leadership in the nonprofit sector. He concluded that at the CEO and senior management levels, there is a clear and compelling shortage of future leaders.

Tierney estimates that the leadership gap may require as many as 640,000 senior managers during the next decade, a disparity exacerbated by all the following factors:

- Increased demand and decreased supply
- The growing number of nonprofits
- The retirement of leaders and managers from the baby-boom generation

The nonprofit organization of the future must understand the impact of this challenge and plan accordingly. Doing so requires elevating talent development to the highest levels in the organization, including the board, to achieve the following goals:

- *All leaders should be accountable for talent development.* Nonprofits need to create a culture that supports talent development as a top priority at all levels of the organization. There should be an expectation that leaders invest in their own development and in professional development of their staff.
- *All leaders should be accountable for succession planning.* Nonprofit organizations need to have a clear succession plan for the leadership of their organization—particularly at the CEO and senior leadership levels.
- *All leaders should be accountable for diversity.* In terms of age, gender, ethnicity, and race, diversity brings richness and strength to an organization. This is not just a "nice-to-do"; it is a strategic advantage for nonprofits.
- *All leaders should be fairly compensated.* Nonprofits need to ensure that their leaders—and all their employees—receive competitive compensation and benefits compared to similar jobs in the community. Nonprofits—yes, nonprofits—should also consider *incentives* to retain their best talent.

Talent development and diversity need to be priorities at board and staff levels in any organization, and they are high on the agenda at Boys & Girls Clubs of America. Given the aging demographic and the competition for board leaders, it is important also to have board-level succession plans, as well as recruitment plans that develop the next generation of leaders. Although these ideas are not new, their degree of significance in the organization of the future is. But there are new ideas, too.

First, the retirement of baby boomers not only creates a challenge but also offers an opportunity. The search for a second, more meaningful career is not unusual among this age group. As boomers search for encore careers, they often regard contributing to their community as more important than compensation. Consider, too, the scope of talent among this pool of individuals: after retiring from corporate, military, and government jobs, they can be a great asset to nonprofits, bringing important skill sets in finance, marketing, human resources, technology, and other areas. This spells opportunity for nonprofit organizations, which with flexibility and creativity can bring much-needed skills to their doorstep at affordable cost.

Another opportunity is to identify and recruit social entrepreneurs, often members of Generation X and Generation Y, who can bring a more youthful demographic to an organization. They can play a leading role in the way we approach social issues (from civic engagement and health to education and philanthropy), and they can challenge conventions, advance the use of technology, and bring new energy and ideas to the marketplace of social change. They can be our innovative breakthrough thinkers.

FUNDING: CREATIVE CONCEPTS

Some years ago, a fiscally conservative member of Congress would regularly interrupt funding debates with the same query: "But where are we going to get the money?" That question—for any of us, certainly for the organization of the future—has not lost its force.

At Boys & Girls Clubs of America, I can first tell you where we do *not* get the money—and that is from our affiliates. We do not believe in charging large dues or fees to our clubs, which often serve children and families from poor and disadvantaged circumstances. (Today, dues from local clubs amount to less than 4% of our annual budget.)

Even so, the financial revenue of our affiliates has increased dramatically over the last ten years, from $450 million in 1996 to more than $1.3 billion in 2006. In that decade, our size more than doubled, and our impact on individuals, communities, and the nation grew exponentially. I'd like to show you why, as I believe that our approach holds lessons for the organization of the future.

A key approach involves what Microsoft chairman Bill Gates calls "creative capitalism," a belief that business can—and should—benefit society. "There are two great forces of human nature," he says. "Self-interest and caring for others." He does not regard these as opposing concepts. Business can profit and do good at the same time.

At Boys & Girls Clubs of America, we're a part of that. One of our key partners is, not surprisingly, Microsoft. Our association began a decade ago with a determination to bridge the "digital divide," a technology gap that in the age of personal computers, was threatening to disenfranchise a generation of young people from low-income backgrounds who lacked access to technology.

To level the playing field, Microsoft helped us pilot tech centers at local clubs, equipping us with a tested technology model (which became known as the Club Tech initiative) to provide our youth with the computer skills they will need to succeed in school and the workplace. The company expanded from there, bringing in other partners, providing BGCA with a multimillion-dollar, multiyear commitment, including $74 million in donated software programs, as well as a national print and television campaign promoting our partnership.

Today, 90% of our clubs have state-of-the-art technology centers—including one on the Oglala Sioux Reservation in Pine Ridge, South Dakota, one of America's poorest communities. Imagine as well the scene in Camden, New Jersey, a place considered one of America's most dangerous cities, where the local Boys & Girls Club has twenty-eight brand-new computers in two tech centers. These life-changing experiences are closing the digital divide for our kids and opening a world of opportunity.

In this relationship and others like it, you see how the non-profit organization of the future can engage with business. The connection is not just that of grantor-grantee, which is the kind of one-dimensional association that begins (and usually ends) by issuing a check. Instead, it involves two forces *working together* to solve a societal problem.

Creative partnerships like this, in Bill Gates's words, "stretch the reach of market forces" in a way that will improve the world. They involve genuine inspiration and engagement. They encompass not only direct fundraising but also in-kind gifts, donations of products or services, the use of skilled volunteers, and employee participation in community service projects.

These connections can enhance a company's reputation, which increases its appeal among customers and investors alike. And as job recruiters seek candidates with meaningful community service among their accomplishments, employees can boost their marketability while also benefiting society.

Partnerships like this helped increase our revenues—at both the national and local levels—over the last decade, which enabled the Boys & Girls Club movement to increase the number of clubs from eighteen hundred to more than four thousand affiliates, and to expand and enhance programs that include educational enhancement programs, learning centers, and other generation-changing programs.

But that expansion was also due to a conscious effort to diversify our revenue streams by reaching out to many sectors of American society, not just the corporate community. For example:

- We built relationships with individual donors—beginning with our own board.
- We attracted government dollars by educating Congress and state legislatures about our work.
- We also strengthened our brand to increase awareness of our clubs, heightening corporate, foundation, and other philanthropic interest in partnering with us.

Diversifying funding streams not only generates more revenue but also provides protection if one or more streams diminish or disappear entirely. Continually focusing on the next quarter is shortsighted and can undermine financial stability. In contrast, a long-term view of finances is the proactive perspective—an increasingly crucial one for the organization of the future.

STRATEGY: COORDINATING RESOURCES

In a globalized age of finite resources, increasing competition, and overlapping service missions, the organization of the future will have to engage in more collaborative efforts.

At Boys & Girls Clubs, we are accomplishing this in a variety of ways, one of which involves partnering with school systems, health clinics, public housing authorities, and many more organizations, thereby surrounding youth with 360° service. Clubs and other institutions share resources (sometimes under one roof) to support the whole child and community—although the approach could just as readily be adapted to serve senior citizens, the unemployed, or another group.

The strategy we use is designed to improve kids' access to key services. This is not only economical but highly effective—and greatly needed, particularly in the area of education. The epidemic of high school dropouts (which is rising to more than 50% in some areas) threatens America's global competitiveness, our workforce of tomorrow, and indeed our very future.

There is no single reason why students drop out. Causes range from a lack of motivation to academic failure, from boredom to fear for personal safety. But the bottom line is that our children are falling behind in math, reading, and science—the very skills the United States needs to stay competitive in a global economy. This crisis should be the focus of national outrage; it continues to undermine the very foundations of our society, threatening nearly every organization of the future.

The situation requires new ways of thinking and acting and new kinds of partnerships. It takes an entire community to bring organizations together and focus collective energy on solving a social problem. In a more competitive world, the organization of the future will have to reach out in this way, engaging others and working with those who have complementary missions. At Boys & Girls Clubs, we seek every opportunity to change and save lives, to show kids that someone cares about them. In so doing, we are determined to engage America.

Bringing HOPE to communities is one example of 360° service. In 2004, Boys & Girls Clubs in distressed neighborhoods of the South Puget Sound region of Washington state were operating at capacity. So the clubs there brainstormed a new kind of expansion strategy.

The result is a concept known as HOPE (Home of Opportunity, Possibility, and Empowerment) Centers. With a club and a school serving as anchors, these 30,000-square-foot centers will be multitenant facilities that promote collaboration among nonprofit agencies to better serve area youth and families. Club kids will have more access to youth and family services, parental support, and job placement services than they would at stand-alone clubs. The first such facility was the Gary and Carol Milgard Family HOPE Center, which opened in September 2007. Six more are in the works.

"The community believed so much in this concept," says Jinnie Hanson, director of special events and marketing for the Boys & Girls Clubs of South Puget Sound. "They voted to pass the district's school construction bond, funding a new elementary school to create an integrated campus with the HOPE Center." Through the centers, club and community partners aim to gain efficiency and quality by sharing facilities, costs, technology, and equipment. The combination of resources saved taxpayers nearly $2 million.

With the first center established, neighboring communities are taking note. "The new HOPE Center sets a great example," says Hanson. "Other school districts are now approaching us, wanting to partner in building additional centers."

A Plan for the Future

This look at the organization of the future would not be complete without a look at the future of the Boys & Girls Club movement, because I believe our situation mirrors that experienced by other organizations. As CEO, I want to leave my successor an organization with a strong leadership corps, solid finances, and a relevant, results-driven strategy. I'd like to share some of that strategy, as it may prove helpful to others planning for the future. Our plan has four distinct areas.

Leading with Impact

Our clubs continually seek to deepen impact on the youth they serve. This means understanding what leads to impact and being able to determine—as well as *quantify*—the results of successful impact, in terms of

- Academic success
- Good character and citizenship
- Healthy lifestyles

Particulars vary from one place to another, but the successful organization of the future needs to know why it matters and how it makes that difference—and it should be able to prove it.

Building Stronger Organizations

The organization of the future has to think ahead about challenges and opportunities and create a climate in which it can continually improve its effectiveness, leadership, and financial strength. Strong professional and board leadership is crucial. So are sound finances, ranging from the creative capitalism envisioned by Bill Gates to diverse revenue streams involving federal, state, and local governments; individuals; foundations; and more.

We must also eliminate redundancies if we are to stay competitive and effective and to continue to make an impact. This can involve mergers (about ten of our clubs do this each year) or consolidation of separate nonprofit organizations and their back-office functions (IT and accounting services, to name two). Some nonprofits may even need to close if a changing environment renders them obsolete.

Going Beyond Our Walls

For Boys & Girls Clubs, "going beyond our walls" means taking what we have learned and sharing it with outside constituencies and communities. Other organizations can doubtless do the same. It is a "push-pull" approach, in which we seek to push out the knowledge we have gained over a century, while pulling in the kind of expertise (in family support, health services, and more) that assists our mission. Pooled expertise creates its own synergy and an enhanced ability to solve problems. Our nation—and our world—will be better for it.

Ensuring Greater Public Trust

One moment of misconduct can undo a century of good works. Impeccable standards for safety, hiring, ethics, financial oversight, and record keeping have become the sine qua non by which we should and must abide. And it is not just a matter of reputation— although the 24/7 news cycle has made sure that no organization can be complacent. We do all this because it is the right thing to do—a moral imperative.

• • •

Taken individually, none of the four areas of our strategy for the future—leading with impact, building stronger organizations, going beyond our walls, and ensuring greater public trust—are ends unto themselves. Rather, they collectively form the working essence of a movement, what *Webster's* defines as "a series of concerted, organized activities or related events working toward some objective." Our movement's objective is to change and save young lives. We have reached a size and scale to do that, to do great things, now and in the future.

TOWARD GLOBAL UNDERSTANDING

I began this chapter with a story of medieval times. I'd like to conclude with a message about the future—my final point about the organization of the future.

It concerns globalization, but it is not a story of world markets or economic competition. It was something I witnessed while visiting a Boys & Girls Club in New Orleans, a place still recovering—three years later—from the ravages of Hurricane Katrina. It was testimony to an understanding that we live in one world.

At the club, I saw a fundraising thermometer on the wall, the kind put up as part of a giving campaign. I asked what it was for, and the children told me they were collecting money for Malaria No More, a cause that purchases bed nets for people in Africa. The nets literally save lives, protecting entire families against the mosquito-borne disease.

Remember that *these kids survived the worst storm ever to strike the United States, and they still have very little of their own.* Yet they care enough to give what money they have to benefit children halfway around the world, whom they will never know.

These are the children I am proud to serve. This is the future we seek—bound by a common humanity, by a belief that we can "do well by doing good." That we can leave the planet better than we found it.

The message is this: we live in an interdependent world. No matter what the mission, nonprofits and businesses alike must understand that—and pave the way for global understanding.

CHAPTER NINETEEN

PIONEERING THE COLLEGE OF THE FUTURE

Building as We Walk

Darlyne Bailey

Darlyne Bailey, founding dean of the College of Education and Human Development, is assistant to the president at the University of Minnesota. Previously, she was vice president for academic affairs and dean of Teachers College, Columbia University, and dean of the Mandel School of Applied Social Sciences at Case Western Reserve University. She has a master's degree in psychiatric social work from Columbia University and a doctorate in organizational behavior from the Weatherhead School of Management at Case Western Reserve University. Dr. Bailey has written numerous articles and book chapters, including Strategic Alliances Among Health and Human Services Organizations: From Affiliations to Consolidations *and* Managing Human Resources in the Human Services. *She recently coauthored, with four women, a book based on the experiences of more than forty women leaders within the for-profit, nonprofit, public, and faith-based sectors of the United States, titled* Sustaining Our Spirits: Women Leaders Thriving for Today and Tomorrow.

The topic for this chapter—the college of the future—is a bit different from others in this book, which are more specifically

---

It must be acknowledged that although this chapter benefited from shared thinking with creative friends and colleagues (most especially with those on our new College Leadership Team), I take full responsibility for accepting the invitation to share this with you here and now.

oriented to for-profits or nonprofit organizations. Nonetheless, although its context is higher education, this chapter shares with the others a core tenet of organization development: in order for all institutions of the future to successfully navigate through our changing world, they must continuously be most aware of and responsive to these changes. It follows, then, that our colleges of the future need to behave similarly to most effectively prepare their graduating students for this world.

Yet the commission to begin to boldly envision the college of the future requires from me a humble observation: simply, all our talk in education about setting "world-class standards," establishing "globalized curricula," and creating organizations that will thrive in our "knowledge economy" is unfortunately becoming more *rhetoric* than *reality*. These and related callings are mired in (if not buried beneath) the structure, systems, practices, and policies of educational enterprises that continue to live in the past. Yes, ironically, although formalized education was designed to facilitate the progress of world leadership, education has largely been conservative and has steadfastly held on to theories and procedures that are centuries old. Indeed, many of these educational theories and procedures emerged from the training and preparation of clergy in the Middle Ages![1]

Although at no time in our recorded history has there been ample food, medical care, and shelter for *all* in our world, our awareness of the increasing prevalence and degree of complexity of these and other issues confronting us has dramatically heightened. However, the institution of education—from elementary school to the academy of higher education—has stayed close to its roots since the founding of the first college here on this continent over 370 years ago, "conceived as phases in the transmission of a civilization."[2] And although it is outside the scope of this chapter to offer any specific evidence for this (apologetic) assertion, it is this contention that provides the foundation for all that follows. So, if you disagree, I urge you to skip these next few pages. If, however, you join me in believing that our children, our families, and our communities here and across the world are in need of a new educational enterprise, then please read on.

The bold yet deserving goal of all our colleges of the future must be to acknowledge, value, provide for, and prepare *all* to be healthy, continuously engaged learners and actively contributing citizens. My wish is that the boldness of even some of the desires and thoughts presented herein becomes absorbed and acted upon so that ultimately it too is known as part of the history of the evolution of our college institutions.

HOW HIGHER EDUCATION IS STRUCTURED TODAY—AND WHY IT NEEDS TO CHANGE

A brief overview of the long-held division of roles, responsibilities, procedures, and ways of organizing in the academy sets the stage for the work to be undertaken by our college of the future. Once admitted, those now determined to be "qualified" students enter classrooms taught by those at different levels in the hierarchy (from part-time instructors to full professors), following a plan of studies developed by the latter. Successfully passing tests of competency, taking courses (again, largely predetermined) in a specific department, the students progress to being graduates with a college degree. Depending on their qualifications and (we hope) desires, some go out into the world of work, while others go on to get "advanced degrees"; some of them getting a more focused master's degree and still fewer earning a doctorate in a specific discipline, which, for most professions, represents the highest degree of expertise in the academy.

All the while, a very strict and specific message about rewards and recognition plays out:

- Students are rewarded for their individual attainment of knowledge as determined by their professors, whose lives in the academy followed the same path.
- Departments (composed of professors who share similar areas of expertise) get rewarded for the numbers of students that they can attract and maintain, while the college is looked on favorably by the larger university (or if a stand-alone, by its "peer institutions," who are actually its competitors) for the largest number of students it can graduate.
- Professors get rewarded in relation to how the students assess their abilities to teach their material—material that the professors have decreed to be the most important.

- In institutions where engaging in research is the highest valued process, the professors are also evaluated (and able either to move up the hierarchy or to move out the door) based on the number of their written works—with single-authored articles in journals read by others in the same discipline being the most highly ranked products, and publications in nonacademic "popular presses" (such as those found in most airport bookstores) being the least rewarded.
- Ironically, professors who spend most of their time actually *working with* our students, or sharing their talents on committees in the college or with groups from the outside communities, or even writing their ideas with others, are usually *not* rewarded by the upward movement through the professoriate. They are sometimes even asked to leave the academy (that is, they do not receive tenure—a form of lifelong employment).
- Staff—the hundreds of employees who are not given guaranteed employment, yet who are charged with keeping all the systems of the whole enterprise running most effectively and efficiently—are the least rewarded in the typical academy of today.

Although I have taken the liberty of perhaps oversimplifying the situation, you get the picture: within academia, students and professors tend to be directed toward working alone (or with those who think just like them), in siloed, clearly circumscribed areas, largely separated from the outside world. A more prevalent irony must be noted, however. This same academy that has instituted the separation of "thought and action" for its faculty views as most forward thinking those college courses that ask students to connect their ideas and their time to the outside world in the form of internships, fieldwork, and service learning![3]

Therefore, the challenges facing the college of the future are quite clear. Artificially subdividing this organization into three domains that I will call function, form, and funding, let us now envision what needs to occur to achieve our aforementioned "bold yet deserving goal"—an educational enterprise accessible to all and valuing of all.

Forward-Moving *Function:* Cross-Stitching the Mission Among Administrators, Professors, and Students

Those of us in academia are privileged to enjoy the gifts of time and space to question and explore some of the major challenges facing our world today. It is our responsibility, therefore, to take our ability to respond and amass our talents to move beyond merely *espousing* and begin *addressing* the many needs that our communities still face. Our college of the future must embrace an appreciation, encouragement, and enactment of *research* and *teaching* and deeply engaged *service* in our local, state, national, and global contexts that transcend disciplines in construction and delivery. We must accept the truth that in our multifaceted world, there is no single perspective or body of knowledge that can inform practice and policies; instead, multiple models of knowledge creation and engagement are necessary.

Multidisciplinarity in academia is actually a reflection of reality—not only life "out there" in the world, but more important, an opportunity for each one of us to live lives that are acknowledging, respectful, and congruent with our personal values and identity. At its core, multidisciplinarity is the mindful appreciation of the science and spirit of connection. I can share with you this perspective because I have "crossed over" and connected the professions of secondary education, psychotherapy, organizational behavior, and community advocacy with academic administration. Although moving across disciplines implies a degree of separateness, healthy boundaries are permeable outlines that create safe holding spaces and opportunities for authentic interconnection and wholeness.

And from this wholeness in academia comes the prospect for even more fully understanding the degree, amount, and complexity of the challenges facing us today, again, as ones that simply cannot be managed or even fully understood by any one discipline or work group alone. The call for multidisciplinarity represents our appreciation of this.

Multidisciplinarity requires increased contact and connection— a coming together of scholars from multiple schools of thought and practice to collectively tear down the barriers that keep us apart. This includes speaking the language of *all* in our colleges. Side-stepping the traps of jargon with which we speak only to ourselves enables us to truly become multilingual. In so doing, we take the risk of being mindful and really seeing. As best described by Peter Senge and colleagues,[4] we are able to move from "seeing our see-ing" (our own assumptions), to really "seeing with the heart"— being and doing from a state of intense compassion, openness, and, yes, connection.

As responsible human beings, we must be intentional about our sight. We generally find only what we seek; and we see only what we look for. Our *intention* brings *attention*. When we attend to someone or something, it becomes more apparent to us, allow-ing a relationship to develop. And as our interactions with others grow, the more we risk showing our talents, our light, which in turn enables others to do so as well. A culture of true multidiscipli-narity requires that all are empowered to shine authentically.

It follows, then, that our college of the future will not expect that we all shine in the same ways. With college administrators closely attending to all of their colleagues (and more to be said about administrators later), let's take a look at how shifts in inten-tion and attention among our professors, staff, and students could be different in the college of the future.

CHANGING THE INTENTION OF PROFESSORS AND STAFF

Tenure. The word alone elicits sighs of relief from those inside today's colleges, while oftentimes prompting questions and even sarcasm from others. What everyone usually forgets are the ori-gins of tenure. Not intended to guarantee lifelong employment, tenure was originally to provide faculty with the freedom to teach what they believe is most germane to their courses, without threat of reprisal for ideas that may differ from the norm.[5] Tenure in the college of the future would either be multidimensional to reflect authentic talents or perhaps not exist at all. With or without tenure as we now know it, faculty *and* staff would be guaranteed to have regularly scheduled, holistic, and formative performance apprais-als. Such reviews would have the goal of continuous improvement in the art and science of scholarly teaching, discovery, and community engagement.

For example, success would be measured by how a professor accomplished the following:

- Took present college course content and translated it for high school students to give them greater college-in-the-schools opportunities
- Facilitated the un-learning of students to free up enough mental space to begin to take in new perspectives and risk new behaviors
- Modeled and rewarded genuine curiosity and questioning
- Provided time for both group and cohort learning and individual reflection for all

And lastly, the college of the future would determine the required faculty-student contact hours or "face time," not by *the course credits to be earned,* but on *the material to be learned.*

Staff would also be recognized and held accountable for their accomplishments. Moreover, rather than focusing largely on faculty and administration, staff would be supported in broadening their attention to encompass their own professional development and the needs of the students and the college as a whole.

Changing the Attention of Students

In addition to recognizing the special talents and desires of faculty, our college of the future must address the needs and development of an increasingly multicultural pool of students, and do so throughout their higher education experience. It must take a holistic approach—from admission of our students, through maintenance of our students, to their graduation into the world of alumni—that attends to its various domestic and international student populations, their successes, and their challenges.

At the same time, as uncomfortable as it may feel at first for our students, we must move beyond the traditional "reach out and touch" approach of teaching to appropriately incorporating more of our technological innovations for distance learning. Although much more could be said about blogs, podcasts, and instant messaging, for now, suffice it to say that our systems of teaching and learning must take advantage of technology—not to be *driven* by technology, but much more effectively *supported* by it.

Despite all the reasons to most closely tie the work of our colleges to the real connections on which our world is grounded, multidisciplinarity has not yet been fully realized in our educational institutions. As we saw earlier, our colleges have historically more highly valued the work done by individuals, not teams or even dyads, as colleges have taken siloed approaches to addressing the questions of society. Our students deserve educational content and processes that reflect the real world in which they live.

The work of our college of the future must be authentically engaged in being multidisciplinary—it must move to become just as market driven as it is consumer driven, mindful of the needs, desires, and assets of the outside world. Only by being open-hearted and open minded will the colleges and the communities they serve together discover and determine the academic programs to be created and those to be let go, always attending to the question best posed by futurists: "What is the content of our curriculum for the next twenty-five years?"[6]

FORWARD-MOVING *FORM:* CREATING NIMBLE CONNECTIONS

Alfred Chandler, former professor of business history at the Harvard Business School, wrote extensively on how corporations and other organizations are structured—and even won a Pulitzer Prize for one of his books on management.[7] Chandler showed that the way we construct organizations often flows from their purpose or content. It follows, then, that the structure of the college of the future must be flat or nonhierarchical to best stimulate, support, and connect the maximum flow of its work, both within its own walls and beyond, as it spans the boundaries of other institutions.

This is not a new idea, but again, one that is more readily espoused than enacted. Our most effective leaders know this. For example, Jim Collins wonderfully describes how Frances Hesselbein (then the CEO of Girl Scouts USA) once arranged dishes and silverware in a series of concentric circles and then pointed to the glass in the middle to poignantly show where she is within her organization, declaring, "I'm not on top of anything."[8] Women and men who lead from the center lead from *their* center, their spirit.[9] College administrators serving as leaders in the colleges of the future must come to know that the synergism of their abilities to be authentic, humble, empathic, patient, courageous and compassionate, faithful, and even loving enables their power to be used to empower all others.

For the most complete diffusion of a leader's power and an organization's mission, all the structural boundaries (that is, those around the internal departments and the organization at large) must be, like the disciplinary ones, flexible and permeable. In the more circular than hierarchical college of the future, this translates into the following characteristics:

- Fewer permanent administrative and academic departments.
- Greater cross-training or job rotation to facilitate the enhancing of skills and interests.
- Work groups that are more task oriented, with clearly understood, specific goals and due dates. These dynamic and fluid units can paradoxically serve as concrete ways to bring faculty, staff, and students together, all as teachers and learners, organizing and focusing their expertise and passions.

Moreover, the actual, physical construction of our colleges of the future will reflect what we now know to be most effective in the delivery of their functions and services. For example, the "community-centric" orientation of the college of the future can be physically reinforced by any or all of the following changes:

- Using more energy-saving technology
- Incorporating "greener" materials
- Creating spacious, sun-filled, and accessible atriums
- Installing flexible seating and setup spaces in both the classrooms and the students' residential halls and dormitories[10]

In short, the structure of our college of the future will accommodate the teaching and learning that takes place, not the other way around.

Accordingly, in this more elastic and adaptable structure, extra care must be given to ensure that an open flow of communication exists. Shared information must be consistent and transparent to all to establish and maintain trust throughout the community. As Gary Hamel suggests, our communication pathways must be vertical and horizontal to ensure "a continuous company-wide conversation."[11]

In our College of Education and Human Development at the University of Minnesota, we are pioneering a new organizing structure that positions us closer to doing just that: our "neighborhoods." The neighborhoods are indeed horizontal clusters of faculty, students, and staff that transcend departmental silos within and across the college and beyond. They serve to operationalize our mission, pulling together our disciplinary strengths and talents toward a shared focus of action, to be reflected in our scholarly research, teaching, and community outreach and engagement activities.

Within the neighborhoods are "blocks," which are smaller groups that develop specific strategies to work on mission-driven goals in teaching, research, and engagement. Here are a few examples:

- In one of our neighborhoods is a block focusing on the STEM subjects (science, technology, engineering, and mathematics education).
- In that same neighborhood, we have a state policy collaboration block, which includes faculty and staff invested in policy management. At the request of both our state senate and house of representatives, an initial project for this block asked our college to provide and then translate research into more valid and meaningful indicators of student achievement than currently used to meet the federal No Child Left Behind mandates.
- In another neighborhood, we have a block working with colleagues in Mexico, collaborating with community members and organizations around issues of migration, citizenship, and the use of technology in teaching and learning across borders.

We are now envisioning a "neighborhood square" to physically accommodate all our neighborhood "residents." Our intent is to have this space go "beyond environmental sustainability to environmental replenishment" in its design and materials.[12]

FORWARD-MOVING *FUNDING:* PRIMING THE PUMP

Our colleges of the future must be well resourced. When we ensure that our teachers and learners (formerly known as faculty, students, and staff) are the best (read: the ones with the demonstrated passion for and commitment to the values evidenced in the functions and form of the college of the future) and have the time and physical space to work together, we must think about funding. Financial compensation for good salaries, recognition and reward, and seeding entrepreneurial ventures must be available and used.

Even today, college leaders know that *no less than one-third of their attention and activity must be devoted to fundraising*—the art and science of helping others see the wisdom of converting their dreams and time into dollars. This money is then entrusted to the leader as it is invested into the college.

As we move into the future, the current distinction between public and private colleges will become just a memory, as more state and federal monies will be sought (despite today's trend of decreasing support), underscoring the college of the future's accountability to its communities. Further, these colleges will be even more effective once individual donors and foundations alike have the majority of their gifts and grants be "evergreen"[13]—that is, continuous investments in our college of the future that enable the leadership to create and re-create as if they had a periscope to see what was coming around their organization's "corner." Although it is regularly reviewed, such reliable funding allows our colleges of the future to be steadfastly committed to the "bold yet deserving goal" described at the outset of this chapter, instead of having its values and actions shaped by following the dollars.

Even with this new way of funding, our colleges of the future, unlike our currently tuition-dependent colleges, will be closer to tuition-free. Why? Because when the community recognizes that the mission, services, and structures of the college of the future are designed to meet the needs of the community, more individual donors and local foundations will invest, enabling those who enroll to do so without funding worries—a true win-win-win.

MOVING FROM HERE TO THERE

By actually moving forward on the function, form, and funding of a college of the future, we venture into new territory: we become pioneers, hopefully leading the way by paving a way for others to follow. Accordingly, we must at a minimum have the courage to embrace five paradoxes, competing truths that I call the "Paradoxes of Pioneering in the College of the Future":

- Paradox 1: although there is much to discover as pioneers, we have to continue to live with the uncertainty of our future.
- Paradox 2: although this uncertainty is frightening, true bravery is having the courage to undertake and make the journey even though we are afraid.
- Paradox 3: the path of pioneering evokes feelings of both thrill and struggle. To continue along the path of discovery, we know we must fight the tendency to back away; instead, we must move toward whatever difficulties rise up along the path or within us.
- Paradox 4: although we began this journey having packed what we wanted and believed we really would need in order to be nimble and not get stuck, we must eventually lighten our load, carrying only that which we know is essential to our lives. And, ironically, the further we travel—that is, the longer we live—the more we recognize that very little of what we're carrying is truly essential.
- Paradox 5: perhaps most important, although pioneering may get lonely at times, we are never really alone. There are always others somewhere like us being "first" in their situation. We in academia need only to seek out and connect with those people, those kindred voyagers who may come from the corporate, faith-based, or even public sector of our world.

Enacting the college of the future as courageous pioneers requires that we make the road as we walk. Yet there are no hard-and-fast answers for how even to look forward. In envisioning the college of the future, we must boldly look out toward the future we cannot see. We must always "plan beyond the plan."[14]

Gloria Anzaldúa—author, poet, and professor of literature—said this so eloquently:

> What to do from here and how? (*qué hacer de aqu y cómo?*) . . . Enough of shouting against the wind—all words are noise if not accompanied with action (*basta de gritar contra el viento—toda palabra es ruido si no está acción*). . . . We are slowly moving past the resistance within, leaving behind the defeated images. We have come to realize that we are not alone in our struggles nor separate nor autonomous but that we are connected and interdependent. We are each accountable for what is happening down the street, south of the border or across the sea. And those of us who have more of anything: brains, physical strength, political power, spiritual energies, are learning to share them with those that don't have. . . . Voyager, there are no bridges, one builds them as one walks (*caminante, no hay puentes, se hace puentes al andar*).[15]

Endnotes

1. Bailyn, B. (1960). *Education in the Forming of Society.* Chapel Hill: University of North Carolina Press.
2. Bailyn, 1960, p. 6.
3. Coleman, E. (2008). "The Thought–Action Continuum in Liberal Arts: A new approach to undergraduate education." Hubert Humphrey Institute Lecture, University of Minnesota.
4. Senge, P., Scharmer, C. O., Jaworski, J., and Flowers, B. S. (2004). *Presence: Human Purpose and the Field of the Future.* Cambridge, MA: SOL.
5. O'Neil, R. M. (2005). "Academic Freedom: Past, Present, and Future Beyond September 11." In P. G. Altbach, R. O. Berdahl, and P. J. Gumport (Eds.), *American Higher Education in the Twenty-First Century: Social, Political, and Economic Challenges* (2nd ed.), pp. 91–114. Baltimore, MD: Johns Hopkins.
6. J. A. Barker, personal communication, March 4, 2008.
7. Chandler, A. D., Jr. (1962). *Strategy and Structure: Chapters in the History of the American Industrial Enterprise.* Cambridge, MA: MIT Press.
8. Collins, J. (2005). *Good to Great and the Social Sectors: A Monograph to Accompany Good to Great.* New York: HarperCollins, p. 9.
9. Bailey, D. B., Koney, K. M., McNish, M., Powers, R., and Uhly, K. (2008). *Sustaining Our Spirits.* Washington, DC: NASW Press; Bailey, D., and Uhly, K. (2008). "Leadership." In T. Mizrahi and L. Davis (Eds.), *Encyclopedia of Social Work* (20th ed.). Washington, DC: NASW and Oxford University Press; Bailey, D. (2006). "Leading

from the Spirit." In F. Hesselbein and M. Goldsmith (Eds.), *The Leader of the Future 2: Visions, Strategies, and Practices for a New Era.* San Francisco: Jossey-Bass.

10.   Oblinger, D. (Ed.) (2006). *Learning Spaces.* Boulder, CO: EDU-CAUSE. www.educause.edu/learningspaces, p. 4.17.
11.   Hamel, G. (2007). *The Future of Management.* Boston: Harvard Business School Press, p. 116.
12.   J. Allan, personal communication, March 4, 2008.
13.   M. Mandel, personal communication, February 22, 2008.
14.   H. Stein, personal communication, March 4, 2008.
15.   Moraga, C., and Anzaldúa, G. (Eds.) (1983). *The Bridge Called My Back: Writings by Radical Women of Color* (2nd ed.). New York: Kitchen Table: Women of Color Press, pp. iv–v. Placement of parentheses modified for this text.

Additional References

Boyer, E. (1990). *Scholarship Reconsidered.* San Francisco: Jossey-Bass.
Buber, M. (1998). *The Knowledge of Man: Selected Essays* (M. Friedman and R. G. Smith, Trans.). New York: Humanity Books.
Cremin, L. (1965). *The Wonderful World of Ellwood Patterson Cubberly: An Essay on the Historiography of American Education.* New York: Teachers College Bureau of Publications.
Hanh, T. N. (1999). *Interbeing: Fourteen Guidelines for Engaged Buddhism.* Berkeley, CA: Parallax Press.
Kabat-Zinn, J. (1995). *Wherever You Go, There You Are.* New York: Hyperion.
Moraga, C., and Anzaldúa, G. (Eds.). (1983). *The Bridge Called My Back: Writings by Radical Women of Color* (2nd ed.). New York: Kitchen Table: Women of Color Press.
Williamson, M. (1992). *A Return to Love.* New York: HarperCollins.

PART FOUR

WORKING TOGETHER

Part Four looks at the people side of organization design by focusing on the age-old problem of getting people to work together more effectively, productively, and nonacrimoniously.

Consultant Lee Cockerell led operations at Disney, Hilton Hotels, and Marriott; in his chapter, he points out that the organization of the future needs to pay as much attention to people and leadership strategies as it does to products and services. In other words, "it's the people, stupid." Therefore, organizations need to create an *inclusive* environment, and this chapter describes ten ways leaders can get started on that path.

MIT/Sloan management professor Edgar H. Schein focuses on another people challenge: managing subcultures, which requires aligning and meshing a diversity of geographic, market-based, functional, and occupational groups. He describes real situations faced by leaders at such companies as General Foods, Ciba-Geigy, and Hewlett-Packard, and he offers suggestions on how to solve this thorny problem.

Finally in this part of the book, management consultant Howard M. Guttman contrasts the traditional hierarchical organization—which he believes is becoming obsolete—and the newer horizontal organization, where people reach across departments to do what they need to get done. He cites examples as diverse as an Australian cooperative of two thousand dairy farmers, a biotechnology company that makes forensic DNA kits, and the Chico's clothing chain, and these case studies show how other organizations can achieve greater success by working horizontally, too.

Chapter Twenty

The Organization of the Future Will Foster an Inclusive Environment

Lee Cockerell

Lee Cockerell recently retired as executive vice president of operations for the Walt Disney World Resort, a position he held for ten years. Before joining Disney in 1990 to open the Disneyland Paris Resort, Cockerell held various executive positions with Hilton Hotels for eight years and the Marriott Corporation for seventeen years. He is credited with developing and implementing Disney's "Great Leader Strategies" for the seven thousand managers at Disney World who lead the fifty-nine thousand cast members (aka employees). Cockerell has developed and teaches a wide range of seminars on time and life management, fostering an inclusive environment, decision making, inspirational leadership, and other topics. His approach to leading is "Learn It . . . Do It . . . Teach It." His first book, Creating Magic: 10 Common Sense Leadership Strategies from a Life at Disney, *was published in 2008. Cockerell currently delivers keynote speeches and leadership seminars around the world in addition to executive coaching, and he serves on several boards. For more information on Lee Cockerell's work, visit his Web site: www.LeeCockerell.com.*

When I consult with major companies, I start by asking them to show me their business strategy and explain it. In most cases, they quickly display a large document and eloquently tell me about their plans for new products and services. They go on and on about how they will use technology and bricks and mortar to improve their services, grow their sales, and expand their organizations' capabilities.

When they finish, I ask them about their people and leadership strategy. Often, they respond with a total silence that lasts way too long while they think about the question. Then they spout a few feel-good remarks like these:

"Our people are our most important product."

"We look for great people to hire, and then we train them in how to deliver great service to our customers."

"We have an annual picnic, a good health care plan, and a tuition reimbursement program, and we give them an annual salary increase of 3 to 4%."

With most companies, that's about the extent of their people and leadership strategy. Unlike their products and services strategies, it is seldom well thought out and documented. Unfortunately, most executives don't see the connection between that missing ingredient and the problems that crop up from time to time—such as having to lay off a bunch of valued employees and creating total insecurity among the ones left standing.

The organization of the future will pay as much attention to people and leadership strategies as it does to products and services.

WOULD *YOU* BE REELECTED TO YOUR POSITION?

Remember the quote that Democratic political strategist James Carville coined for Bill Clinton's campaign in 1992? *"It's the economy, stupid."* Americans agreed and promptly voted George H. W. Bush out and Bill Clinton in. Similarly, in organizations the motto should be, *"It's the people, stupid."* And maybe if business leaders had to run for reelection every four years to keep their jobs, they'd wake up to that fact.

On the day after 9/11, my boss, Al Weiss, who was then president of Walt Disney World, said, "We have to reduce costs significantly, but we are not going to lay anyone off." That one single piece of clear direction from Al put the focus of our entire executive team right back to where it had to be: on the company's number one ground rule, that our people are the most important factor in creating Disney magic.

In the aftermath of the tragedy, with the travel and resort business in a nosedive, it was very hard to get our costs in line without a layoff. But our leadership team not only worked hard together but also solicited ideas from people at every level of the company, top to bottom. We accomplished our goal because the direction was clear from day one and because we got quick, enthusiastic buy-in across the board. All fifty-nine thousand cast members (Disney World's term for employees) already knew they were valued, respected, and needed. As a result, they were fully committed to the company's purpose: to make sure that every guest has the most fabulous time of his or her life.

DOCUMENT, TEACH, ROLE-MODEL

After forty-one years in the hospitality industry (eight years at Hilton Hotels, seventeen at Marriott Hotels and Resorts, and sixteen at Walt Disney World Resort), I'm absolutely convinced that *the secret to success for organizations in the future is positive, inclusive leadership*. Back in 1995, when I was executive vice president of operations at Disney World, I spent much of the year working with my team to produce a document titled "Disney Great Leader Strategies." Disney World's ultimate goal is to create magic for our guests, and we knew that the best way to make that happen was to also create magic for our cast members, because they are the ones who deliver the magic. Our intention was to build strong leaders at every level of the company, and the document we created was used to train all seven thousand managers in the expected leadership behaviors. The message that was (and still is) constantly repeated to cast members was this:

IT IS NOT MAGIC THAT MAKES THE WALT DISNEY WORLD RESORT WORK. IT IS THE WAY WE WORK THAT MAKES IT MAGICAL.

That belief, that philosophy, is so important to any organization that I used it to open my new book on leadership. Having total clarity about expected leadership behaviors and making sure those behaviors are modeled consistently will be a vital ingredient in the organization of the future.

THE SECRET OF GREAT ORGANIZATIONS

One morning many years ago, as I walked out the door to go to work, my wife, Priscilla, told me, "Lee, be careful what you say and do today, because people are watching you and judging you." This might have been the best piece of advice I ever received. I remembered it every day for the rest of my career, and I made sure to remind all the leaders at Disney of the vital importance of conducting themselves as professionals every minute of every day.

The great organizations of the future (and great families, neighborhoods, houses of worship, and any other collection of people) will have great leaders in place at every level. They will understand that leadership is not a question of someone's position, title, or salary. Leadership is more than a role, it's a *responsibility*. A big one. Being a leader means doing what has to be done, when it has to be done, in the way it *should* be done, whether you like it or not. It means making the right things happen by bringing out the best in others.

The organization of the future will have caring, humble, inclusive leaders who understand what is expected of them and who are held accountable for conducting themselves professionally and serving their employees. That requires leaders to do all of the following:

- Make their fellow employees feel special
- Appreciate how difficult their jobs are, both physically and mentally
- Treat them as individuals
- Show employees total and complete respect
- Provide every opportunity for appropriate training and development

YOU ARE A MANAGER, A LEADER, AND AN ENVIRONMENTALIST

When people asked me what I did as executive vice president of operations for the Walt Disney World Resort, I told them my title should be changed to "chief environmentalist." Good leaders are environmentalists: their responsibility is to create a sustainable business environment—that is, one that is calm, clear, crisp, and clean, with no pollution, no toxins, and no waste—in which everyone flourishes. At Disney, we reminded every manager that he or she was an environmentalist for his or her cast members.

I came to this conclusion a long time ago when I went through a major transition in my management style. I had been a take-no-prisoners manager who could meet any deadline and was expert at getting done what had to be done. What I was *not* good at was creating an environment where my team woke up in the morning excited and energized about coming to work, as opposed to having that dreaded feeling of "I have to go to work because I need the paycheck." After some rude awakenings, I learned what a huge difference those two environments can make in every measure of performance. I eventually learned to use my authority and my position to change the toxic environment that exists in most organizations to one with blue skies, radiant sunshine, and warm spring rains, where workers at all levels are happy to come to work.

I learned to focus most of my time on a few crucial environmental activities and to let other leaders—who were carefully selected for their skills and professionalism—take care of the financial details and other technical necessities for creating and maintaining a successful, healthy organization. Because the buck stopped at my desk, I decided that my chief priority was to create a truly inclusive workplace, where every employee contributed to the best of his or her ability. To accomplish that goal, I outlined ten main tasks for myself. I later taught them to others, because focusing on these ten things can help anyone move from being just another manager to being a respected, inspiring, trusted leader.

TEN WAYS TO FOSTER AN INCLUSIVE ENVIRONMENT

The next sections outline these ten ways to create an inclusive environment. They work because they go right to the heart, and it's through the heart that you get to a person's brain. Whether you're a senior leader, a rising star, or the newest kid on the team, if you aspire to leadership in the organization of the future, I suggest you put them into practice and get other leaders to do the same in their domains. Regardless of your position, never underestimate the impact you can have on your organization's culture.

1. KNOW YOUR TEAM

I mean really know them. Know all about them. Know their past work experiences. Know what skills and talents they possess. Ask them about their aspirations, their short- and long-term goals. Sometimes people do not recognize their own potential and sell themselves short. Leaders in the organizations of the future will look for that potential, nurture it carefully, and help employees grow. Many of us are where we are today because someone saw the potential in us and took an interest in helping us develop that potential.

Also get to know your employees as people. For example, I'll never forget the wounded expression of an employee who told me that her manager of ten years did not know whether she had a son or a daughter. It would have made a tremendous difference to that woman's work performance if her boss had shown a genuine interest in her family. You can't imagine how much it can mean to employee morale when a leader says, "How did Bobby do on that exam?" or "Did Judy's team win that soccer game?" instead of just "Good morning."

2. ENGAGE YOUR TEAM

This means asking for their opinions about the business and making it clear that you sincerely want to hear their points of view. Don't wait for them to volunteer their thoughts; instead, solicit them actively by asking them,

"What do you think?"
"Do you think this is the best way?"
"Is there anything else I should think about before I make this decision?"

This doesn't just make people feel needed; it produces great ideas. I can't count the number of improvements we made at Disney World based on the suggestions of cast members at every level.

For example, I once asked a group of frontline people how we could improve our organizational structure. One young man raised his hand and said, "I have some ideas." I invited him to come to see me. One of his suggestions was to eliminate a whole level of supervisory positions. It sounded radical at first, but once the management team worked out the details and made sure we could move people to different jobs so that no one would suffer, we put the idea into practice—and we ended up saving millions of dollars a year.

3. Develop Your Team

When he was fourteen, my son, Daniel, told me, "Dad you can't fire your children; you have to develop them." If more companies thought that way, their employees would do a whole lot better job.

Developing employees is one of a leader's main responsibilities. It starts with selecting great people to begin with. Then, by getting to know each of your team members really well and staying engaged with them on an ongoing basis, you come to know where each person can benefit from training, mentoring, and other forms of development.

For example, not long ago, I received a letter from a woman who worked in the dining room of a Marriott Hotel I had managed more than twenty years ago. It was a thank-you letter for helping her learn important lessons in professionalism and leadership. When she worked for me, I had forced her to pay close attention to certain details that she considered unimportant. I was tough on her, holding her to higher standards than she held herself. Now she was thanking me for it. She said those tough conversations enabled her to develop as a professional and reach the executive position she holds today. I did not remember the specific incident she recalled in that letter, but she never forgot it. That's what happens when you help people develop their full abilities.

4. Greet People Sincerely

This advice might sound like your mother talking, but I assure you that if you don't pay attention to the little things, you'll have more big things to worry about. And this is an easy one for leaders to mess up. You get so caught up in your work that you become preoccupied and stop noticing other people. But when you walk past employees without greeting them, they'll decide either that you are a jerk or that you just don't care about them. Believe me, everyone notices. So stay alert.

For example, I owe much of my success at Disney to my reputation as a leader who cared and was always available. I earned that reputation by getting out and about every day, and stopping to chat with my fellow cast members as I moved around the operation. I even consulted my DayTimer before setting out, so I knew the names of the people I was likely to run in to. If you do this and other little things that you might think are trivial, people will say nice things about you behind your back—and that's a good sign that they're willing to follow where you lead them.

5. BUILD COMMUNITY

Think of your team as a community. Each one of your team members has different motivations, ideas, priorities, preferences, and dreams. They come from different backgrounds and live in different neighborhoods. Get to know them well so that you can leverage these dynamics. Build a team that looks and thinks like the different parts of the community. The more perspectives you have, the more successful you will be.

When you create an inclusive environment where everyone matters and they know it, you soon have an organizational community that looks like the real community we live in. In contrast, if you are in meetings and everyone looks like you, you are in trouble and out of touch.

I really learned over the years the value of having diversity at the table when we made important decisions. For example, one cast member who was a single mom gave me great perspective about our policy around the use of sick time when her child was sick and how we should change that policy. She had a perspective I would not have thought of as a married man with a wife at home who took care of our son when he was sick.

6. LISTEN TO UNDERSTAND

As Stephen Covey says, "First seek to understand before being understood." The first step to good listening is to position yourself to listen. Get out from behind your desk, sit close to the other person, and give him or her your complete attention—no distractions, no interruptions, no multitasking. Then listen intently to what the other person is saying—and to what he or she is *not* saying but is expressing with facial gestures and body language.

You might not have an immediate solution for the person's concerns, and you might not be hearing anything you haven't heard before, but by simply letting your employees know that you care enough to listen, you are earning the kind of loyalty that money can't buy. But make sure to follow up, or you'll lose what you've gained by listening. Leaders have to walk their talk.

For example, when I retired from Disney World, I received a lot of adulation, but the acknowledgment I remember best was a note from a cast member who said, "Lee, I will never forget how you took the time to get involved in my termination when no one else would listen, and how you worked until it got straightened out and I was put back to work."

7. Communicate Clearly, Directly, and Honestly

Good communication is clarification. So use ordinary words, say exactly what you mean, and make sure you've been understood. I often received very positive feedback from fellow employees for telling it the way it was. For example, I told one executive, "If your negative attitude continues, I am going to terminate your employment in 180 days." He said, "Can't you just write in a warning that there will be consequences?" I said, "No, I want to be crystal clear about what I am saying." He went on to become one of our best executives, and he thanked me for my honesty.

But don't sacrifice decency and compassion in the name of clarity. I wasn't always a good communicator; I learned that skill early in my career after being passed up for a key promotion because I was blunt and intimidating.

8. Hear All Voices

Everyone has an opinion. Most everyone can speak, but most people do not have a voice unless you, the leader, allow them and encourage them to have a voice. A single mom, a high school dropout, a new employee, a long-term employee, a young employee, and an old employee all have different voices. Get to know them and where they are coming from.

For example, I sat down with a secretary who worked in my office and had young children. I told her that we would work with her during school breaks and adjust her schedule so that she could get out on time to be home with her children when they got home from school. She ended up being one of our best employees because we heard her voice, which was expressing her concern for her children.

Every manager learned to practice the "Four Cast Member Expectations" to build trust so that each cast member would have the confidence to let us hear his or her voice. These four expectations are as follows:

1. Make Me Feel Special
2. Treat Me as an Individual
3. Respect Me
4. Make Me Knowledgeable, Develop Me, and Understand My Job

These are the basic principles for leading employees in any organization.

9. Speak Up When Others Are Excluded

When you are in a leadership position, you need to be on the lookout for people who are being excluded for one reason or another. Maybe they are new and being ignored by long-term employees. Maybe they are being made fun of through inappropriate jokes because they look or dress differently. Maybe they are introverts and find it difficult to speak up. Maybe they feel insecure because they don't speak the language well. Maybe they have low self-esteem and low self-confidence. The reasons can be many, and some forms of exclusion can be very subtle, so keep your eyes peeled.

For example, I once noticed a very introverted employee who seemed to have the potential to become a manager but did not believe in herself. I noticed that when I asked her a direct question, she had great answers and was willing to give her opinion.

I became her mentor and spent a lot of time encouraging her, getting her into the right positions and training, and then giving her a shot at management. She turned out to be a great manager. I still hear from her often about her successes with her career. She has gone from being introverted to being a self-assured professional manager. She just needed some encouragement and someone believing in her.

10. Be Brave

This trait separates the great leaders from the average and good ones. It might also be the most important one. By "brave," I don't just mean being willing to take business risks or to try out new ideas. That kind of courage is very important, of course, but I'm talking about being brave enough to do the right thing.

One of the biggest problems most organizations face is that people are afraid to speak up when they see something wrong, whether it's people slacking off or wasting resources or treating people inappropriately or committing a serious ethical or legal violation. It is absolutely critical that you as a great leader create an environment in which people get braver and braver, meaning that they will do the right thing, knowing that you have their back.

For example, I remember on one occasion a manager coming to me to tell me about some inappropriate behavior by the manager's boss. This person told me that the main reason he was willing to let me know what was going on was that he trusted me 100%. There are lots of things employees are keeping from leaders because they just do not trust them; many of these things would dramatically improve the organization.

Get Started Now

During the time I led Walt Disney World Operations, the results of our annual anonymous leadership survey improved year after year as people throughout the company made the transition from being great managers to being great managers *and* great leaders. They learned that they would be evaluated not just on what they accomplished, but on *how* they accomplished it. That "how" meant getting things done by creating an environment where their fellow

employees weren't just interested in their jobs but were fully committed to them because the employees felt valued and respected
as individuals.

There is a big difference between interest and commitment.
At Walt Disney World, we thought of commitment as "Going all
the way." That's the kind of commitment that Martin Luther King
Jr., Nelson Mandela, Susan B. Anthony, and other courageous
leaders had. If you make people feel special, treat them as individuals with total and complete respect, and train and develop
them so they can have a brighter future, they will be committed
to you—and they will go all the way for your organization, your
customers, and your bottom line. If you want greater productivity,
higher customer satisfaction, and improved business results, focus
on leadership that inspires that kind of commitment.

I think most employees in most organizations will give 25
to 50% more than they currently do if leaders can release their
energy by practicing these leadership behaviors. Your fellow
employees want exactly what you want, so give it to them and
watch your environment become a breath of fresh air that people
can't wait to get to in the morning. In a truly inclusive environment, employees raise the bar themselves, setting high standards
for how they serve their customers.

It took twenty years or more to pollute Lake Erie and twenty
years or more to clean it up. Fortunately, you can clean up your
organization's environment much faster than that. Still, moving
from a good environment to a great one does take time, so you need
to get started today. You might even run into some resistance. If any
leaders in your organization do not believe in the values you wish to
put into practice, you need either to change their minds or to move
them out. Role modeling is everything for leaders, and it's absolutely critical at the top levels of an organization. You simply cannot
become the organization of the future unless everyone on your team
is focused on positive, respectful, professional leadership.

As your inclusive organizational culture takes shape, you will
see quick results: your fellow employees will make your customers
feel more special, treating them as individuals, showing total and
complete respect to all of them, and using the knowledge you gave
them through training and development to exceed customers'
expectations. As a result, word of mouth about your business will

soar, and so will both new business and repeat business. It's a quadruple win: you win, your employees win, your customers win, and your bottom line wins.

I hope you can now see why your people and leadership strategy has to be just as strong as your products and services strategy. This may sound like common sense, and it is, but I assure you it is not common practice. Leadership is not hard. It is, in fact, quite simple. Great leaders worry more about their fellow employees and their customers than about their salaries, titles, stock options, company cars, and other perks—just as great parents worry a whole lot more about their children than they do about themselves. If you have children, you know this. If you don't have children, ask any parent.

But it is strange how managers, once they go to work, forget all the wise things their parents and grandparents taught them about how to treat other people. That's why I often give speeches titled "Manage Like a Mother." Great parents are disciplined, tough, and sensitive. They know what the goal is, and they know that they have just a few years to prepare their children to be good, productive citizens. So they start creating the right environment from day one.

You need to do the same, starting today. You can begin by earning the trust of your employees. Every year on Disney's anonymous leadership survey, I received a perfect score on the question "Do you trust your leader?" Of all my accomplishments, this is the one I'm proudest of, because I earned that trust by being *trustworthy*. If the leaders in your organization are not trustworthy, employees will smile to their faces and despise them—and maybe sabotage them—behind their backs. They will give only 50% of themselves, and you will never know the difference. If, in contrast, people trust their leaders, they will do anything for them.

At the end of each working day, I figured that if I spent most of my time creating an inclusive environment and providing the right training and development for employees, everything else would fall into place much easier. That is exactly what happened at the Walt Disney World Resort. You can do the same by creating an environment where everyone matters and they know it. If you get that right, you'll start a positive chain reaction: you take great care of your employees, they take great care of their customers, and the customers reward you with repeat business for decades to come because you will have become the organization of the future.

CHAPTER TWENTY-ONE

THE LEADER AS SUBCULTURE MANAGER

Edgar H. Schein

Edgar H. Schein is the Sloan Fellows Professor of Management Emeritus at the MIT Sloan School of Management, where he has taught since 1956. He received his PhD in social psychology from Harvard in 1952. His teaching and research focused both on the individual through research on career anchors, and on organizations through research on organizational culture and process consultation. He was a process consultant to major corporations both in the United States and overseas. Schein's most recent books are The Corporate Culture Survival Guide; Process Consultation Revisited; Organizational Culture and Leadership, 3rd ed.; *and* Career Anchors, 3rd ed. *He is currently finishing a book on helping.*

One of the things one learns if one hangs around long enough is that good insights and ideas don't die; they just evolve into new forms. Therefore, it's not surprising that researchers Paul Lawrence and Jay Lorsch identified more than fifty years ago the two central problems of organizational growth: how to differentiate into meaningful subunits, and, once differentiated, how to integrate the different subunits into coherent corporate action.[1]

Both differentiation and integration are central tasks of the leader. Both are difficult to accomplish and are getting more so because we have begun to see more of the effects of national, organizational, and occupational subcultures.

So what is new? Why bother rehashing all of this? What are leaders supposed to learn that they did not already know? The most important "news" is that the integration problem is much more complicated if you view the units into which the organization has differentiated itself as *subcultures* rather than as just groups or as just structural components of a larger corporate culture. What we have learned in recent decades is that the corporate culture covers only a limited number of central values and assumptions and that the actual functioning of the organization, its effectiveness, is more a product of *good alignment* of the subcultures.[2] A strong corporate culture does not guarantee such alignment; therefore, *the leader of the future must learn how to align and mesh strong subcultures.* This is a much more difficult task of integration.

In other words, the problem of differentiation is one of how to divide up the labor between the various geographic, market-based, functional, and occupational subcultures. The problem of integration is to create enough of a corporate culture to fight the centrifugal forces of subculture differentiation and competition and then to mesh the subcultures and get them aligned around a common purpose.

The word *culture* entered managerial thinking in the 1980s, but the notion that employees who worked together and had common occupational backgrounds would form strong common values and norms was known from the earliest studies of organizations.[3] In fact, it is surprising that not more of this is grasped in today's leadership literature. We know perfectly well that the union and management have different cultures, yet we ignore the equally obvious reality that every echelon and every functional and geographic unit of the organization has a different subculture.

There is a growing acceptance of the idea that a central function of leadership is culture management, not in the trivial sense of "creating" a culture of something or other but in the profound sense of realizing that culture arises from a combination of leader actions and environmental responses. What has not yet been grasped sufficiently is that culture management also involves aligning the activities of the subcultures with organizational goals.

It is important to note that this is not *culture creation* or *culture change;* instead, it is *culture evolution,* because any organization with any history will have not only an entrenched top management and corporate culture but also an existing distribution of subcultures that will have learned to work with each other in a certain fashion that they will not easily give up. Cultural evolution then involves both new elements of the overall corporate culture and possibly new alignments among the subcultures.

Aligning Subcultures at General Foods

Years ago, I worked with the director of management development of General Foods (GF), Betty Duval. Our immediate focus was on management development, but the context in which this had to occur was among the cultures we observed within GF. The dominant subculture was "marketing," defined by the style and technology of product management. Product managers were young hotshot MBAs who saw themselves as the key to GF's future and were the pool from which crown princes were recruited. This subculture was built around market research through surveys, choosing the right kind of advertising, and intensive product development.

A second but subordinate subculture was "manufacturing," defined by reliability and cost effectiveness. This subculture had special significance because some of the greatest innovations in the human side of manufacturing were made in the GF organization at that time, built on the group dynamics insights of Kurt Lewin and his students.[4]

A third and also subordinate subculture was "sales." The members of the sales force were out in the supermarkets, observing how store managers placed products on shelves and how customers responded to where products were located on the shelves. They often brought back what they regarded as key insights on how products were viewed and how they should be advertised, but it was notable how consistently the product managers would ignore those data in favor of what they learned from their own market survey research. I watched many a meeting where experienced salespeople would walk away in frustration and disgust after an inexperienced hotshot MBA product manager ignored their advice. This was a case where the organization consistently lost information because these subcultures were not aligned effectively.

Was there an overarching corporate culture within General Foods? Indeed there was, and it was a kind of blending of the marketing subculture and the financial subculture, manifested primarily in the annual marketing plan ritual that every product group had to undergo. This ritual was a presentation to corporate senior management of the marketing plan for the product of each group. The success of this presentation could make or break young product managers, so as much as a half year or more would go into the development and fine-tuning of not only the plan itself but also the actual presentation.

The plan was evaluated by senior management on both its marketing quality and its financial analysis. And, not so surprisingly, senior management arrogated for itself the final decision about how the product would be *priced*. On almost every other aspect of the plan, the product managers made recommendations, which might be fine-tuned but were generally approved. But on pricing, senior management kept a tight rein, often to the frustration of the product managers.

Conflicts among the product subcultures were minimized by giving them maximum independence and by carefully selecting managers who could compete but who were also willing to be good corporate citizens. Thus Maxwell House, Birds Eye, Jell-O, and several other divisions could develop subcultures that reflected the technologies that underlay their products. These differences should not be minimized, because the making of coffee and the making of Jell-O and peas are, in fact, quite different processes, relying on some important technological differences. But by keeping key financial decisions—such as pricing—centralized, senior management had the leverage necessary to minimize the destructive elements of competition.

A further mechanism to keep the subcultures aligned was intensive rotation of high-potential managers around the units. Most product managers felt that if they did not receive a promotion within two years of being in a given job, they were failing. By moving people across the different product lines, senior management was assured that each of the subcultures would be understood and taken into account when corporate decisions had to be made.

As GF grew, it expanded both nationally and internationally— which created cultural issues around geographic and national variations in norms, working habits, and consumer habits. As I reflect on it, the presidents of GF who grew up with these changes had an enormous culture management and evolution job on their hands. This was illustrated in the 1970s, with a major organization development exercise that Alan Sheldon of the Harvard Business

School was asked to conduct in order to help senior management resolve some strategic conflicts that had arisen.

The president had several senior vice presidents who could not agree on whether GF should grow by becoming primarily a domestic food company, an international food company, or an innovation-oriented food company. Each of these alternatives was passionately backed by one of the VPs, and the president realized that they represented cultural units that did not really understand or appreciate each other. Months of arguing did little to dispel their differences because they argued from different cultural assumptions.

The president decided that they needed a process that would create a common language and common understanding. To create this commonality, a Delphi process was designed. Each major alternative was carefully described, followed by a questionnaire that required each participant to make predictions on the consequences of following each alternative. The key was that they could not make these predictions responsibly without studying each plan. The predictions were then circulated, and an intensive discussion process was launched.

After the discussion and the discovery of how each VP felt, another set of predictive questionnaires was again launched. This whole process was carried out over a six-month period, at the end of which another major strategy retreat was held. This time, the group was able to come together because by now they had built a common base of understanding. Instead of the decision resting on who had the best *argumentation* skills, it now rested on all of them carefully *analyzing the consequences of each strategic alternative.*

Warring Subcultures at Other Companies

Kaiser Permanente. When I worked for a time with Kaiser Permanente in Oakland, I found that this organization had two completely different subcultures that were in a kind of war with each other. The insurance side of the organization was a traditional hierarchy built around financial assumptions, whereas the doctors' organization was built around a democratic system in which each unit elected its chief. One of the questions had to do with which of the two subcultures would "win" as the total organization evolved. Not surprisingly, the financial subculture won because it was much better aligned with the larger financial culture in which the whole organization was embedded.

Hewlett-Packard. HP is a case where subculture issues led to a splitting of the company. The original company built around measurement and instrumentation grew into computing and discovered that the culture of computing was very different in style and orientation from the original culture built around instrumentation. Both were engineering cultures, but they were built on *different core technologies,* which led to differences in engineering and management style.

These differences eventually led to the breaking off of Agilent, which represented more of the original culture, while the name of HP remained with the growing computer side of the business. Agilent and HP are today very different kinds of companies.

Digital Equipment Corporation. DEC is a case of creating an environment that fostered independence and the growth of subcultures around different engineering groups.[5] Ken Olsen, one of the founders and the long-term leader of DEC, was a genius at creating a climate in which strong creative engineers could flourish. He also believed in internal competition and letting the market decide which of several competing products should survive and be supported.

The extraordinary success of the company for twenty-five years made the engineering leaders very powerful, and they created groups around themselves that became strong subcultures. When the market evolved toward commoditization and the need for efficiency and cost control, Olsen discovered that the subculture conflicts could not be managed, nor could they resolve issues among themselves. As a result, the company could not focus its resources and compete in the changing marketplace, leading to its failure as an economic entity. Paradoxically, the culture that had spawned the strong subcultures continued to be highly revered by ex-DEC managers.

Ciba-Geigy. An interesting example of a subculture causing cultural indigestion for the corporate parent comes from Ciba-Geigy back in the late 1970s. In order to learn how to be better at "marketing," corporate management asked the U.S. subsidiary to acquire a consumer goods company. It acquired Airwick, a company that specialized in removing unpleasant odors from carpeting, furniture, pets, and so on.

The subsidiary became financially successful after several years both in the United States and in many countries in Europe, yet Ciba-Geigy sold Airwick to Reckitt and Coleman because of the obvious discomfort of senior management with the image that the product created. Ciba-Geigy saw itself as a high-tech, science-oriented chemical company devoted to solving the world's "big" problems—such as curing starvation through agricultural chemicals and curing diseases through new pharmaceuticals. The notion of being identified with merely an air freshener clearly created cultural discomfort. I had the feeling that being identified with Airwick might even have offended the Swiss sensibility because "Swiss air was clean." In any case, the financial and marketing arguments to keep Airwick did not win out over the technical image arguments.

THREE CRITICAL TYPES OF SUBCULTURE

The case studies mentioned previously show how specific subcultures based on functions or occupations influence organizational outcomes. More recent research has revealed that all organizations have within them three generic subcultures, which must be aligned if the organization is to function at all. This cultural structure is clearest in high-tech manufacturing facilities (such as a nuclear or chemical plant), but some version of each of these subcultures can be observed even in voluntary or nonprofit organizations.

1. An *operator culture* that is built around the day-to-day operations and the management of the inevitable surprises that arise in even a carefully designed system; the members of this subculture take great pride in being able to handle whatever contingencies arise in getting the job done.
2. An *engineering culture* that is built around principles of the design of the work and the organizational structure; ideally the designers would ultimately prefer to automate everything, on the assumption that it is people who are ultimately the problem because they make mistakes.

3. An *executive culture* that is concerned primarily with economic survival and is built on the assumption that if financial affairs are not managed properly there will be no organization in the first place.[6]

The dilemma of all organizations is how to maximize the contribution of each subculture by aligning them instead of trying to judge who is right and who is wrong. "Humanizing" the engineer or the CEO does little good, because for optimum innovation the engineer should use his most creative ideas and the CEO should do his best in managing the financial affairs. What is most critical for leaders, then, is to learn how to manage the dynamics of the various subcultures to align them for optimal performance.

SUBCULTURE DYNAMICS

Subcultures derive from two forces—occupational socialization and shared history. For example, the engineering or R&D department of a company has a culture by virtue of the education and training that the scientists and engineers received before coming to the company and the shared experiences they have had within the company. The members of the headquarters financial organization have a culture by virtue of their education, their career experiences climbing the finance ladder, and their shared history in keeping the company's finances in order.

Once these subcultures are established, they are reinforced by the role that they are to play in the company. The R&D function is supposed to maintain its values of creativity and innovation, allow and encourage its members to be individualistic, and even permit violation of some company norms, such as dress codes and working hours. The finance function is supposed to keep the banks, the investors, and the analysts happy, so they learn how to translate all decision issues into financial cost-benefit terms,[7] develop a whole language and conceptual structure around these issues, and often appear to be disconnected from some of the "human" issues that others in the company feel.

The line organization (which may include sales and manufacturing) develops its subcultures more around shared history than occupational origin, and in many organizations, each echelon or hierarchical level will develop its subculture around its tasks and roles. Thus you will find different subcultures at the hourly employee and union level, the first-line supervisory level, middle management, and senior management.

In all the examples described earlier, the distinguishing feature is that the problems could not be solved by either power or logic. You cannot *order* a culture to think differently. If people speak different languages and have different assumptions because of the underlying technology of their work or their educational background, you cannot order them to agree.

BUILDING SUBCULTURE ALIGNMENT

Leaders have to think about how they can build cross-cultural understanding and alignment. Probably the most important principle was provided recently by the HR manager of the joint-venture oil company formed by British Petroleum and the Russian counterpart. This manager was asked how she got the Russians and Brits to begin to understand each other, to which she replied "forced interaction." If the members of the subcultures don't get to know each other, they will never understand each other enough to work in alignment.

I would add to that two more principles: a *common problem* and *dialogue* (instead of discussion or debate).[8] What I mean by dialogue is interaction that minimizes arguing and debating and maximizes trying to understand why the "other" holds the view that he or she holds.[9] The forced interaction and common problem alone won't produce mutual understanding without this kind of dialogue and the climate it creates.

What leaders need to do, then, is to create vehicles—task forces, committees, after-action reviews—that enable members of different subcultures to work together on something. Then, either by example or by getting the right kind of facilitation, leaders must ensure that the common work is done in a dialogue fashion that stimulates understanding.

The Delphi process at General Foods was an interesting example of how to create dialogue through a very formal process. It is to be hoped that leaders can invent other, simpler ways of getting cross-cultural dialogue going within their organizations. In any case, leaders must realize that the management of their organizations will depend increasingly on *recognizing and managing the subcultures* within those organizations.

Endnotes

1. Lawrence, P. R., and Lorsch, J. W. *Organization and Environment.* Boston: Harvard Graduate School of Business Administration, 1967.
2. Schein, E. H. "Three Cultures of Management: The Key to Organizational Learning." *Sloan Management Review*, 1996, *38*, 1, 9–20; Schein, E. H. *Organizational Culture and Leadership.* (3rd ed.) San Francisco: Jossey-Bass, 2004.
3. Argyris, C. *Integrating the Individual and the Organization.* Hoboken, N.J.: Wiley, 1964; Dalton, M. *Men Who Manage.* Hoboken, N.J.: Wiley, 1959; Hughes, E. C. *Men and Their Work.* Glencoe, Ill.: Free Press, 1958.
4. Walton, R. "Improving the Quality of Work Life." *Harvard Business Review*, May/June 1974, p. 12ff.
5. Schein, E. H. *DEC Is Dead; Long Live DEC: The Lasting Legacy of Digital Equipment Corporation.* San Francisco: Berrett-Kohler, 2003.
6. Schein, 1996.
7. Donaldson, G., and Lorsch, J. W. *Decision Making at the Top.* New York: Basic Books, 1983.
8. Schein, E. H. "On Dialogue, Culture and Organizational Learning." *Organizational Dynamics*, 1993, *22*, 40–51.
9. Isaacs, W. *Dialogue.* New York: Random House, 1999.

CHAPTER TWENTY-TWO

THE NEW HIGH-PERFORMANCE, HORIZONTAL ORGANIZATION

Howard M. Guttman

*Howard M. Guttman (hmguttman@guttmandev.com) is the principal of
Guttman Development Strategies, Inc. (www.guttmandev.com), a Mount
Arlington, New Jersey–based management consulting firm specializing
in building high-performance teams, executive coaching, strategic and
organizational alignment, and project implementation. He is the author of*
When Goliaths Clash: Managing Executive Conflict to Build a More
Dynamic Organization. *His latest book is* Great Business Teams: Cracking
the Code for Standout Performance.

In many respects, business organizations are like living organisms; their survival and success depend on similar evolutionary forces. Failure to adjust to changing conditions renders both organizations and organisms unfit to survive.

Since the Industrial Revolution, most business organizations have been hierarchically structured entities in which authority and decision-making responsibility emanated from a central hub at the top of the organization. As in the military, to which it bore more than a passing resemblance, "command and control" was the paradigm of the hierarchical organization, which flourished, in large part, due to the high degree of control its leaders were able to exercise. In the last half of the twentieth century, however, the traditional business organization fell under attack by the four horseman of the revolution around us: globalization, the growth of information technology, new forms and intensity of competition, and pressure for rapid innovation. Today, the hierarchical model is quickly becoming something of a dinosaur, unable to cope with the requirements of the postindustrial marketplace.

DEVELOPING AND DRIVING THE HORIZONTAL VISION

The need for a high-speed, "intelligent" enterprise is making obsolete the hierarchical organization, with its multiple layers, slow-motion decision making, and dependence on the personality of the leader. The most successful business organizations of the future will be characterized by fewer levels and decentralized decision points. Exhibit 22.1 contrasts the distinguishing characteristics of the once-predominant hierarchical organization with the horizontal one that is taking its place.

Many leaders have discarded the traditional hierarchical organization and replaced it with the new, horizontal model. For example, here's how one of them, Robert Gordon, CEO and managing director of Dairy Farmers of Australia (DF), defines the emerging horizontal model: "a horizontal organization means moving to an . . . action- and results-driven workforce at every level—not one that waits around for instructions or trips over functional boundaries. It means giving employees the opportunity and skills to decide who needs to be involved in solving problems and making decisions, dividing responsibilities, then stepping aside to allow people to implement."

DF, a cooperative owned by over two thousand farmers, was established more than a hundred years ago. With facilities across Australia, each year DF processes approximately 1.25 billion liters of milk, which is sold as fresh milk, flavored milk, yogurt, and cheese. DF's annual revenue is U.S.$1.3 billion.

When Gordon moved into his position in 2004, his goal was to turn around the financial performance of the business and provide a process to attract external investment at fair value. It was a tall order that required a shift from a *production* mind-set focused on owner-suppliers to a *performance* culture based on financial returns. In addition, DF was facing dramatic market and organizational challenges. Consumers were becoming more sophisticated, dairy production

EXHIBIT 22.1. HIERARCHICAL VERSUS HORIZONTAL ORGANIZATION.

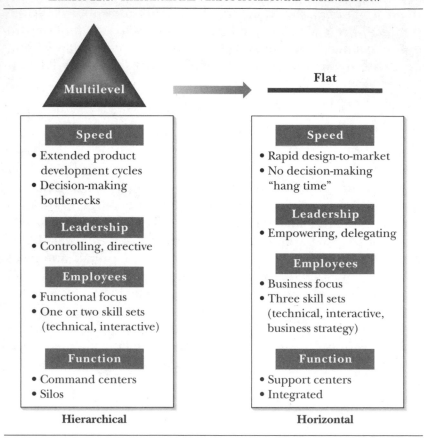

was declining, international farm gate milk prices had skyrocketed, and global fuel costs were at an all-time high. Internally, operating expenses were unsustainable. The company not only was offering too many products but also had too many factories and distribution depots and had become involved in several ancillary businesses that were draining resources from its core operations.

And then there were the rigid silos, each of which operated as an individual hierarchy. One function would make a decision with little or no input from other departments. For example, marketing got a new product idea, then handed it off to R&D for input; R&D weighed in, then passed the decision on to engineering, and as the decision moved from one function to another, assumptions were built in at each step, constraining those further down the chain and eventually making the original decision unworkable. By the time marketing's bright idea hit the plant floor, manufacturing discovered that it just didn't have the processing capability to commercialize it. As Gordon observes, "the head of sales stated that, in his time with the business, the company had never launched a new product on time and to specification."

Given the fragmentation, it is not surprising that resources were distributed without regard to strategic priorities. All the plants received equal budget allocations, so that those supporting high-growth categories didn't have sufficient resources, while those that were producing low-volume products continued to survive.

Gordon realized that it was time for radical change: "I was convinced that our best bet—indeed, our *only* bet—was to go horizontal." He replaced the silos with four cross-functional business teams, one for each of DF's categories: dairy foods, impulse beverages, cheese, and white milk. Each category team is made up of a team leader plus a representative from each of the following functions: marketing, sales, finance, innovation, manufacturing, logistics, and category management. In addition, one member of the executive management team serves as a mentor to each team. Each team is accountable for the profitability of its category and operates fairly autonomously, bringing in the executive team only when there are significant resource allocation issues or additional substantive funding is needed.

By the end of 2007, DF had eliminated much of the complexity that was eating into its profits:

- It reduced its total product portfolio by more than one-third, shifting resources to high-growth product categories.
- It increased total revenues by about 20%.
- It closed four processing facilities, seventeen depots, and all of its noncore businesses.
- Time to market for new products was reduced significantly, enabling the company to win the New Line Launch of the Year award from the largest retailer in Australia; and DF led the growth rate in every retail market in which it participated and improved market share in every category.

THE HIGH-PERFORMANCE TEAM: HALLMARK OF THE HORIZONTAL ORGANIZATION

In the modern enterprise, work gets done largely by teams. In horizontal organizations, high-performance teams have become the driving force of the new structure. They embody the vision that Gordon and many other new-style leaders are striving for.

Applied Biosystems (AB) provides a good example of the power of high-performance teams. AB is the company that created every instrument used in the sequencing of the human genome; it also makes the forensic DNA kits used by law enforcement agencies.

When Catherine Burzik became president of AB in 2004, the company had been stagnant for several years, with little revenue growth and falling stock prices. Despite significant R&D expense, there were few new products in the pipeline. Both Wall Street and AB employees had turned sour.

Burzik's mission: work with her executive team to put in place a strategy to reenergize the company. She quickly moved to align the team (a process discussed later in this chapter), and team members began to evolve from a group of independent, functionally oriented managers into a mini board of directors—willing and able to accept responsibility for the success of the entire company.

Burzik began to push decision making down from her office to the team, and soon speedy decision making and implementation began to replace bottlenecks and impasses. As the senior team took on more responsibility for operational issues, Burzik was freed up to deal with the strategic issues that had been holding the company back. And as more and more high-performance teams were created throughout AB, the advantages grew exponentially. As a result of the process, business accelerated:

- AB's stock price nearly doubled, as did its market cap.
- Revenue began to grow, and the bottom line has seen double-digit performance.
- After several years of no acquisitions, two significant ones were successfully completed.

High-performance teams within horizontal organizations are pools of energy that subvert traditional ways of operating. The old top-down model, with its silo thinking, has been swept away and replaced by players who are asked, often for the first time, to assume individual and collective responsibility for business results.

A NEW KIND OF LEADER

High-performance teams fundamentally redefine both what it means to be a leader of a team and what it means to be team member, or player.

"Born leaders"—those who single-handedly shape the destiny of their organization—are more myth than reality. The high-performance leaders we know are not Lone Rangers; instead, they are deeply committed to the team model. Their espousal of teamwork is not driven by ideological notions of "shared" decision making or "engagement," but by strictly utilitarian considerations. They are convinced that they are more powerful and effective—and that their organizations create greater value—in the presence of high-performance teams that function horizontally.

High-performance leaders are all about leveraging talent, which is why they put considerable energy into answering such questions as

- Who are the key players? And how can I enroll them in my vision?
- What additional competencies must we develop or acquire to create a high-performance organization?
- What role do I play in bringing this about?

In the process of building a high-performance team, the leader redefines three fundamentals of leadership—the leader-follower relationship, accountability, and power—which are described in detail in the following sections.

REDEFINING THE LEADER-FOLLOWER RELATIONSHIP

In the new model, the leader continues to assume ultimate strategic decision-making responsibility. But the leader-follower dynamic changes: the leader is no longer a breed apart, but *primus inter pares*—first among equals. As Brian Camastral puts it, "A high-performance team is not a leaderless team, but a team of leaders."

He should know. Camastral is regional president, Latin America, for Mars Inc., the international producer of food, snack, and pet care products. When Camastral took over the Latin American division in 2005, growth had been stagnant amid a population of more than 560 million potential customers. Many millions of dollars had been invested in the division, with no return. Leadership was practically nonexistent. The entire executive level of the organization was rife with churn, as stars fled faster than they could be promoted. Not surprisingly, any notion of team cohesion had long since evaporated: executives in each unit didn't understand that some issues cut across geographical boundaries, and they had no interest in working together. They were content to keep running their units as independent "fiefdoms." As a result, Mars Inc. Latin America was starving in a land of plenty.

Camastral's top agenda: make his organization flat, fast, and team driven. When Camastral arrived, Latin America was divided into three units: the Caribbean, Mexico, and South America. Camastral quickly divided the territory into seven smaller, more manageable areas. A senior team of seven executives was created to lead each, with the exception of Brazil (which had nine executives on its senior team: a general manager; VPs of finance, HR, R&D, sales, manufacturing, and purchasing; and the heads of marketing for two categories, pet food and snacks).

The teams were aligned and given the skills training and coaching they needed to function in the new, high-performance environment. Because one of the major roadblocks to progress had been the players' failure to see the need for collaboration, during the alignments, the teams were asked to examine their decision-making processes. Each player was asked to list his or her accountabilities, the decisions he or she was responsible for making alone, and those he or she was expected to make in consultation with others.

The results opened eyes. The lists of collaborative decisions were very short. Not so the lists of decisions the players felt they could make unilaterally. And when they compared the latter, they saw that they had all laid claim to the same decision-making areas—for example, when asked who was responsible for ensuring the quality of products and service, the general manager, the VP of manufacturing, and the VP of R&D all thought it fell into their bailiwick—when it actually was the responsibility of all three.

This was an *aha!* moment for the teams. It suddenly became apparent that the way to achieve the best solutions to quality issues (and other vital business issues) was to break out of their unit-specific thinking and begin collaborating. The new divisionwide esprit de corps paid off. Turnover became a nonissue, and more than 70% of management-level openings have been filled from within the company. In just twelve months, the division began experiencing double-digit growth, as the agile teams of leaders met all earnings targets and blew away bottom-line expectations.

REDEFINING ACCOUNTABILITY

This new leader-player paradigm requires a major change in mind-sets—beginning with that of the leader. Part of the challenge involves the leader's ability to put aside ego and insist that team members hold him or her accountable for promised results.

For example, consider Scott Edmonds, CEO of Chico's FAS, Inc., one of the most successful chains of women's clothing stores in the United States. To make the transition to a high-performance, horizontal approach, he had to revamp his own and his organization's mind-set related to accountability. That mind-set change was put to the test after Edmonds had spearheaded the acquisition of Fitigues, a small specialty clothing chain. It became his pet project, and he was soon devoting a great deal of time and energy to it. He didn't realize that his emotional commitment outweighed his business sense until members of his senior team called him on it. They told him, point blank, that the acquisition had become his blind spot and was draining his time away from core business issues. Their input enabled him to regain his perspective. He thanked them for their feedback, assessed Fitigues's performance objectively, and closed the business.

REDEFINING POWER

In hierarchies, power is vertically defined. It flows, in diminishing amounts, from the top down. It is a mechanism for control and compliance, using a variety of carrot-and-stick strategies.

The emerging high-performance leader favors influence over control, commitment over compliance. To the new-style leader, power is a value-neutral concept. The essential question he or she asks is, "In order to achieve results, who needs to be empowered?" High-performance leaders favor "distributive power"—putting as much of it as possible in the hands of team members—provided the team is aligned, the ground rules in place, and the players sufficiently evolved to deliver maximum payoff.

One of the major ways in which a team leader distributes power is by relocating decision-making authority. Recall that one of the first things Cathy Burzik did as president of Applied Biosystems was to push decision making down to her senior team:

- A division presidents' council became the forum to raise and resolve tactical issues common to all; this council is made up of the presidents of AB's four global business divisions.
- An executive strategy team was created to identify and evaluate possible mergers and acquisitions: this team is headed by the VP of strategy and includes the four global business presidents, the VPs of HR and R&D, and Burzik.
- A third subteam was chartered to keep a close watch on the numbers—making sure that the businesses were running well and that financial commitments were being met. This team is run by the VP of finance and includes fifteen members of the executive staff.
- A fourth team focused on the R&D pipeline and made decisions regarding the allotment of R&D dollars among the four divisions. This team is made up of the same members as the executive strategy team and is led by the VP of R&D.

This minimalist approach to decision making—fewer decision makers per issue and more decision making per capita—along with greater individual accountability freed up Burzik to pursue the next round of competitive advantage. For example, the executive strategy team developed a mergers and acquisitions pipeline and succeeded in making two very strategic acquisitions for the company, broadening its portfolio in the areas of consumables and next-generation DNA sequencing. Both were critical acquisitions that strengthened AB's business and were lauded by customers, investors, and employees.

A NEW KIND OF TEAM PLAYER

Perhaps the most significant change that sets high-performance teams apart from their hierarchical counterparts centers around accountability. In hierarchical organizations, accountability is narrowly defined to include results achieved by individuals and those within their span of control. In hierarchical organizations, employees rarely climb above the first and second rungs of the accountability ladder shown in Exhibit 22.2.

In contrast, on a high-performance team, the goal is for everyone to reach the top rung. On the third rung, peers hold peers accountable for delivering promised results—and this is where high performance kicks in. Instead of depending on the leader to deal with underperforming colleagues, players confront one another head-on on issues ranging from lackluster performance to unproductive behavior.

On the surface, peer-to-peer accountability sounds relatively straightforward. Yet it is one of the most difficult breakthroughs a

EXHIBIT 22.2. THE ACCOUNTABILITY LADDER.

Accountability Ladder

Rung 5 — Individuals accountable for the success of the organization

Rung 4 — Individuals accountable for their leader's success

Rung 3 — Individuals accountable for peers

Rung 2 — Individuals accountable for direct reports

Rung 1 — Individuals accountable for their own performance

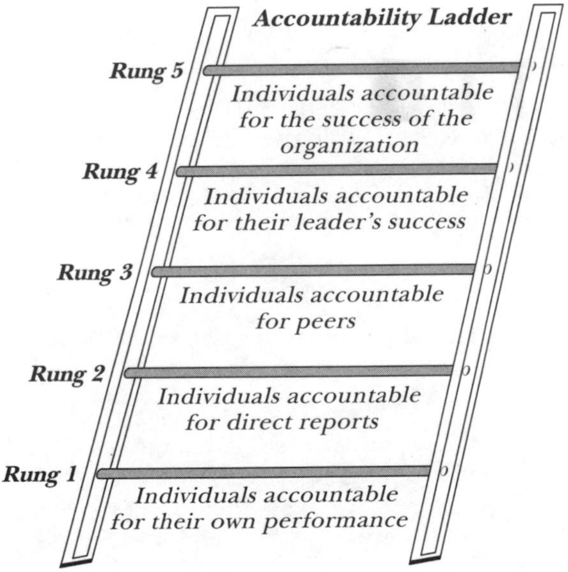

team must achieve. After all, it runs counter to the ingrained habits of the hierarchical culture, typified by statements like these:

"Other people's areas of responsibility are not your business."
"You don't criticize a coworker in front of others."
"If you confront a colleague, you'll destroy your working relationship."

It is even more difficult to break through the mind-set that "you don't critique the leader," which is what is needed to move up to the fourth rung of the accountability ladder. Yet it can be done, as our example of Scott Edmonds illustrated.

ALIGNMENT: THE KEY TO HIGH PERFORMANCE

The logic of the horizontal organization, with its breaking apart of silos and its distributive approach to power and decision making, requires that all its teams be aligned. Alignment entails being in sync, in five key areas, as shown in Exhibit 22.3.

A team alignment, centering as it does on these five areas, presents a leader and team with the opportunity to redefine the new playing field for performance:

1. What's the *business strategy*, and how committed are we to achieving it?
2. What key *operational goals* flow from the strategy, and how do we make sure these goals drive day-to-day decision making?

EXHIBIT 22.3.   THE FIVE KEY ALIGNMENT AREAS.

Strategy

| Goals/Business Priorities/Focus |
| Individual Roles/Accountabilities |
| Protocols/Rules of Engagement |
| Business Relationships/Mutual Expectations |

3. Are we clear on *roles and accountabilities?*
4. What *protocols*, or *ground rules*, will we play by as a team?
5. Will our *business relationships and interdependencies* be built on honesty and transparency?

The alignment process puts the leader's ability to build a new set of relationships with his or her team to the ultimate test.

FROM A HIGH-PERFORMANCE TEAM TO A HIGH-PERFORMANCE ORGANIZATION

In the move toward the horizontal model, the senior executives we know have not followed the typical path of embracing some mega change initiative. Their approach to organizational change is significantly different, in the following ways.

First, the vision is horizontal. Burzik, Edmonds, Camastral, and Gordon realized that without radically changing the way they did business, their organizations would never be able to meet the short- and long-term challenges they faced. Experience had taught them that the horizontal model was simply the best way to leverage the brainpower within their organization to meet those challenges. If throughout the organization they could break down hierarchies, eliminate silos, distribute decision making, and create a sense that everyone was equally accountable for results, then high performance would follow. And it did.

Second, the goal is squarely on business results. Change per se is not a key objective of the high-performance horizontal approach. The fuel for the effort is a significant business challenge that must be met. It is often the need to get a stagnant business moving again, as Gordon, Burzik, and Camastral did. In other cases, it's the need to react quickly to a competitive threat or a significant new opportunity. Whatever the challenge, the forces for change are a burning business issue and an obsession with achieving ever-higher results.

Third, the focus is on tight targeting. High-performance leaders shy away from large-scale interventions aimed at transforming entire organizations in relatively short order. Instead, they set their sights on the molecular level of organizational life: the performance and the interaction of teams. Leaders like Burzik, Camastral, Edmonds, and Gordon begin changing the way their organizations do business by aligning their senior team. Only when that team ratchets up its performance does the leader move to align additional teams.

Fourth, the emphasis is on building organizational momentum. Ideally, the transformation of an organization to a high-performance horizontal entity begins with the senior management team. But aligning itself is just the first step a senior team must take to achieve excellence. For an organization to reach high performance, teams everywhere in the organization must also turn in a stellar performance, which makes "multitier alignments" an imperative.

For example, at Chico's, CEO Scott Edmonds and his direct reports were the first to move to the high-performance team model. Then they cascaded the model to the second tier of management, and the new mind-set has taken root throughout the company. The changes in this group's way of thinking have been dramatic. "In the past," says Chuck Nesbit, Chico's executive vice president and COO, "they might have waited for direction. Now, they have stepped up to the plate and begun taking action. More managers are getting out into the stores, listening to the customers, bringing back feedback and their interpretation of what they have learned. I hear people say, 'We didn't buy enough inventory to take advantage of this opportunity. It's clear that we could sell more. Here's what I suggest we do.' A real sense of cross-functional ownership has replaced the silo mentality."

Perhaps the best evidence of the high-performance momentum that now drives teams throughout Chico's was the company's reaction on November 26, 2006: Black Friday, the day that retailers count on to move their balance sheets from red to black. On Black Friday 2006, more than $622 million was spent each minute. Every second that a retail cash register stayed silent on that day was a major loss. In Chico's five hundred clothing stores, traffic was slow. The company had planned a nationwide marketing event, with an easel in front of each store advertising "40% off already marked-down merchandise." But the customers just weren't buying. Store managers were calling the company's Florida headquarters looking for direction—and fast.

At eleven that morning, the head of marketing picked up the phone to ask his store leadership team, "Is our marketing approach working? Is that easel out front getting shoppers into our stores instead of Talbot's or Ann Taylor?" "No," he was told, "most of the store managers report that it's not working." So the marketing department swung into action and called the stores with a new strategy: bring in the easels and replace them with tables outside each store to display accessories, with new signs that read, "Buy one accessory, get the second one 50% off." The five hundred outlets and their teams moved swiftly to execution.

"We changed our nationwide marketing approach before noon," says Edmonds. "That change delivered strong same-store sales. It saved Black Friday for Chico's, and it happened in the snap of a finger."

END THOUGHT

At a time when the drumbeat of economic bad news gets louder each day, and as organizations continue to be buffeted by the forces of globalization, hypercompetitiveness, and technological change, a growing number of executives are casting aside the hierarchical model.

To meet the new set of performance and value-creating challenges, these executives have opted to build a radically different organization that is horizontal in structure, that redefines the nature of leadership, and that is driven by high-performance teams that are aligned, accountable, and focused on achieving an ever-higher measure of results.

Call it evolution, natural selection, or survival of the fittest, but count on high-performance horizontal organizations to be the ones that make it to the future.

LEADERSHIP

Part Five looks even more closely at what's required of the *leaders* of the organizations of the future.

David G. Thomson advises companies on how to achieve exceptional growth, and in his chapter, he describes the "7 Essentials" that leaders need to do to create "Blueprint Companies"—that is, wildly high-performing companies. One critical factor is having "dynamic duos" as leaders, and he offers two detailed examples—from a spin-off of DuPont and from Microsoft—and if you thought you knew everything about this company, think again.

Professor and consultant Noel M. Tichy and researcher and consultant Christopher DeRose believe that "judgment is the essential genome of leadership," and the three most important judgments leaders make concern who's on and off their teams, what the strategy is, and how to handle crises. As evidence, the authors cite examples of leadership failures and successes at Dell, Litton Industries, PepsiCo, Merrill Lynch, and P&G.

William A. Cohen is a retired major general of the U.S. Air Force who now runs the Institute of Leader Arts. In his chapter, he writes how leaders can't delegate responsibility; all they can do is delegate authority. He offers four tactics for how to influence without giving direct orders—as well as some advice on what to do when a tactic fails.

Finally, leadership adviser Debbe Kennedy writes about the need for leaders to learn by doing, and how *practicing* leadership is the key to successful leadership. She describes four critical skills and five distinctive qualities that leaders need to have. The first of these is to make it truly a priority to achieve diversity in your organization—accomplishing this goal leads not only to success in your organization but also to a better world overall.

CHAPTER TWENTY-THREE

THE LEADERSHIP BLUEPRINT TO ACHIEVE EXPONENTIAL GROWTH

David G. Thomson

David G. Thomson is the chairman of the Blueprint Growth Institute (www. blueprintgrowth.com), which is dedicated to advising companies to achieve exceptional growth. Serving midmarket companies and new business units of large corporations, he transforms organizations into exceptional-growth teams. He is the author of Blueprint to a Billion: 7 Essentials to Achieve Exponential Growth, *which was ranked the number four best-selling book at 800CEOREAD.com for 2007 and a top management book by Soundview Book Summaries for 2006. Thomson has been featured in* Leader to Leader, *the* New York Times, Investors' Business Daily, *and* Fortune Small Business *and on CNBC, ABCNEWS.com, and MSNBC.*

Why do we aspire to create organizations of the future? Peter Drucker pointed out that a totally different approach is emerging that says the purpose of an organization is to get results *outside*, that is, to achieve performance in the market.[1]

One of the ultimate dimensions of this "performance" calling is the building of businesses that enhance our everyday lives, create a great place to work, and develop the leaders of the future. Where might we find these unique opportunities in one place? In the *businesses of the future.* But the probabilities of failure for these companies are greater than the odds of success! Therefore, the business of the future must take the form of an exceptional-growth company that executes what it takes to sustain growth and to change the lives of its customers for the better.

How do you build an exceptional-growth business despite the odds against it? And is there an actionable blueprint to follow?

To answer these questions, I launched a multiyear study to identify the success pattern of America's highest growth companies. *Blueprint to a Billion: 7 Essentials to Achieve Exponential Growth* became the first quantitative identification of the success pattern of these consistently high-performing companies. Although just about all companies aspire to achieve exceptional, even exponential growth, the real surprise is that of the seventy-five hundred American companies that went public between 1985 and 2007, only 5% have achieved $1 billion in revenue! That's only 387 companies. Yet these exceptional companies—I call them Blueprint Companies— account for 56% of employment and 64% of market value created by all IPO companies. The disproportionate success of the Blueprint Companies shows that they are the heart of America's innovation and growth: these are the new companies to work for and invest in. They are the organizations that shape our future.

Look around and you will find Blueprint Companies everywhere. Their products enhance our everyday lives. Every time you use Microsoft software; use the Internet (which rides on Cisco equipment); search the Web using Google; sip a Starbucks latte; shop on eBay or Amazon.com; purchase products at Williams-Sonoma, Staples, or Home Depot; take medicine made by Amgen, Genentech, or MedImmune; use financial services from Charles Schwab; or ride your Harley-Davidson motorcycle, you use products from a Blueprint Company.

You may think every company is unique. And it is. But there is something that the minority saw about what to do so as to create a business of the future, which the rest of us are missing. The numbers prove it. Underneath the numbers, there are what I call 7 Essentials (listed at the end of this chapter) that underpin this unique pattern of exponential growth. One of the most important of these essentials is the leadership team, which is the focus of this chapter.

To get started on the journey to the business of the future, we need to ask this question: What kind of management does it take to propel a company to a billion dollars in revenue in only a few years? If you look at the covers of business magazines, you might think it only takes an all-star CEO to run a Blueprint Company. But this is not what my colleagues and I found; no single CEO can possibly keep all the essentials in motion without help. That may sound self-evident, yet I learned that blueprint-to-a-billion management is actually significantly different from that in regular-growth companies.

Back to the Future: Bill Gates Didn't Build Microsoft Without Help

Back in 1983, when Microsoft was at an inflection point at $50 million in revenue, the company was outgrowing its small-time style faster than Bill Gates could handle. Gates had been trying to take personal charge of five product lines. As a result, he paid little attention to tailoring programs to customers' needs. Key planning decisions were often delayed or not made.[2] Fortunately, Gates recognized his own shortcomings. He tried to hire a president, but the individual didn't work out. He tried again in August 1983, and this time he hit gold with Jon Shirley, a twenty-five-year career veteran at Tandy Corp., who had known Gates as a customer.

Shirley recalled, "The company lacked a lot of systems that it needed to grow, to become big. It was nothing like an ideal organizational setup, and it had no MIS system. They were using a Tandy Model 2 for the general ledger." Shirley also discovered that Microsoft lacked key statistical data about its products, its markets, and its sales. "We were totally out of manufacturing space, and we had no one who knew how to run the manufacturing side," he recalled, adding that he threw himself into developing "a whole lot of structures and systems that would give us the tools we needed."

Shirley had performed many of the same operations for the much larger Tandy and felt comfortable operating within Microsoft's corporate culture. Shirley viewed his role as one of building up the support side of the business, hiring the CFO (Francis Gaudette, who would later play a critical role in shepherding Microsoft's IPO through Wall Street in 1986), and honing the management team, most of whom were hired from within.

In August 1984, the management team took serious action. It reorganized around two divisions: systems software (the programs that control a computer's internal operations) and business applications (programs that tell a machine to do specific tasks, such as word processing). Four years later, in 1988, Microsoft restructured its applications division into five business units. The business units would have P&L responsibility for their product lines and would be responsible for marketing and documentation of their products, said Shirley. "It gives them a great deal of control to run as a small business," he noted.[3]

Analysts give Shirley credit for quarterbacking many of the key strategic alliances that helped catapult Microsoft to industry prominence (although Shirley modestly said they naturally evolved from simple customer relationships). In contrast, Gates focused externally on the market, establishing standards leadership and shaping the technologies for various product areas. "Gates and Shirley absolutely occupied different ends of the business," said Arthur Block, Manufacturers Hanover Trust VP in charge of end-user support. "Bill focused on the IBM alliance while Shirley focused on HP. Gates talked to user groups while Shirley talked to the financial community. Gates linked product/market opportunities to technology while Jon applied structure and process to the business so that it could scale."[4]

On the day-to-day level, Shirley mirrored a management style that is supportive and didactic, well suited to Microsoft's campus ambiance. "I believe in delegation and teaching," Shirley said. "You've got to give people sufficient authority to make mistakes."[5]

Shirley retired in 1989—after Microsoft passed $800 million in revenue (on the way to $1 billion the next year). He had essentially guided the company from the inflection point to $1 billion as Bill Gates's "Mr. Inside."

THE IMPORTANCE OF DYNAMIC DUOS

In my study of Blueprint Companies, I found that a great many of the star performers were driven by *dynamic duos*—two individuals who worked tightly together to build the firm from dreams to a billion dollars in revenue.

Dynamic duos are the stuff of corporate legend: Hewlett and Packard, Sears and Roebuck, and Walt and Roy Disney. But what

I found is that in Blueprint Companies, it's more than corporate myth—Blueprint Companies do spring from such pairings.

There were more surprises as I drilled deeper into this finding. For example, I learned that for the duo to be dynamic, one of the two had to excel in the *public* part of the effort—in marketing and sales. Meanwhile, the other one had to be the *insider*—keeping the operations purring or perhaps inventing a better wrinkle in the new product. Together they had to explore and innovate continuously—whether it was in product or marketing innovation. They had to make swift decisions and correct their mistakes quickly. Most important, they had to have complete trust in and respect for one another.

The Shirley-Gates combo at Microsoft is typical of what I found in the top Blueprint Companies: an inside-outside leadership pair, working in partnership with the founding team, who managed to execute all the essentials simultaneously. This pair, like many others in Blueprint Companies, had a unique chemistry—and a unique *synergy* that electrified the evolution of the product and the marketing of Microsoft as well. Cisco, eBay, Nike, and Starbucks are established examples, and such new billion-dollar companies as Research in Motion, NutriSystem, and Endo Pharmaceuticals have and are applying the same leadership pattern.

Again, these dynamic duos benefit from having complementary strengths. They are the yin and yang, the weave and warp, the Lerner and Lowe, the bacon and eggs—and without this dynamic, their companies could not have made it to the top.

THIS DYNAMIC DUO CURES YOUR PAIN

In contrast to Microsoft in the 1980s, Endo Pharmaceuticals is a wonderful case study of a similar management pair in today's world of new billion-dollar companies. Endo will be exceeding a billion dollars in revenue in 2008 as a leading supplier of new drugs and therapies for the treatment of pain. More than 20% of Americans suffer from acute pain. Almost everyone has a family member or knows someone who is affected by pain. Endo Pharmaceuticals improves the quality of life.

Like Microsoft, Endo originally had a dynamic duo. While Carol Ammon was the chairman and CEO and Mariann MacDonald was the executive vice president of operations, they were really referred to as the Dynamic Duo by all who knew them. This dynamic duo was connected by a friendship that had been built on their favorite mantra, "Check your ego at the door." Carol and Mariann met each other when they were in their twenties while working at DuPont. Carol worked in research, and Mariann worked in new product development. Mariann tended to follow Carol through each department: they seemed to be walking on the same set of stepping-stones, and through this career path, they became very good friends.

THE DYNAMICS OF TEAMWORK

As friends often discover, Mariann and Carol each had strengths and weaknesses that complemented each other—truly the basis for a lasting dynamic duo relationship. As all duos would testify, the two women truly feel that they did their best work when they worked together. Here's some of what Mariann and Carol told me about their unique relationship and approach to teamwork:

Carol: "Everyone has strengths and weaknesses. If you can pair up with a person who blends perfectly and matches where your weaknesses are with their strengths, the two of you together make that powerful third person. We think of it as a three-legged stool."

Mariann: "We never had big egos. Carol was never afraid to say 'I don't know this, and can you please help me with this.' We were really friends, and when you have somebody as your friend, there is no obstacle you cannot overcome. We were very open with each other. If we had challenges, we could talk to each other. In business, that is not always the case. We were never threatened by one another. We could go into an office and yell at each other, then give each other a hug and go out as a team. There was never a time that we lost that friendship even though we were business partners. We could never have done this without each other."

Dynamic duos form their relationship on the basis of trust, friendship, and complementarity. They really care about each other. Their bond grows over the years.

By 1994, Carol and Mariann had become part of a team put together by DuPont Merck (in a joint venture) to determine what to do about some old pain medications, such as Percocet, which had been launched in the mid-1970s. The patents had long expired, and the products were now losing sales to cheaper generics. Faced with the choice of either investing in these drugs to expand their markets or selling them, the recommendation was to sell. In effect, Dupont Merck wanted to cast off its pain management franchise, an area to which Carol had devoted much of her career.

Carol recognized that pain management was an underserved area, neglected by major pharmaceutical firms in search of high-margin sectors. But she also observed a changing attitude in the public about pain management that presented a niche opportunity for a small company willing to focus on it. Prior generations, hardened by the experience of the Great Depression and World War II, were far more stoic about enduring pain than members of the baby-boom generation, who were less interested in pleasing a doctor and more than willing to acknowledge when they were experiencing uncomfortable pain. Also, in the early 1990s, pain management became a specialty, and physicians could now take their residency in it. Moreover, hospitals were now rated on how well they assessed and treated pain.

FINDING YOUR OTHER HALF IS A LIFE-CHANGING DECISION

Is it ever that easy to start a company? Patience and wisdom are necessary virtues if one is to turn a million-dollar business into a billion. According to a company profile, "Ammon recalls how she ran into the office of her colleague and longtime friend, MacDonald. . . . 'Look, we can buy these products. Do you want to?' MacDonald's answer, 'Yes.' 'Maybe you want to go home to talk to your husband? We may not have a job if this doesn't work out.' MacDonald didn't hesitate. 'No, I'm in.'"[6]

But that isn't the real story. In 1994, Mariann had breast cancer and was going in for surgery. Carol called to check on Mariann—and to ask her to join her in building Endo. As Mariann explained, "Carol just wanted me to come work with her when[ever] I was ready. I said, 'You have to be crazy . . . I am in the hospital. I don't know when I will be back.' And Carol said, 'I will wait. You will be back.'" It was a short wait: Mariann asked the doctors if she could have her chemotherapy on Friday so that she could be at work on Monday.

The next week, they focused on raising $277 million in equity investment and loans. In August 1997, they bought thirty-five medicines from DuPont Merck along with the Endo name, and in November they incorporated Endo Pharmaceuticals Holdings Inc.

THE ONE VOICE OF THE HEART AND THE HAMMER

If you ask everyone on the outside, Carol is described as loving, huggy, gracious, very smart, funny, witty: a leader with heart. Mariann, in contrast, is the driver, is pragmatic, has a get-it-done attitude, is the dirty-work "guy," and is not so huggy: she's the hammer. Carol was a master at inspiring armies to follow Endo; Mariann was a master at battling the corporate army. Carol relates a story of Mariann at her best: "We were negotiating with Merck and DuPont . . . to get our company started. There were different agreements being negotiated simultaneously. You have to have credibility at the table, but you are outnumbered. . . . We went into a negotiation regarding manufacturing rights with fifteen people on the other side from different groups. We had Mariann, [but] she knew more about the points than anyone in the room. Our equity partners were bowled over by Mariann: they called her the perfect balance between Mother Teresa and Attila the Hun!"

On the inside, the relationship between Carol and Mariann was different from what others saw from the outside. As Mariann described it, "When it came to making important decisions, Carol would say I am being too hard, and I would push back that Carol is being too soft. . . . We would move to the middle: to be balanced with the head and the heart. We would debate 'What is the right decision [for the business]? What is the right decision for everyone?' We were first and foremost friends. We would give each other a hug . . . and go out as a team and speak with one voice . . . [with] a balance between the heart and the hammer in every decision we made."

Those decisions not only improved the quality of life for thousands of people in pain; for employees and investors, this dynamic duo built a billion-dollar business by leveraging the essentials to achieve exponential growth. They leveraged their brand names and attracted marquee customers and opinion leaders in pain management, including neurologists, oncologists, physiatrists (doctors of rehabilitative medicine), and pain doctors. To promote company growth, they created alliances and offloaded non-core functions to partners, including Pharmaceutical Product Development for clinical trials, UPS for distribution, Novartis for manufacturing, and others. They diversified their product lines, and they stacked their board not with investors but with CEOs who had grown businesses. The result was a cash-flow-positive business that has scaled to a billion.

WHY AREN'T THERE MORE DYNAMIC DUOS?

Once you have grown a business to a billion, you have a chance to look around and ask "Why me?" As Carol said,

> I think it goes back to the time and place when we came of age in our careers. It was a time when DuPont wanted opportunities for women. We had to work hard to get the opportunities, and we made sure that when we got there, we worked hard to succeed. We weren't in a position to gloat about ourselves. We had to work hard and had no time for that ego stuff. This made us different. Every job we had, we were never brought in as the manager. We had to learn the job and get the hands-on experience in order to become the leader. We trusted each other and built teams that valued trust. We could see that in competitive situations, in order to get the top job, others are pitted against one another. These competing situations motivate leaders to not build relationships based on trust and mutual success.

The cure for a competitive situation where there is a lack of trust? Find your other half! Not one with the same skills you have.

THE BOTTOM LINE

To become a leadership team for the future, follow this handy leadership formula:

Blueprint leadership = focus on people and product
× drive for exploration and innovation
× ability to manage 7 Essentials simultaneously

Why multiply the three leadership dimensions rather than add them? We found that multiplication illustrates the compounding nature of Dynamic Duo leadership effectiveness. Alternatively, if leaders don't achieve the performance required on each of these dimensions, the business fails. Therefore, each of these dimensions is necessary to achieve success.

Ever see a "hands-off" leader who focuses only on process, with little understanding of the details of the business? Ever find leaders who are focused only on cost reduction at the expense of growth? Ever find leaders who are simply maxed out, with no time to manage all the moving parts? Not a leader for a Blueprint Company—the business of the future.

THE 7 ESSENTIALS OF BLUEPRINT COMPANIES

These seven essentials are the common management practices utilized by America's highest-growth companies—independent of industry or economic cycle. Utilizing one or more of these essentials will improve your business, organization, team, or yourself. Utilizing five or more will truly turbocharge your business to achieve exponential growth.

• • •

1. Create and Sustain a Breakthrough Value Proposition. A value proposition states the benefits customers receive from using a company's products or services in terms that the customer understands. The best Blueprint Companies not only created but sustained breakthrough value propositions. For example, Starbucks delivers you a coffee experience and provides a social location that is the third place, to home and work.

2. Exploit a High-Growth Market Segment. Opportunities exist in a lot of industries; some industries have more opportunities than others. However, specialty retail stores generated the highest number of Blueprint Companies, with eighteen firms: AutoZone, Staples, Tractor Supply, Williams-Sonoma, PetsMart, and others. This occurred because there were multiple market segments to address within this industry. In contrast, there are numerous cases where a single company arises out of an industry to become the only player to achieve $1 billion in revenues—witness Harley-Davidson.

3. Develop Marquee Customers to Shape the Revenue Powerhouse. Customers can be more than customers. The best of them can serve as an extension of your sales force—they become your most effective sales team! I call these *marquee customers*—that is, customers who shape the company by testing and deploying the product, recommending the company to their peers, and simply providing exponential revenue growth on a per-customer basis. For example, eBay has a large base of "PowerSellers" as marquee customers.

4. Leverage Big Brother Alliances for Breaking into New Markets. The complement to marquee customers is a "big brother–little brother" alliance relationship. These alliances, in which a bigger company helps a smaller one, provide credibility to the little brother, give it market intelligence, and lead it to marquee customers. Microsoft's early alliance with IBM is a perfect example.

5. Become the Masters of Exponential Returns. Blueprint Companies serve to illustrate what it takes to create the highest value per company. On average, they were cash-flow positive early and sustained this positive cash flow to $1 billion revenue. Shareholder returns for being a top-performing and exponential growth company are more than compelling: an average of 87% returns to their shareholders while exceeding analysts' expectations 80% of the time! Do you remember Google beating expectations as it rapidly grew to a billion? In contrast, today's fairly common management behavior suggests that overinvesting and utilizing debt is the best financial approach to fuel growth.

6. Develop the Top Management Team with Inside-Outside Leadership. One of the pivotal essentials that enables the other essentials to be simultaneously executed is a dynamic leadership pairing in which one leader (or team) faces outward toward markets, customers, alliances, and the community, while the other leader (or team) is focused inward, to optimize operations. Contrary to the somewhat popular belief that one leader is *the* leader, this inside-outside leadership pair is highly prevalent among Blueprint Companies: Microsoft, eBay, Yahoo!, and Tractor Supply, to name just a few. For example, at Tractor Supply, Joe Scarlett was

Mr. Outside to Jim Wright, who was the inside-facing leader. In the early days of Yahoo, it was Koogle and Mallett.

   7. Develop Your Board with "Essentials Experts." Blueprint boards are not packed with investors, as one would think. Instead, Blueprint Companies recruited customers, alliance partners, and other blueprint CEOs to the board, and that made a big difference. I call them "essentials experts" because their role is linked to the shaping and execution of one or more of the essentials. Because most investors have not scaled Blueprint Companies to $1 billion revenue, CEOs of Blueprint Companies were often recruited to provide insight into exponential growth. In contrast, boards with only investors and management tended to be associated with struggling companies. Even today, Tom Stemberg, the founder and former chairman of Staples, is still on the board of PetSmart. Similarly, Howard Schultz served on the board of eBay as the company ascended to a billion.

Endnotes

1.   Drucker, P. F. "Introduction." In F. Hesselbein, M. Goldsmith, and R. Beckhard (Eds.), *Organization of the Future.* San Francisco: Jossey-Bass, 2000, pp. 4–5.
2.   Levine, J. B. "Microsoft: Recovering from Its Stumble Over 'Windows'—Embarrassed by Problems with the Computer Program, Management Is Reforming." *BusinessWeek,* July 22, 1985, p. 107.
3.   "Microsoft Divides Applications Division." *Computer System News,* Sept. 5, 1988, p. 65.
4.   Pelton, C. "For Bill Gates, Micros Are Personal: Microsoft's Founder Is a Sharp Businessman, but Can He Overcome Slow OS/2 Acceptance and Unix Growth?" *Information Week,* Aug. 14, 1989, p. 18.
5.   "Microsoft Campus Booms Under Three Deans." *Computer Reseller News,* July 11, 1988, p. 2.
6.   "Endo Pharmaceuticals History." Business & Company Resource Center [online service]. www.gale.cengage.com/BusinessRC.

CHAPTER TWENTY-FOUR

LEADERSHIP JUDGMENT
The Essence of a Good Leader
Noel M. Tichy and Christopher DeRose

Dr. Noel M. Tichy is a professor of management and organizations at the University of Michigan's Ross School of Business. Previously, he taught at Columbia University Business School for nine years. In the mid-1980s, Dr. Tichy was head of GE's Leadership Center, where he led the transformation to action learning at GE. He has written numerous books and articles, including his most recent book, Judgment: How Winning Leaders Make Great Calls *(coauthored with Warren Bennis). He consults widely in both the private and public sectors for such clients as Best Buy, GE, PepsiCo, GM, Nokia, Nomura Securities, 3M, Daimler-Benz, and Royal Dutch Shell.*

Christopher DeRose is an active researcher and consultant in the area of organization change and leadership. He teaches executive education with Noel M. Tichy at the Ross Business School, and he has consulted and taught around the world with such companies as Royal Dutch Shell, Intuit, Intel, 3M, and HP. His research and consultation in the areas of leadership, organization change, and growth have taken place in the automotive, telecommunications, publishing, e-commerce, software, financial services, biotechnology, pharmaceutical, energy, semiconductor, retail, and beverages industries.

Judgment is the essential genome of leadership. Ultimately, a leader is judged by others on the performance of his or her organization. The three most important judgments leaders make are about

1. People—determining who is on the team or off the team
2. Strategy—setting a course to make the organization successful
3. Crisis—handling the inevitable organization-endangering, usually unexpected threats

Unfortunately, the leadership landscape is cluttered with failed leadership judgment. Take the example of Dell Inc. from 2005 to 2007, a time when company founder Michael Dell was acting as chairman, and his longtime friend, Kevin Rollins, was CEO. Rollins had led Dell to a market capitalization much bigger than HP in 2005. By April 2008, Dell had lost more than half its value, dropping to $38 billion in market capitalization, whereas HP was worth $116 billion, a total reversal of positions in three short years. Rollins and Dell exercised bad leadership judgment by missing the rebirth of HP under Mark Hurd's leadership. In 2007, Dell's board of directors fired Rollins and installed Dell as chairman and CEO, even though the two shared offices and Michael Dell had remained involved in the business throughout Rollins's tenure. Although the prescription was Rollins's ouster, the underlying malaise had been the failure to see the change in the competitive landscape.

Bad judgment also cost Stan O'Neal his job as CEO of Merrill Lynch in late 2007 amid the subprime mortgage meltdown. In this case, poor leadership judgment should be attributed to Merrill's board of directors. O'Neal was not the right CEO; many had said he did not listen, did not get data from his people, and failed to build teamwork with his board of directors. Although he was successful for a time, these attributes left O'Neal without an internal constituency to help him handle a crisis.

Chuck Prince also lost his CEO job at Citigroup due to the subprime meltdown. The root cause of Citigroup's problems was similar to those at Merrill Lynch, in that Prince was probably not equipped as a lawyer to run complex Citigroup during a crisis. When a crisis hit, the board made its judgment call to get a new CEO.

As we journey further into the twenty-first century, and the competitive landscape intensifies with enhanced global competition, geopolitical uncertainty, and environmental challenges, good leadership will become the scarcest asset on the planet. Leaders who exercise good judgment and who are able to correct course to steer their organizations in times of turbulence will be the great talent scarcity in decades to come.

The good news is that there are some leaders who are showing the way. For example, Indra Nooyi, CEO of PepsiCo, is transforming the food and beverage company to a global powerhouse with new, more healthy products. Understanding consumer trends as she further globalizes PepsiCo, Nooyi has made an underlying strategic judgment to invest in R&D to create healthy snacks. This led to a *people* judgment: PepsiCo has hired its first global R&D leader, Dr. Mahmood Khan, a seasoned leader from the pharmaceutical industry.

Nooyi herself is the product of an outstanding people judgment made by PepsiCo's board of directors. Her career was changed when her talent was discovered by former CEO Roger Enrico in an intensive leadership program that Enrico personally led and taught. Nooyi was already recognized as high potential, but her strategic mind differentiated her during Enrico's program and led to high-profile development roles, such as CFO, to help her prepare to become CEO.

Another leader demonstrating outstanding judgment is David Novak, CEO of YUM! Brands (which includes such powerhouse brands as Taco Bell, Pizza Hut, KFC, Long John Silver's, and A&W). He has exercised great leadership judgment in dealing with crises, ranging from SARS in China to *e. coli* in U.S. lettuce to the bird flu globally.

Another leader with outstanding judgment is A. G. Lafley, who has successfully transformed P&G and taken it out of the doldrums in 2000 with great strategic judgments as well as world-class people judgments. Such massive turnarounds are rarely the result of one single judgment but more often the cumulative result of numerous decisions. Taking Lafley as a case example, he showed great composure after being installed as CEO at a time when analysts and the media were questioning whether P&G should be acquired by a competitor. He calmed the organization and set forth a strategy in which the "consumer is boss," which resulted in new innovation.

Lafley also made very difficult people judgments. In one instance, Lafley put thirty-eight-year-old Deb Henretta in charge of the $8 billion baby care business. Despite the fact that baby care had been male dominated and manufacturing focused, Lafley recognized Henretta as a good marketing leader who could transform the business. Henretta's subsequent success not only fixed the baby care business but identified her as a leader capable of running bigger operations.

This chapter presents a framework for guiding leaders in making good leadership judgments regarding people, strategy, and crisis. As leaders make such judgments, they should also consider how to develop the next generation of leaders in the process. The chapter draws heavily on the five years of research conducted with Warren Bennis and presented in the book *Judgment: How Winning Leaders Make Great Calls.*

LEADERSHIP IS A DYNAMIC PROCESS

We make a distinction between judgment and decision making. Much of the academic literature and popular notions of decision making culminate in a single moment when the leader makes a decision. In this chapter, we focus on judgment as a process that unfolds over time. Analysis of this process has either been absent, leaving leaders to unconsciously pick a course of action, or it has been unrealistically linear. In our experience, the judgment process is actually more like a drama with plotlines, characters, and sometimes unforeseen twists and turns. A leader's success hinges on how well he or she manages the entire process, not just the single moment when a decision is made.

Key leadership judgments encompass several dimensions—time, domain, and constituency—which are described in the following sections. Exhibit 24.1 shows how these dimensions play out in the judgment process.

TIME

There are three phases to the judgment process:

1. *Preparation:* what happens before the leader makes the judgment call. This includes sensing the need for change, gathering data, and working with stakeholders.
2. *The call:* what the leader does as he or she makes the judgment and how the leader works with others to help ensure that it turns out to be the right call.
3. *Execution:* what the leader must do to make sure the call produces the desired results, including ongoing assessment, learning, and resetting the course.

EXHIBIT 24.1. THE LEADERSHIP JUDGMENT PROCESS.

Cognitive Processes Span All Phases →
Emotional Processes Span All Phases →

	Preparation Phase			Call Phase	Execution Phase	
	Sense/ Identify	**Frame/ Name**	**Mobilize/ Align**	**Call**	**Make It Happen**	**Learn/ Adjust**
Good Judgment	• Early identification in the environment • Mobilize to act • Energized about the future	• Able to cut through the complexity and get to the essence • Clearly sets parameters of a problem • Provides context and language	• Identify key stakeholders • Engages and energizes around framing • Taps best ideas from anywhere	• Exercise yes/no judgment • Clearly explains judgment	• Leader stays in the game • Supports those making it happen • Sets clear milestones	• Gets feedback • Makes adjustments • The feedback is continuous
Bad Judgment	• Cannot read the environment • Fails to see reality • Not following your gut	• Frame the wrong decision/judgment • Ultimate goal is not clearly defined • Stuck in old paradigm	• Don't set clear expectations • Wrong people • No self-correction	• Still make bad call/wrongheaded • Failure to see how things intersect and are likely to play out • Avoid dillydallying in making the call	• Leader walks away • Bad info • Failure to see all factors	• Resistance by organization • None or wrong metrics • Lack of operating mechanisms for dealing with changes

Redo (between Frame/Name and Mobilize/Align)
Redo (between Mobilize/Align and Call)
Redo (between Make It Happen and Learn/Adjust)

Not Following Gut Can Span All Phases →

These phases do not always happen in a clean linear fashion; instead, good leaders self-correct by using "redo loops," repeating earlier phases to correct errors or adjust for oversights.

DOMAIN

In addition to three phases of decision making, there are also three critical domains in which many of the most important calls are required:

1. Judgments about people (who is on the team or off the team)
2. Judgments about strategy (where the organization is headed)
3. Judgments in time of crisis (when things go wrong)

CONSTITUENCIES

A leader's relationships are the sources of the information needed to make a successful call. They also provide the means for executing the call, and they represent the various interests that must be attended to throughout the process. A leader must interact with different constituencies and manage those relationships to make successful calls. In addition, to improve judgment making throughout the organization, the leader must use these interactions to help others learn to make successful calls.

IT'S WHAT HAPPENS THAT COUNTS

A leader's report card is ultimately a reflection of how he or she fared in the making of major judgments that impacted the well-being of the institution. As noted earlier, if we look at Dell Inc.'s loss of market share and capitalization, the judgment of its leaders can only be deemed poor from 2005 to 2008.

Exhibit 24.1 lists factors that contribute to good or bad leadership judgment. The leader can make mistakes and still have a good judgment outcome by using the redo loops to continuously self-correct. The test of leadership is how well the leader adapts during the process to drive a successful outcome. There is no such thing as a strategy that's good in theory but lousy in execution. A leader sets the organization on a course based on the premise that it will lead to success. Recognizing execution limitations during the judgment process is as vital as having intellectual clarity about a potential breakthrough strategy. Similarly, people judgments rest on whether the people put in leadership positions are able to do the job with integrity and courage as they deliver results.

For example, Bill George, former CEO of Medtronic and currently a Harvard professor, shared a story during an interview that encapsulated this sentiment. Reflecting on a wildly successful career that included growing the company from $1.1 billion in market capitalization to more than $60 billion, and the market introduction of lifesaving technologies along the way, George shared what he called his "greatest failure." Prior to his years at Medtronic, George had been a promising senior executive at Litton Industries. While there, George actively groomed someone for three years to ultimately be his replacement. "Every year I would present him as my successor and everyone said 'yes, yes, yes!'" But when George left Litton, the CEO stepped in and selected a production leader who George described as "in totally over his head. He destroyed the business, literally destroyed it. Eventually, they tried to sell it, and two thousand people along the way lost their jobs."

George's self-assessment—that is, that this was *his* failure, even though it was the CEO who made this bad decision—is candid, honest, and, in our view, correct. His succession judgment failed because although George's succession candidate likely would have been better than the CEO's choice (it's hard to imagine much worse), George wasn't able to make it happen. It would have been easy for George to let himself off the hook on this judgment call, even to have felt smug about the correctness of his analysis. After all, the CEO intervened, and George had no real ability to campaign after he left the company. However, George holds himself accountable for his inability to get his people judgment implemented, and he realizes that the eventual closure of the business was related to that failure. In short, George knew long ago that the measure of a successful judgment isn't how *well-reasoned* it is; only the *outcome* matters.

As we've noted, however, this doesn't mean that a leader must make the right call on the first try. Rather, as Exhibit 24.1 depicts, the leader can go back to earlier stages of the judgment process to correct mistakes. We call these redo loops. This openness to learning and self-correction should not be mistaken for lack of commitment. As Bill George said of his many later successful judgments: "My style is I don't second guess myself. . . . I may be wrong and we may have to change it, but I don't say, 'Why didn't I do that?' or 'Why did I go for that?' You don't know if something's going to work until you go. . . . You just have to hang in there because you don't know."

As mentioned, another leader who has exercised good judgment is the CEO of PepsiCo, Indra Nooyi. Her strategic judgments include rapid acceleration of the development of healthy products and a ramping up of globalization. Nooyi has built an aligned team around her, including the unusual appointment of Cynthia Trudell as head of human resources. Trudell was the former CEO of Saturn at GM, then CEO of Brunswick, and on the board of PepsiCo. Trudell was not at all thinking of taking a job inside PepsiCo when, as Trudell described it, Nooyi asked her "out of the blue" to become head of HR at PepsiCo. Trudell's appointment has resulted in a thoughtful reconsideration of how PepsiCo develops talent and aligns the company to further globalize. In short, Nooyi's unconventional and unexpected selection of Trudell for the HR role—a wise people judgment—set the stage for subsequent calls by Trudell that will be critical to implementing PepsiCo's strategy.

In summary, exercising good judgment is the most important attribute of good leaders. The traditional management literature is too static and limiting in its view of leadership decision making. We have taken a judgment process view, which we feel reflects the real world of leadership. Exhibit 24.2 summarizes the differences between these two views.

A JUDGMENT STORYLINE

Making judgments about the future requires leaders to use their past experiences to help them anticipate the future. To do so, leaders develop a storyline for what their organization will do, how their team will act, and the role that they will personally play. When leaders possess this capability, it plays out as a drama in their imagination. They envision the actions that they will take, imagine how competitors might respond and the dialogues between key actors in the drama, and they write themselves into the script.

EXHIBIT 24.2. COMPARISON OF THE TRADITIONAL VIEW OF JUDGMENT AND
JUDGMENT PROCESS VIEW.

Characteristic	Traditional View	Judgment Process View
Time	Single moment, static	Dynamic process that unfolds
Thought Process	Rational, analytic	Recognition that rational analysis happens alongside emotional, human drama
Variables	Knowable, quantifiable	Interactions among variables can lead to entirely new outcomes
Focus	Individual—heroic leader persona who makes the tough call	Organizational—a process that the leader guides but that is impacted by many actors and subsequent judgment calls
Success Criteria	Making the best decision based on known data	Ability to act and react through judgment process that guides others to a successful outcome
Actors	Top-down; leader makes the key decisions	Top-down-up; execution influences how judgments are reshaped
Transparency	Closed system in which decision makers hold information, and rationale for judgments not explained	Open process in which mistakes are shared and learning is used to adjust
Capability Building	Unconsciously happens through experience or luck; reserved for top leadership	Deliberate development at all levels

For example, Lafley at P&G had a storyline developing in his mind for the baby care business, one that envisioned a business focused on the customer, not the engineers focusing on the machines and cost savings. His fuzzy storyline of the future was the platform for selecting Deb Henretta, a customer-focused marketing person, to be the key actor in his storyline.

Like the director's cut on a DVD, however, the story often includes multiple endings. As the leader writes his storyline, he can see the twists and turns that may lead to different outcomes, some desirable and some less so.

As a leader, you need to have your own storyline for your organization. A critical component of self-knowledge is conscious awareness of this storyline. The storyline is the leader's vision of the future—a reflection of the leader's hopes and dreams for what the leader's organizational, team, and personal accomplishments will be and for how the leader will achieve them. Successful leaders have vivid storylines that run like movies in their heads. These minidramas are only bounded by their imagination. The stories may enable leaders to visualize the moment that they'll beat out their competitor and close the big deal with their customer, or the newspaper headline announcing an anticipated acquisition.

For others, the storyline is a vague notion of where they would like to be, more directional than definitive. Some people experience the storyline on an emotional level without the imagery. They may not be able to put it into words, but they have a sense of what they want—or at least a gut reaction when they feel that they are off course.

This storyline can propel leaders, whether consciously or otherwise, toward action and can sometimes cloud their judgment. That is, they often make judgments that try to preserve the storyline they desire. This can lead to their conforming data to fit prejudices, or to selectively neglecting data that may contradict their desired storyline. For those who are not conscious of the storyline they have written, they may fail to sense and respond to critical changes in the world around them.

On the positive side, a storyline can also prepare leaders to make challenging judgments by helping them anticipate potential outcomes and interactions among the many actors and factors that may affect them. Those leaders who are able to imagine a dynamic storyline for themselves and their organizations are able to shape the living drama that plays out over the course of a judgment call.

Another example of a storyline is the one Jeff Immelt, CEO of GE, created around the theme of "ecomagination," which captures the use of GE innovation to solve ecological environmental issues. GE has been a pioneer in the commercialization of wind technology and has driven emissions reductions in its manufacture of jet engines, turbines, appliances, and lighting. GE's emphasis is twofold: it strives not to only create less pollution during manufacturing but also to innovate new products that are more environmentally friendly. Ecomagination was a storyline Immelt started creating in 2006 to guide strategic judgments on new products, services, distribution channels, and customer segments globally. It is an unfolding drama and storyline that has guided billions of dollars of investment and new products for GE.

Starting with Your Teachable Point of View

The first step is making your personal storyline explicit. This starts with having a "teachable point of view" about where your organization is going in the future. Simply put, a teachable point of view is an articulation of the ideas that will help your organization be successful, the values required to be on your team, and how you will energize people along the way. These components—ideas, values, and emotional energy—become your guideposts for making judgments. The ability to face reality and make such judgments is what Jack Welch, General Electric's former CEO, called "edge."

Leadership judgments are made in the context of the storyline based on the building blocks of a teachable point of view, as illustrated in Exhibit 24.3.

Judgment Built on Deep Knowledge

A leader's teachable point of view is shaped through experience. Every leader makes some bad judgments, but great leaders learn from these and don't repeat them. They manage the judgment process so that outcomes are successful and people are involved and developed along the way. Doing this requires the leader to

EXHIBIT 24.3. TEACHABLE POINT OF VIEW AND STORYLINES.

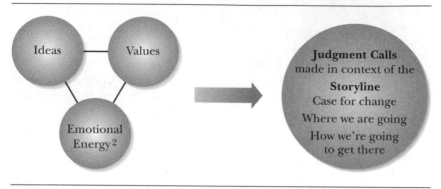

have knowledge that spans beyond a "just the facts" analytical capability. It requires deeper knowledge in four areas:

1. **Self-knowledge:** awareness of your personal values, goals, and aspirations. This includes recognition of when these personal desires may lead to a bias in sensing the need for a judgment or interpreting facts. It also includes the ability to create a mental storyline for how judgments will play out and the results they lead to.

2. **Social network knowledge:** understanding of the personalities, skills, and judgment track records of those on your team. This includes how they supplement or bias your judgment process.

3. **Organizational knowledge:** knowing how people in the organization will respond, adapt, and execute. This also includes personal networks or mechanisms for learning from leaders at all levels in the organization.

4. **Contextual knowledge:** understanding based on relationships and interactions with stakeholders, such as customers, suppliers, government, investors, competitors, or interest groups that may impact the outcome of a judgment. This knowledge entails anticipating not only how they will respond directly to a judgment but how they will interact with one another throughout the judgment process.

DEVELOPING JUDGMENT

Too often, judgment is viewed as one of those ineffable leadership qualities that a person either has or doesn't have. It is true that some people do seem to possess inherent leadership characteristics that enable the judgment process. To name only a few of these characteristics,

- They develop broader and deeper relationships.
- They empathize with others.
- They are future oriented.
- They have courage to act in the absence of full knowledge.

Obviously, though, judgment is built on life experience, and it is a capability that can be developed and improved through practice so judgment becomes a conscious process. Development of judgment capability in organizational life starts with discussions of the judgment process and deliberate activities to develop leadership judgment within your organization. Take the test in Exhibit 24.4 to assess where you and your organization stand.

EXHIBIT 24.4. JUDGMENT SELF-ASSESSMENT.

Building Blocks	Not at all		To a great extent		
1. **Process Orientation:** Judgments are conscious, deliberate processes rather than single-moment decisions.	1	2	3	4	5
2. **Involvement:** Judgment calls involve the team, organization, and stakeholders in an open, transparent process.	1	2	3	4	5
3. **Teaching Environment:** The judgment process helps everyone understand how, when, and why a judgment call is made so people can learn from the experience.	1	2	3	4	5
4. **Learn and Adjust:** Knowledge comes from all levels of the organization to help assess and adjust judgment calls so they drive a successful outcome.	1	2	3	4	5
5. **Development Process:** Judgment capability is an explicit part of the assessment and development processes.	1	2	3	4	5
6. **Succession Planning:** Leadership roles go to those who consistently demonstrate good judgment capability.	1	2	3	4	5

CHAPTER TWENTY-FIVE

THE LEADER OF THE FUTURE

William A. Cohen

William A. Cohen is president of the Institute of Leader Arts (www.stuffofheroes. com). In 1979, he became Peter Drucker's first executive PhD graduate and continued a relationship with Drucker that lasted more than three decades. Cohen is also a retired major general from the U.S. Air Force Reserve and the author of several books on leadership. His latest book is A Class with Drucker: The Lost Lessons of the World's Greatest Management Teacher *(AMACOM, 2008).*

When Frances Hesselbein invited me to write a chapter on my views of the organization of the future, she suggested I might want to follow the method of her friend and my doctoral professor, Peter Drucker. When asked how he was able to make such accurate predictions, he had told her, "I just look out of the window and report what I see." I promised her I would try to follow Peter's methodology. As I looked out the window, I was reminded not only of the "Father of Modern Management's" wisdom but also that I would do well to report what the leader of today could do about what he or she sees through the window and what was in store for the leader of the future, which today's leaders will ultimately become.

LEADERSHIP HAS NOT CHANGED

The first thing I noted while looking out the window was that the trends leading to the future are clear and that the leader of the future had better be ready and able to adapt to them. However, contrary to what some have said, the day of the responsible leader is not over.

Leaders will not be relegated to practicing "laissez-faire leadership," whereby organizational members will make all their own decisions while the "leader" does little except make assignments and monitor results. Total self-direction is neither desirable nor essential in order to meet the challenges of the future.

The so-called new approaches for self-direction do not abrogate a leader's responsibilities. In fact, no leader can delegate *responsibility;* a leader can only delegate *authority.* Effective leaders understand this. Delegating the authority to a subordinate to perform a task or lead an organization under your overall authority and responsibility doesn't change this. The leader is, and will always be, responsible for everything his or her organization and its membership does or fails to do. This is true even after authority to do something is delegated. The subordinate may be responsible to you, but you, and no one else, are responsible for what this individual does or fails to do.

Being a responsible leader does not mean that workers or managers reporting to you won't have a role in making decisions. For thousands of years, leaders have been admonished to tell those they lead what needs to be done, not how to do it, and whenever possible to get input from those led as well. However, this never meant that followers went about doing their own thing. Drucker discovered this in what he called "the first systematic book on leadership, and still the best." This was a book called *Kyropaidaia.* It was written two thousand years ago by the Greek general Xenophon about the leadership education of Cyrus the Great of Persia. If you want to be amazed by the number of "cutting-edge" leadership techniques already in use and recommended millennia ago, I recommend reading this book. As Drucker stated emphatically, "Without someone in charge, you have a completely permissive organization without anyone at the helm. This will invariably lead to chaos." The basics of leadership haven't changed. What then has?

FUTURE CONDITIONS AND CHALLENGES

About the time that I graduated from what was then Claremont Graduate School and is now the Peter F. Drucker and Masatoshi Ito Graduate School of Management, only one in seven American companies sold its products abroad. In contrast, today you would be hard pressed to find organizations that don't export or have one or more foreign divisions or representations, aren't joint venturing with an organization in another country, or aren't in some way dealing globally. Globalization is making major demands on today's leaders, and increasing globalization fueled by politics and advancing technology will make these demands even more challenging in the future.

Life would be simpler if globalization were the only challenge for leaders of the future, or if the globalization that has occurred would be frozen in time and develop no more. In addition to the challenges that leaders of the future will face, unfortunately there are simultaneous changes in other areas, and globalization itself as a trend hasn't leveled off. Globalization will continue to increase further and will interact with other changes—for example, in demographics and the frequency and ability to switch jobs over a single career.

A long time ago, I spent some time as an executive recruiter. There was a new phenomenon in that industry that was affecting business. Whereas in the past most employees spent an entire working life with a single company, suddenly they now worked, on average, in four different companies during their careers. That was thirty years ago. Today some employees may work in as many as twenty different companies over a career. No wonder Drucker also told us that leaders must treat all employees as volunteers. With this kind of mobility and so many alternatives, volunteers are exactly what they are. In the workplace of the future, employees will have even more options. They will be able to work elsewhere, and it will be a lot easier for them to change jobs than it is even today.

Technology and companies assisting both companies and job seekers already abound. When I wrote my first book, *The Executive's Guide to Finding a Superior Job* (AMACOM, 1978, 1983, and now out of print), I explained a technique of job finding whereby a job seeker could line up out-of-town interviews paid for by the hiring company in just a few weeks. A few years ago, I described the method while teaching a graduate class at the Drucker School in Claremont. A student took my method, used e-mail rather than "snail mail," and got a paid, "fly-out" interview the next day. Clearly, even though the method of communication has changed, the method hasn't!

It was once true that a leader could give an order and it would be obeyed or else. This was the "carrot-and-stick" approach. It worked, but had its drawbacks even in ancient times. Xenophon wrote that Cyrus had a discussion with his father on the carrot-and-stick approach. His father agreed that such a process worked in gaining obedience through force. However, he went on to say that there was a far better way of leading, through which others would obey him with great pleasure and without having to use the "stick." All Cyrus had to do was to pay more attention to how he led and give more to his followers than he took for himself.[1]

In the future, leaders who use only the carrot-and-stick method when all workers are volunteers will barely qualify as leaders. Volunteers must be led differently. Leaders of the future who don't change what I call their "influence tactics" are going to have serious problems, and they deserve them.

As a new leader, I was taught that I had to be willing and able to do any job that I expected one of my subordinates to do. In practice, it was not unusual for me to demonstrate to those having difficulty exactly how to do a particular job properly. I could perform any one of the jobs done by those who worked for me. Today, however, many times this isn't possible, and that will be even more often the case in the future. This is not because of a leader's incompetence or laziness, but because many jobs require specialized training or education. It is the day of the knowledge worker. These aren't just words concocted by Drucker. Tasks that were once very basic are now performed more efficiently and effectively through the use of technology. The trouble is that employing this technology requires complex tools to be mastered by those who use the technology and perform these tasks. As a result, the leader of the future will be able to perform some, but certainly not all, of the jobs done by those whom they supervise. This too will demand a change in how leaders interact with those led.

There was a time when the leader dealt with a boss, with followers, with customers or those who were the beneficiary of products or services within the overall organization, and occasionally with leaders of collateral organizations. That was about it. Top management may have interacted with a few others. Yet in the future, a trend that started fifty years ago will increase dramatically. All leaders in the organization will be expected to interact with, and sometimes lead, not only those mentioned but also media, governmental officials, leaders in other companies that are joint-venture partners, and more. Clearly, the leader of the future must be adept at ways of leading these others that have little to do with simple direction or what has erroneously been called command-and-control leadership. This is an erroneous term because *command and control* is a military term referring to a commander's authority to have a legal order enforced; it has nothing to do with leadership, and there is no such term as "command-and-control leadership" in the military.

Increasingly, I've been asked to help organizations develop leaders who can maximize the advantages and avoid the pitfalls of diversity. More recently I've even been queried by foreign companies on this issue. This is because it's not only equal opportunity laws that fuel a trend toward increasingly diverse organizations. Demographics, globalization, and the international mobility of workers are also forces. When you have a corporation spread over many countries and many cultures, with employees, even senior managers, speaking several different languages and from different backgrounds, you have a truly diverse organization, and the leader of the future had better be able to deal with the challenges that result. The leader of a diverse organization has to understand how to respond to the varying needs of a wide range of human beings. Some aspects of this response are very basic. For example, all workers want to feel important. This will be true especially of the highly trained and educated worker who has already entered the workforce, as opposed to those who are just entering the workforce now.

TODAY'S LEADER NEEDS TO PREPARE FOR THE FUTURE

These developments make the future environment tremendously complex for the leader. Still, nothing will defeat the leaders of the future if they are prepared. But prepare they must, for I do not see these leaders being relegated to figureheads or glorified cheerleaders. The critical role of leaders will still require their being in charge and actually leading their organizations despite the increasing complexity due to the interrelated and interdependent trends of globalization, technological innovation, sociological change, demographics, and more. The leader of the future will still be the leader in name as well as fact. He or she will still be responsible. How then should today's leaders prepare today for their new and more challenging role tomorrow?

THE RIGHT WAY FOR LEADERS OF THE FUTURE TO LEAD

We've known how to motivate people properly for thousands of years, and I'm not talking about the carrot-and-stick approach. I am talking about the universal need for a sense of importance. Every person wants to feel important, and it is crucial for the future leader to understand this. Strangely, many leaders, intentionally or not, do things that have the opposite effect on followers. For example, I once witnessed a senior company officer make a speech clearly intended to prove his own superiority over the engineering division he led. As might be expected, the speech had an effect exactly the opposite of motivating his division to high productivity. The leader did prove his own importance, but this was accomplished by denigrating the importance of those most needed for his organization's success.

The most successful leaders nurture a feeling of an individual's importance among their subordinates. Cyrus held the power of life and death over his followers. Yet this powerful king never challenged any in a skill that he knew himself to be superior. He never went out of his way to prove his superiority over one of those who followed him. When he competed with his soldiers, as he frequently did, he usually did so in a competition requiring skills with which he was untrained and unfamiliar. Consequently, he was often bested by them. When this happened, he would laugh at himself. No one "threw the game" to make the boss look good.[2] Their sense of importance was increased, but this did not diminish the respect they held for Cyrus or their willingness to follow him. Those increased.

Two thousand years later, Mary Kay Ash (who with a mere $5,000 built the billion-dollar Mary Kay Cosmetics company) also emphasized the value of making others feel important in all relationships. Every day, she imagined that everyone she met wore a huge sign reading "Make Me Feel Important." Similarly, Andrew Carnegie, the Scottish immigrant to the United States who became a self-made multimillionaire steel czar in the nineteenth century, even carried this idea to his grave when he had the following engraved on his tombstone: "Here lies a man who was able to surround himself with men far cleverer than himself." Carnegie knew who was important in his organization.

You cannot make anyone feel important by simply ordering them around, nor will you be able to surround yourself with men or women far more clever than yourself by simply giving orders. That's not leadership. The leader of the future will find that the correct way of influencing those led will have an even greater impact than it does today. Consequently, leaders of the future must develop an array of influence tactics by which they lead in an environment that is ever more complex, with many new challenges and in which their followers are knowledge workers with an especial need for recognition of their own importance. The day of simply giving orders—that is, of using the directive influence tactic in all situations—is over.

How to Influence Without Giving Direct Orders

Of course, there is a time and a place for just telling someone what to do. But for the reasons previously stated, in the future, you should be prepared to get things done by less direct methods. There are an infinite number of influence tactics that are alternatives to simply ordering people around. An effective leader can be cold, warm, upbeat, a recluse, open, secretive, well liked, hated, funny, you name it. These traits have to do with a leader's style. And the leader's style is unimportant.

What is important is that the leader *be effective*. Being effective in the future world of far greater complexity means employing an appropriate influence tactic for the appropriate situation at the appropriate time. Let's look at a few of these other influence tactics that the leader of the future must master to be effective. Although not all of the following examples are drawn from work, they clearly illustrate each tactic well, and leaders of organizations of the future should bear them in mind in their own situations.

THE INDIRECTION TACTIC

Children frequently use indirection. They know how to get things without asking. When my youngest son was ten years old, he became interested in computers and took a special course during the summer to learn how to operate one. One day, we saw that he had rearranged his room. A bare card table was flanked by two other tables. A chair faced the card table. "What's that for?" I asked. "For my computer, when I get it," he responded. "I'm saving my allowance." My wife and I calculated that saving the amount needed would take him many years. On the next holiday, he got his computer.

If you look around, you probably can spot leaders who lead using the same principle my son once did. Recently, I heard someone say when referring to his boss, "You just have to do what he says; you just can't refuse him." I knew this person's boss, so I was able to observe the boss's actions firsthand. He rarely gave orders directly, yet he always got others to follow his lead. Maybe my son took lessons from someone like this man's boss.

THE ENLISTING INFLUENCE TACTIC

When you enlist influence, you simply ask for what you want. It works in situations where you don't have power—or you may have the power, but you may not want to use it. Just asking works in more situations than you might think.

Not too long ago, a social scientist looked at how people motivated others to do things. He found that frequently the logic for persuading is unimportant. Instead, the person doing the persuading only has to *give a reason* for wanting the action performed. During one study, this scientist discovered that many people would allow someone to cut ahead of them in line to make copies on an office copier simply if a reason were given. Did the reason have to be compelling? Hardly. The person had only to say, "Can I go ahead of you because I have to make copies?"[3] This is hard to believe. The researcher felt that the key was simply including the word "because." I think that the key was simply to give a reason and that people want to help.

In general, I don't think you should follow the copier example, but there are times when you need a special effort. Then you want to explain it and say, "We need your help." For example, what stirs American patriotism more than the words "Uncle Sam wants you!"?

THE NEGOTIATION INFLUENCE TACTIC

Negotiation can be an influence tactic and a very effective way of leading. This tactic is especially useful when leading others who are at your level and of equal power. George Washington used this influence tactic to win the Battle of Yorktown and American independence. In 1781, Washington faced Lord Cornwallis and his army at Yorktown, Virginia. Another British army was poised to link up with Cornwallis. If successful, they would outnumber Washington's army, and force him to retreat or surrender. Washington wrote to the French Admiral François de Grasse, who commanded the French fleet supporting Washington, and asked him to leave port and sail for Yorktown to prevent the two British armies from coming together. Admiral de Grasse agreed that this would work, but he deemed it too risky given the severe storms along the Virginia coast during that season.

So Washington responded with a negotiation influence tactic. "Bring the fleet, support our troops, and blockade the coast. If we don't defeat the British by November, I'll release you to return to safe ports before the most dangerous part of the season sets in." De Grasse did this. The two British armies were not able to come together. With French help, Washington defeated the British, and Lord Cornwallis surrendered, bringing a successful end to the American Revolution and securing our independence.

INVOLVEMENT AS AN INFLUENCE TACTIC

Involvement is one of the most effective influence tactics for leading subordinates, other managers at the leader's level, leaders of outside organizations, and just about anyone. It just means getting the person you are interested in leading involved in what you are doing. Drucker said that when it is used correctly, this influence tactic is very powerful.

For example, a few years ago, the English actress Judi Dench played seventy-year-old widow and theater owner Laura Henderson in a movie based on a true story that unfolded in London during World War II. To save her theater, Mrs. Henderson proposed that the responsible government official, Lord Cromer, allow her actresses to perform in the nude, as the Follies Bergères did in Paris. Such a thing was unheard of in 1940s England: after all, England was not France. Yet Mrs. Henderson received permission to do this by getting Lord Cromer *involved* in the issue and in solving her problem. It was finally decided that nudity was acceptable if, like classic paintings containing nude figures, the actresses did not move. Thus was born the Windmill Theatre, which ran continuously until 1964.

WHAT TO DO WHEN A TACTIC FAILS

Which tactic the leader of the future uses depends on many factors in the situation, including these:

- The relative power of the leader
- The urgency or the time available
- The personalities involved
- The general mood
- Rules and regulations

In some cases, a particular tactic won't work. Then the leader of the future must shift and try another. The difference between effective and ineffective leaders will only be that the effective leader will do what the ineffective leader will not.

CONCLUSION: DEFINING THE LEADERSHIP OF THE FUTURE

The definition of leadership of the future, indeed any leadership, was expressed by Peter Drucker some time ago. It has not changed: "Leadership is the lifting of a man's vision to higher sights, the raising of a man's performance to a higher standard, the building of a man's personality beyond its normal limitation."[4]

Endnotes

1. Wayne Ambler (Ed. and Trans.), *Xenophon: The Education of Cyrus* (Ithaca: Cornell University Press, 2001), p. 52.
2. Ambler, 2001, p. 34.
3. Robert B. Cialdini, *The Psychology of Influence, Rev. Ed.* (New York: William Morrow, 1993), p. 4.
4. Peter F. Drucker, *Management, Tasks, Responsibilities, Practices* (New York: HarperCollins, 1973), p. 463.

CHAPTER TWENTY-SIX

LEADERSHIP BY PERPETUAL PRACTICE

Debbe Kennedy

Debbe Kennedy is founder, president, and CEO of the Global Dialogue Center and Leadership Solutions Companies, an award-winning enterprise since 1990 that specializes in custom leadership, organizational, and virtual communications solutions. She is a pioneer and innovator in people-focused leadership and employee communications using Web 2.0 technologies and social media. Formerly, Kennedy had a distinguished leadership career with IBM Corporation for more than twenty years. She is the author of Putting Our Differences to Work: The Fastest Way to Innovation, Leadership, High Performance *and the creator of the online resource center for leaders at www. puttingourdifferencestowork.com.*

Aristotle left a piece of forward-thinking wisdom for us to consider as we look to the future. He said, "For the things we have to learn, before we can do, we learn by doing."[1] I think he was on to something that is more relevant today for organizations preparing leaders for the future than at any time in recent history: the idea that it is day-to-day *practice* that develops a leader's skill and the essential mastery of positive influence. It is through the learning and development experiences of work and life that leaders are discovered, developed, and called. Aristotle also noted this truth when he said, "men become builders by building; lyre-players by playing the lyre; so too we become just by doing just acts, temperate by doing temperate acts, brave by doing brave acts."

In adapting this sage advice for a new time and new circumstances, leaders of the future will be groomed best by living and working in an environment that, by design, fosters a leader's growth—not just by simply delegating additional tasks, expanding responsibilities, or giving out titles, or even by leaving the necessary skill building to the traditional training and development programs we have long relied on for the mainstay of what we considered *leadership development.*

Developing leaders for the organization of the future calls for something more immediate and consciously ongoing than ever before. At best, we will use a hybrid approach to leadership development that encompasses important lessons learned from the hallmarks of leadership style and effectiveness, such as management by objectives and management by walking around. At the same time, we need to elevate the importance of a constant polishing of discipline, skill, and habits to meet the challenges and opportunities of new frontiers. It calls for an accelerated practical, ongoing priming of leaders at all levels of the organization, defining the essential style for a new generation: *leadership by perpetual practice.*

NEW REALITIES OF LEADERSHIP PRACTICE

There are compelling reasons for reevaluating our approach. Times have changed. Things are different. The stakes are higher. It is clear that the landscape for leadership is also very different as we look to the future in any organization. It is as local as the individual sitting at a desk and as global as time, distance, and technology can take us. The very nature of changes in our work suggests that the pace of our dynamic, troubled, and changing world demands a fast, flexible, adaptable, and reliable means of achieving leadership mastery.

The leaders of the future need an essential set of attributes for *being* leaders of character that have a passion for *doing*—getting things done with a conscious intention to deliver positive results. Dr. Martin Luther King Jr. invited all of us to be leaders of character and passion in our own right, framing it simply, "Whatever your life's work is, do it well."[2] Imagine the benefits of an organization with all its members seeing themselves as leaders on a mission to influence a positive outcome wherever and whenever they are called.

A respected leader once shared with me that the word *leadership* has a Germanic origin meaning to "find a new path." For organizations of the future, these new paths will be found by collections of leaders at all levels. They will be created by first changing the prevailing rules for how leaders think, behave, and operate their organizations. These fundamental changes are necessities in order to respond, heal, enrich, and transform both business and society. *Are you ready?*

There is a compelling reason for the organization of the future to make learning to lead a top priority and day-to-day practice for every leader, at every level. Joel A. Barker, futurist, filmmaker, and author of *Paradigms: The Business of Discovering the Future* says it best: "You can and should shape your own future, because if you don't, someone else surely will."[3]

A first step stands out: our acceptance that everything is up for renewal and change. This is a big one for most of us in any organization, because we have difficulty letting go of the familiar and willingly stepping into the unknown. There is risk involved, and those haunting questions *Can I? Will I be able to . . . ?* seem to whisper in the background unexpectedly even for the accomplished leader, as well as for new leaders stepping up to begin their important work. The challenge for leaders who are opening the way for a new era of leadership and organizational success is that there is no roadmap. Uncharted territory and uncertainty will be constants. This means we will have to be comfortable with "cutting the brush" for a new trail. Sometimes it may even mean "being the trail" that others trust enough to follow and pass over in order to discover new choices and deliver innovative contributions to our organizations and those we serve.

Consider this wisdom from the forward-thinking founder of what is today Kyocera Corporation in Japan, who blazed such a trail at age twenty-seven with little money and a great passion for success of his organization. Kazuo Inamori, now chairman emeritus, describes the disciplined work of the leaders of organizations of the future in his book on business philosophy for the twenty-first century, *For People and for Profit:* "It is much harder not to depend on the established order but to blaze a new trail. . . . In taking up a challenge that conventional wisdom holds to be impossible, the first requirement is courage and a strong will."[4]

He goes on to remind us of the role of perpetual practice in fulfilling our mission, not by implementing grandiose programs, but by taking many small steps, refining as you go along, letting one sure step inform the next: "Proceed step by step, like an inchworm. This is the way to take up the challenge of great things."

Organizations of the future not only operate in a climate of uncertainty but also find themselves face-to-face with a diverse, connected, and complex world. This demands developing leaders who know how to understand and respond to the realities of an extremely diverse workplace, marketplace, and community. The dire need for change in all aspects of business and society doesn't allow for long, complicated processes, years of study, and theoretical approaches. Not now. There is a sense of urgency that is hard to escape. *Learning while doing* must be an integral part of the future leader's and future organization's work across industries and sectors. We are the ones—the leaders, the innovators, the aspiring leaders, and individual contributors—who will create the organizations of the future, setting a new direction that will transform business and society as we know it today. These new realities beg two questions:

1. What critical skills do we need to develop in leaders in order for the organization of the future to thrive?
2. What new leadership qualities are essential?

Critical Skills for Leaders in Organizations of the Future

Our most critical skills aren't trendy or brand new, and I believe that they are the same regardless of profession, industry, or sector. They were taught to me by an IBM executive when I was an up-and-coming leader. I never knew why he offered the advice, but I remain grateful for it. I was visiting his location on a mission from our regional headquarters. He called me into his office, asked me to sit down, and went on to offer his wisdom. What he taught me set my direction, and it has helped many other organizations and leaders over the years, passing the test of time. His words still echo in my mind:

> You must always remember that jobs, missions, titles, and organizations will always be in a constant state of change. There are four critical skills that you will need to be successful in the future anywhere, anytime, and in any assignment. They are

1. The ability to develop an idea
2. The ability to effectively plan its implementation
3. The ability to execute second-to-none
4. The ability to achieve superior results time after time

Seek opportunities and experiences that will help you master these critical skills. Forget what others do. Work to be known for delivering your own brand of excellence. It solves problems. It speaks for itself and it opens doors.

At the time I had no idea how profound his mentoring was. But couple these four skills with a pioneering spirit, and you have a great formula for leadership development for any organization. What's new and challenging for the organization of the future is that these critical skills need to be developed in everyone, so that its leaders at all levels are both skilled at working alone and adaptable to working in collaborative, connected situations that move across many dimensions.

Interestingly, I've discovered that these skills also serve as a reliable yardstick for recruiting and evaluating leaders at all levels. These four critical skills can be practiced by leaders in entry-level assignments as well as by leaders in the highest positions of influence. The first two skills are more common. However, it is *execution* and *achieving superior results* that are nurtured in an environment that encourages "leadership by perpetual practice." As leaders grow and change, they raise the bar for new levels of contribution for themselves. When organizations don't value the second two critical skills by setting expectations for them, they end up measuring *efforts* instead of the *results* the organization needed.

So here are a few suggestions for developing these critical skills in your organization:

- Practice deliberately seeking assignments that offer the opportunity to refine your skills for developing, planning, implementing, and achieving superior results. Also recognize that every assignment (even your day-to-day business routine) holds opportunities to develop these skills as well.
- Develop a conscious habit of setting expectations with leaders at all levels that include the leader working to improve, refine,

and demonstrate their skills for developing, planning, implementing, and achieving superior results in all assignments.

- Talk often with your team about these critical skills, even if doing so seems awkward at first. Define for yourselves what each skill means in the context of your environment.
- Use a simplified "after-action review" to evaluate progress; ask yourself
  - What's going well?
  - What isn't?
  - What am I [are we] going to do about it?

FIVE DISTINCTIVE QUALITIES OF LEADERSHIP FOR ORGANIZATIONS OF THE FUTURE

What leadership qualities will be essential to ignite the real power in the critical skills we've just identified? In my book, *Putting Our Differences to Work: The Fastest Way to Innovation, Leadership, and High Performance*,[5] I introduce five distinctive qualities of leadership that invite all of us to strengthen our portfolio of skills with this purpose in mind. The "research and development" behind these five qualities emerged from years of exploration, experimentation, and independent practice. They were also notably enriched in collaboration with my longtime colleague, Joel A. Barker. For more than a decade, we've consciously used our collaboration to try, test, vet, refine, and prove their relevance by perpetual practice with our work and independently in our own businesses, as well as in our work with clients. They took form as what we call the Five Distinctive Qualities of Leadership in response to the growing number of organizations and individuals all over the world that are discovering that putting our differences to work is the most powerful accelerator for generating new ideas, creating innovative solutions, executing organizational strategies, and engaging everyone in the process.

These leadership qualities are described in the next sections of this chapter. Together they put a spotlight on how we think and behave as leaders—considering that every word spoken, every thought expressed, every attitude revealed has a powerful influence on achieving results. Living these qualities as part of "leadership by perpetual practice" becomes an ongoing leadership development experience. As you consider each of them, think about how your organization would benefit from them if leaders at all levels mastered them and adapted the qualities to serve the unique needs, opportunities, and style that define your brand of excellence.

Leadership Quality 1: Make Diversity an Organizational Priority

This quality flips everything we've been conditioned to believe; it reaches beyond "Let's put our differences aside." "We are more alike than we are unalike." "Look at all we have in common." It values these truths, but when we stop there, our differences are made secondary and sometimes brushed away as if they don't matter. The bigger oversight is that differences aren't even recognized as an advantageous stockpile of kindling to ignite new ideas and breakthrough thinking, which are the drivers of innovation, more creative problem solving and decision making, and invention.

In an interview some time ago, Sue Swenson, president and CEO of Sage Software, North America, shared how she builds considerations of diversity and inclusion into mainstream business. Recently, we talked again, and she reflected on how her own form of leadership by perpetual practice has passed the test of time. Her approach serves as a forward-thinking example of how this first distinctive quality of leadership can be put into action. She described her practice this way:

> I guess I'm not only a fairness fanatic, but also a pragmatist. The values of diversity and inclusion are part of the way we do things as a business. My job is to make it simple and integrated. It is not simply a program. My belief is that the only way to sustain anything is to build it into the organization's business processes and culture.

> The Hoshin planning process[6] helped me do this. It is a simple way to help everyone understand and participate in the success of the business. To help create shared ownership, employee satisfaction has always been the first goal. The focus: continuous improvement. This means that achieving business goals, including employee satisfaction, is everyone's responsibility. What each of us does to contribute

to it may be different at every level, but everyone is engaged in creating it. Over time, I've made it a priority to integrate employee satisfaction into performance management, staffing and development, strategic planning, new hire orientation, and a regular part of employee meetings.

A common protocol of behaviors helps create the environment, especially when it is expected across the company. When you describe to people how you want them to do things and you articulate the expectations around behaviors, it is incredibly powerful in creating a culture that integrates the values of diversity and inclusion, as well as being a place where customers enjoy doing business.

Leadership Quality 2: Get to Know People and Their Differences

This quality expands our thinking to see the many dimensions of diversity in a new light. Putting our differences to work means consciously developing a curiosity, a reservoir of knowledge, and a day-to-day practice that masters how, when, and where to tap into these invaluable human resources. The process offers the opportunity to discover and learn from unique ethnic origins, cultural perspectives, generational insight, global know-how, marketplace understanding, fresh new thinking, challenging new motivations, creative talents, and a wide range of life experiences—all of which are shown in Exhibit 26.1.

Through day-to-day practice, this quality opens a whole new world of possibilities. I've always had an interest in people, or so I thought. However, I've learned that there is a difference between having an interest in people and developing a genuine *curiosity* about them.

One specific influence continues to help me develop a more conscious curiosity about people, as well as to affirm why this leadership quality is so important to organizations in the future. It was one of those *ah ha* moments when I realized how limiting labels can be in describing who we are and what we have to offer the world. Each of us has multiple dimensions of difference that reach far beyond the traditional diversity considerations and enrich the mix with such strengths as generational perspectives, cultural wisdom, and how we think and operate based on our experiences and habits. It is at these

Exhibit 26.1. Dimensions of Difference.

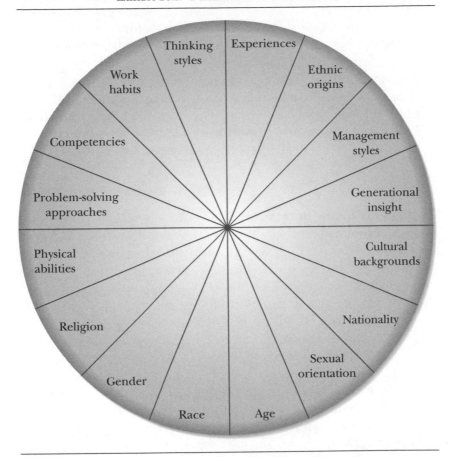

Source: Debbe Kennedy, *Putting Our Differences to Work: The Fastest Way to Innovation, Leadership, and High Performance* (San Francisco: Berrett-Koehler, 2008).

unique intersections of our differences that the value lies. In his groundbreaking 2000 film, *Wealth, Innovation, and Diversity,* Joel A. Barker introduced what he termed a "surprising discovery": that diversity has a direct connection to innovation and innovation to the creation of new wealth of many kinds. He presents a compelling business case that affirms the importance of developing this second distinctive quality of leadership, when he concludes that "societies and organizations that most creatively incorporate diversity will reap the rewards of innovation, growth, wealth, and progress."[7]

To begin expanding your reservoir of knowledge of differences,

- Let your good intentions shine; be friendly and approachable—be someone others want to get to know.
- Start asking more questions.
- Take time to listen to what others have to say.
- Reach out in a more deliberate way to people who are different from you.
- Look for the value and opportunities to innovate at the intersections of differences when you partner and collaborate.

LEADERSHIP QUALITY 3: ENABLE RICH COMMUNICATION

This quality defies the notion of unilateral streams of thought; through openness, people move far beyond the two-way communication of the past. Rich communication relies on approaching problems with a "beginner's mind"—even as an expert. It places a new, higher value on what others have to say and on the responsibility and openness to listen with a new consciousness of mining for the better idea. It adds a requirement of trusting ourselves, and each other, enough to engage in action-directed dialogue, across disciplines—welcoming outsiders.

Bert Bleke was a superintendent of Lowell Public Schools in Michigan when I met him at a Leader to Leader Institute conference. Two lessons came from a conversation with him that remind us how much we can learn from each other and how to build a rich communication through dialogue that engages everybody. Although our missions may be different, the process of engaging people is universal:

> It is interesting how easy it is for most of us to think that our organizations are unique. I've been lucky to have had experiences in education, business, nonprofits, and churches—and I have realized there are many more similarities in the challenges we face than there are differences. The greatest similarity I see—one we tend to forget—is that all our organizations are about people with the same basic needs and desires. The only thing that is truly different is our unique end product. Consequently, we should be able to learn from each other about leading change and making our schools and organizations, businesses, and communities better places for everybody.

For us, change started by people coming together: three hundred people—students, parents, teachers, administrators, and clergy. In a period of a few hours, we came up with five character traits we felt would be the most powerful influence on kids, our organization, and community: responsibility, integrity, compassion, honesty, and respect. We chose the words based on everyone's input, but we did not define them.

Then over a period of the next year or so, we let our schools gradually talk about them and ask themselves, "What do these core values mean to us? How can they be important for us?" We have worked diligently to instill these character traits not only into our kids but also saying to our employees, our parents, our churches, our community, "This is a partnership. Together, we can model these kinds of traits."

The process has enabled us to start talking with each other about character and values—it has given us a common language for change.

LEADERSHIP QUALITY 4: HOLD PERSONAL RESPONSIBILITY AS A CORE VALUE

This quality acknowledges the shift from employees having "institutional loyalty" in the past to being "free agents" or perhaps other more fluid, mobile kinds of arrangements we've not yet imagined in the marketplaces, workplaces, and communities that are in a continual state of churn. What we must add to our way of operating as individuals is the essential quality reflected in Nelson Mandela's words: "With freedom comes responsibility." A sense of *personal responsibility* needs to be part of our portable portfolio that goes with us when we move from one job to another or wherever our freedom takes us.

Recently, I was taken aback by a young innovator who had just entered the workplace, fresh from college. I was talking to him at an online Skypecast about this fourth quality of leadership that holds personal responsibility as a core value. I shared that what had been instilled in me as a leader was that leadership isn't about power but fundamentally about responsibility, and that we needed more leaders with a sense of responsibility to others. He said, with genuine sincerity in his voice, "I hear what you are saying about leaders in the twenty-first century, but I don't feel this way. I really don't care about anyone else. I know this sounds gross, but I just want to make money and live a good life." He went on to share that this was how many of his friends felt also. I listened and I asked questions; when the session was over, I felt deeply sad. What I know for sure is that all signs indicate that this mind-set is not so uncommon today, and that it is not one that will sustain organizations of the future or our global family.

Organizations of the future need to develop a new mind-set in leaders at all levels—one that creates a continuous "value-chain" that comes from everybody's commitment to personal responsibility; one that stays with leaders as they navigate their way through a dynamic career. Nana Luz, a small business owner and a self-described global citizen, tells how a leader can most effectively demonstrate commitment to personal responsibility: "I recommend this be done mostly by example, rather than official announcement."

To begin incorporating this quality of leadership,

- Consciously incorporate personal responsibility into your leadership mind-set, then work to imprint the habit of personal responsibility into your decision making and actions.
- Support, inspire, and encourage others to take personal responsibility, leading by example and by constructively coaching and acknowledging others' actions.

LEADERSHIP QUALITY 5: ESTABLISH MUTUALISM AS THE FINAL ARBITER

This quality adds a new guide for decisions, problem solving, products, services, programs, and profit making: *everyone benefits; no one is harmed.* In other words, it creates win, win, win: I win, you win, we all win. Building the future organization on a foundation of mutualism changes everything we do. It demands that we consciously make a routine practice of evaluating our actions, behavior, decisions, thinking, and new ideas with, *first,* a thoughtful inspection of their implications and benefits for all concerned. It adds a new element of consideration to every business or strategic plan, and provides a whole new measurement for equitable collaborations and partnerships.

The need for this distinctive quality of leadership emerged from the mistakes, poor judgments, greed, exploitation, and unintended

consequences we've all witnessed in recent years in some organizations and every region of the world. Many leaders have become
good at implementing the best strategies and trendy new means of
yielding a fast return on investment, but their sometimes thought-
less, sometimes rash decisions have had sweeping influences on
organizations and on others' lives.

For example, Jerrold V. Tucker shared a story with me a while
back about his first day as chief learning officer at GTE Service
Corporation. It highlights the need for a more mutualistic kind
of thinking on the part of leaders and underscores three related
leadership lessons for organizations of the future:

> Our center was out of control by any business measurement at the
> time. I was brought in to turn the situation around—to implement
> the recommendations from a consultant. On my first day, we laid off
> nineteen people. If I had to measure the way I handled it, I would
> have to say it was poor. The methodology was to call people up to
> one of the conference rooms. The message was "your job has been
> eliminated." Then we directed them into the next room to hear
> about their benefits, followed by security escorting them out the
> door. It was a terrible process. Most of all, the recommendations
> from the consultant didn't fit our company. It was a family-oriented
> organization. Laying people off in this manner was not part of our
> culture. Afterwards, the rest of the organization was paralyzed in
> fear. We reduced the budget. We reduced headcount—but instead
> of making improvement, we set the organization back further.
>
> This mistake took about two years to fix. We started by first chang-
> ing our focus to customer service and making sure every person
> understood their important role in our success—every dishwasher,
> curriculum developer, waiter, administrator, housekeeper, manager,
> and faculty member. What we did best was unleash the talents of
> our diverse team of people, a dynamic group representing over
> fifteen countries and cultures. Together, they created one of the
> premier management development centers in the world.
>
> There were many leadership lessons learned. Three stand out:
>
> 1. Listen to input, but decide for yourself what is right to do.
> 2. Preserve human dignity in all situations.
> 3. Put your trust in people; they have the answers.

The distinctive quality of leadership that establishes mutualism as the final arbiter requires a conscious day-to-day practice, as do each of the five distinctive qualities of leadership described in this chapter (and in more detail in my book). Dr. Martin Luther King Jr. highlights the importance in this wisdom: "We are all caught in an inescapable network of mutuality, tied into a single garment of destiny. Whatever affects one directly, affects all indirectly."[8]

Leading the Way for an Organization of the Future

How do we begin this more conscious kind of leadership by perpetual practice that will drive the success of the organization of the future? A universal truth shared with me by a close friend when I once asked her a similar kind of "how-to" question states it clearly: "You get up in the morning and you start." This is the way all transformations, *big and small*, begin.

One of the strengths organizations of the future have to draw on is the knowledge, know-how, and timeless wisdom of all that came before them. At the same time, they have to be adaptable and willing to embrace the uncharted territory that bears their name. One of my cherished books is *Take a Second Look at Yourself*.[9] I discovered it a few years ago in a used book store. It was published more than fifty years ago. The author, John Homer Miller, may not have instant name recognition today, but I've learned that he was a forward-thinking leader with many contributions and influences in another time. He affirms the kinds of change we've discussed about developing leaders for the organization of the future—leaders who become masters of the human dimension of change through leadership by perpetual practice: "You want [a better organization,] a better world. What you need to help make [your organization better or] to make the world better is not more education of your intellect. What you need is something spiritual and ethical added to your knowledge. You need educated emotions and a dedicated heart. Shakespeare once said that we can always tell a wise man by the fact everything he says or does smacks of something greater than himself. Great leaders start from within and move out."

Endnotes

1. Aristotle, *Nicomachean Ethics*, translated by W. D. Ross (Whitefish, MT: Kessinger, 2004), p. 18.

2. King, Martin Luther, Jr., "Facing the Challenge of a New Age," in James M. Washington (ed.), *A Testament of Hope: The Essential Writings and Speeches of Martin Luther King, Jr.* (San Francisco: HarperSanFrancisco, 1986).

3. Barker, Joel A., *Wealth, Innovation, and Diversity*, video with written workshop by Debbe Kennedy (St Paul, MN: Star Thrower Distribution, 2000), www.starthrower.com; *Paradigms: The Business of Discovering the Future* (New York: Collins Business, 1993).

4. Inamori, Kazuo, *For People and for Profit: A Business Philosophy for the 21st Century* (Tokyo: Kodansha International, 1997), pp. 149–150.

5. Kennedy, Debbe, *Putting Our Differences to Work: The Fastest Way to Innovation, Leadership, and High Performance* (San Francisco: Berrett-Koehler, 2008), www.puttingourdifferencestowork.com.

6. "Hoshin Kanri is a step-by-step strategic planning process that assesses breakthrough strategic objectives against daily management tasks and activities. It provides a visual map at all levels of the organization [and] provides clear strategic direction. . . . Hoshin Kanri methodology ensures that everyone in the organization knows the strategic direction for the company. Creating a working communication system means everyone is working towards a common goal!" This definition is from Karen Becker, iSixSigma Dictionary, www.isixsigma.com (2005).

7. Barker, Joel A., *Wealth, Innovation, and Diversity*, video with written workshop by Debbe Kennedy (St Paul, MN: Star Thrower Distribution, 2000), www.starthrower.com.

8. King, Martin Luther, Jr., "Facing the Challenge of a New Age," in James M. Washington (ed.), *A Testament of Hope: The Essential Writings and Speeches of Martin Luther King, Jr.* (San Francisco: HarperSanFrancisco, 1986).

9. Miller, John Homer, *Take a Second Look at Yourself* (Nashville, TN: Abingdon-Cokesbury, 1950).

INDEX

R

Rao, S. S., 2, 37
Real Change Leaders (Katzenbach), 98
Realignment News bulletin (GSUSA), 213
Reengineering the Corporation: A Manifesto for Business Revolution (Champy), 3
Reengineering Management (Champy), 3
Reichheld, F., 45
Reinventing Strategy (Pietersen), 207
Repacking Your Bags (Leider), 112
Research in Motion, 289
Respect at work, 79
Responsibility
  core value of personal, 331–332
  leadership, 311
  See also Social responsibility
Responsibility Gap, 127–129
Retirement
  finding new purpose during, 118–119
  "new elders" in, 113–114
  organizations which will re-create, 116–118
  re-creating concept of, 112–113, 114–115
  Working on Purpose seminar on moving beyond, 115–116
Reward system support, 195–197
Reynolds and Reynolds, 183
Rickitt and Coleman, 264
Ritz Employee Promise and Credo, 71–72
Ritz-Carlton Hotels, 2, 64, 71–72, 73
Rockwell Collins Display Systems, 33
Rollins, K., 298
Ross, F., 148
Rowe, J., 101, 102
Ryan, K., 165
Ryan, M. J., 71

S

Sabia, M., 106–110
Sage Software, North America, 327
Salamon, L., 218
SAP, 183
Sarbanes-Oxley Act (2002), 135
SAS, 58
Saturn, 304
Savvy Source for Parents, 166
Scarlett, J., 295–296
Schein, E. H., 243, 258
Schmidt, E., 121
Schramm, C., 162
Schultz, H., 73, 132, 134, 296
Self-interest concept, 41
Self-knowledge, 308
Senge, P., 66, 68
Shakespeare, W., 334
Shaping School Culture (Deal and Peterson), 132
Share Our Strength, 171
Shareholders
  how organizations of the future treat their, 47–48
  value maximization for, 40
Sheldon, A., 261
Shirley, J., 287, 288, 289
Shooting magazine, 11

Shultz, H., 57, 103
Siebel Systems, 199
Siebel, T., 199
Significance concept, 141–143
Sinegal, J., 56
SIs (systems integrators), 183
Sisodia, R., 47
Skype, 161
Smallwood, N., 13
SMARTHINKING, 159
Smith & Wesson Company (S&W), 9–12
Smith, A., 92
Smith, D. K., 98
Social network knowledge, 308
Social responsibility
  "corporate social opportunity" for, 38, 126–127
  growing interest in, 123–125
  growth in social sector/nonprofit organizations and, 125–126
  lasting importance of, 129–131
  "Responsibility Gap" in, 127–129
  See also Community; Ethical issues; Responsibility
Solomon, R. C., 135
Something to Live For: Finding Your Way (Leider), 112
Sonicbids.com, 68
Southwest Airlines
  authorship approach of, 137, 138
  formal and informal integration by, 102–103
  "informal organization" approach of, 99
  talent management approach by, 195
  treatment of employees by, 58, 134, 147
Spillett, R., 158, 217
Spot management, 65–66
SRC Holdings, 58, 61
SSM Health Care (SSMHC), 70–71
Stability issue
  assumptions related to, 189
  change management and, 190–191
  effectiveness relationship to, 190
  organizational design and, 189–190
Staples, 296
Star Model, 184e–186
Starbucks, 57–58, 59, 103, 132, 147, 169, 194
Steelcase, 150
Stemberg, T., 296
Strategic Alliances Among Health and Human Services Organizations (Bailey), 228
Strategic learning capability, 215
Strategic unity
  definition of, 16
  three agendas for creating, 23–24
Strategists, 18
Strickland, B., 76, 145
Students
  changing the attention of the, 234–235
  MBC model helping disadvantaged, 151–153
  redefining at-risk, 149–151
  See also College of the future; Higher education; Vocational education
Subcultures
  building alignment of, 266–267

dynamics of, 265–266
engineering, 264
executive, 265
General Foods (GF) alignment of, 260–262
operator, 264
organization differentiation into, 259
other organizational examples of warring, 262–264
See also Culture
Suppliers, 46–47
Sustainability, 140
Sustaining Our Spirits: Women Leaders Thriving for Today and Tomorrow (Bailey, and associates), 228
Swenson, S., 327–328
Systems thinking
developing a learning organization using, 67–69
making the organizational change to, 72–74
origins and description of, 66–67
overcoming the accountability hurdle, 69–71
as value driven, 71–72, 74

T

Take a Second Look at Yourself (Miller), 334
Talbot's, 281
Talent
attracting, 163–164
definition and formula of, 16
developing, 18, 164–165
Low-Labor-Cost strategy barrier to hiring, 55–56
mature workers as essential, 112–119
organization design to manage, 195
as organizational capability, 16–17
retaining, 165
See also Employees
Talent (Lawler), 188
"Talent mindset," 162–163
Tandy Corp., 287
Teach For America, 121–122
Teams
GSUSA bridging change using "gap," 210
high-performance, 272–273, 277e–278
leadership redefined through high-performance, 273–276
strategies for creating inclusive, 250–255
Teams at the Top (Katzenbach), 98
Technological communication aids, 312
Temple approach, 76, 141–143
Tenure (higher education), 233–234
Tesco, 179
Theft by employees, 55
The Theory of Moral Sentiments (Smith), 92
Thomson, D. G., 285
"Thoughts for Today" (BBC radio segment), 88
360-degree feedback
Leadership Practices Inventory questionnaire for, 27
of organizations, 25
Tichy, N. M., 297
Tierney, T., 219
Timberland, 169

Today (BBC radio program), 88
Tolstoy, L., 207
Tractor Supply, 295–296
Training value, 82–84
Transparency, 42
Transparency (O'Toole, Bennis, and Goleman), 49
Treat People Right! (Lawler), 188
Trilogy Software, 164
Trudell, C., 304
Trust
BGCA focus on ensuring public, 226
"Four Cast Member Expectations" practice to build, 254
as progressive organization quality, 42
Tucker, J. V., 333
Turnover rates, 55
20% rule, 165

U

Ulrich, D., 13
The Ultimate Question (Reichheld), 45
UN Global Compact, 121, 122
Unfreezing model, 190–191
Unilever, 96
Unionization, 55
University of Minnesota, 228, 237
University of Pittsburgh, 148
University of Pittsburgh Medical Center, 150
Untethering trends, 166–168
UPS, 58, 293
U.S. Constitution, 95
U.S. Secret Service, 192
USMC, 103

V

Value proposition
Blueprint Company breakthrough, 294
leveraging learning for, 193–194
mastering exponential returns for, 295
of mature workers, 112–119
of ongoing training, 82–84
Value-based systems approach, 71–73, 74
See also Organizational values
Vanourek, G., 157, 159
VARs (value-added resellers), 183
Venture philanthropy, 171
Vioxx scandal, 133
Vision
of constituents, 32–34
developing and driving the High-Involvement model, 269–271, 279
forward-looking leadership as, 27–36
Girl Scouts of the USA (GSUSA), 207
"ideal job," 39
leadership as lifting a man's, 319
See also Mission
Visionary change
MinuteClinic as example of, 3–6
Smith & Wesson Company (S&W) example of, 9–12
Sonicbids.com as example of, 6–8
Vocational education
changing future of, 148–149